Travels in Southern Europe and the Levant, 1810-1817. The Journal of C. R. Cockerell

THE JOURNAL

OF

C. R. COCKERELL, R.A.

TRAVELS IN SOUTHERN EUROPE AND THE LEVANT, 1810–1817. THE JOURNAL OF C. R. COCKERELL, R.A.

EDITED BY HIS SON

SAMUEL PEPYS COCKERELL

With a Portrait

LONGMANS, GREEN, AND CO.

39 PATERNOSTER ROW, LONDON

NEW YORK AND BOMBAY

1903

PREFACE

My father, Charles Robert Cockerell, whose travels the following pages record, was the second son of Samuel Pepys Cockerell, a man of some means, architect to the East India Company and to one or more London estates. He was born on the 27th of April, 1788, and at a suitable age he went to Westminster, a fashionable school in those days. There he remained until he was sixteen. He was then set to study architecture, at first in his father's office, and later in that of Mr. Robert Smirke. His father must have had a great faith in the educational advantage of travel, as already in 1806, when he was only eighteen, he was sent a tour to study the chief architectural objects of the West of England and Wales. The sketches in the diary of this journey show him already the possessor of so light and graceful a touch in drawing that it is evident that he must have practised it from very early years. This no doubt was followed by other similar excursions, but his father's desire was that he should see foreign countries. Unfortunately, in 1810 most of the Continent was closed to Englishmen. Turkey, which included Greece, was, however, open. As it chanced, this was a happy exception. The current of taste for the moment was running strongly in the direction of Greek architecture; Smirke himself had but lately returned thence. When a scheme for making a tour there came to be discussed, Mr. William Hamilton, then Under-Secretary for Foreign Affairs, an intimate friend of the family, who had himself travelled in those parts, took a great interest in it, and offered to send him out as King's messenger with despatches for the fleet at Cadiz, Malta, and Constantinople. Such an offer was too good to refuse.

No definite tour had been or could be marked out in the then existing conditions of European politics. The traveller was to be guided by circumstances; but nothing approaching the length of absence, which extended itself to seven and a quarter years, was contemplated at the time of starting.

As far as possible I have used my father's own words in the following account of his journeys; but the letters and memoranda of a youth of twenty-two, who disliked and had no talent for writing, naturally require a great deal of editing.

His beautiful sketches form what may be called his real diary.

I should add that accounts of some of the episodes recorded in this Journal have seen the light already. For instance, the discovery of the Ægina Marbles and of the Phigaleian Marbles is narrated in my father's book, 'The Temples of Ægina and Bassæ,' and in Hughes's 'Travels' as well. Stackelberg gives his own account of the excavations at Bassæ in ' Der Apollotempel zu Bassae &c.' So that I cannot flatter myself that the matter is either quite new or well presented. But in spite of these drawbacks I have thought the Journal in its entirety worth publishing. Sympathetic readers will find between the lines a fairly distinct picture of what travel was like in the early years of the last century, and also the portrait of a not uninteresting personality.

Samuel Pepys Cockerell.

CONTENTS

CHAPTER VI

CHAPTER VII

CHAPTER VIII

CHAPTER IX

CHAPTER X

CHAPTER XI

CHAPTER XII

CHAPTER XVIII

CHAPTER XIX

FRONTISPIECE

TRAVELS IN SOUTHERN EUROPE AND THE LEVANT

CHAPTER I

" I STARTED from London on Saturday, April the 14th, 1810, with 200*l.* in my pocket to pay expenses. By the favour of Mr. Hamilton I was to carry out despatches to Mr. Adair, our ambassador at Constantinople, so I had in prospect a free passage in fair security to the furthest point of my intended journey. As my good friend and master in Art, Mr. R. Smirke, accompanied me to Salisbury, we loitered there a little, but for the rest of my journey, night and day, I lost not one moment. Nevertheless I had forgotten that when on Government duty one has no business to stop at all anywhere, and when I was cross-examined as to my journey by the Admiral of the Port at Plymouth, I felt extremely awkward.

B

On the morning following my arrival, viz. April 16th, I embarked on board the vessel which was to carry me.   She was a lugger-rigged despatch boat, hired by Government, named the *Black Joke*.   She was very old, as she had been at the battle of Camperdown in 1797, but I was charmed with her neatness and tidiness.   We had ten guns, thirty-five men, one sheep, two pigs and fowls.   The commander's name was Mr. Cannady, and we were taking out two young midshipmen to join the squadron off Cadiz.

We did not set sail till the 19th.   Once out in the open sea the two young midshipmen were very ill and so was our commander.

On the third day out, Sunday, April 22nd, while we were at dinner the boatswain suddenly sang out, ' Sail ahead ! '   We ran up to see what it might be, and the ship was pronounced to be a merchant brig.   At the same time, to be prepared in case of deception, all things were cleared for action.   It was not long before we came up with her, and the master went aboard. Presently we heard the report of two pistols.   Great was our astonishment, and the expression of suspense on every face was a study till it was relieved by the voice of the master bawling through a trumpet that she was a British merchantman, the *Frances*, from Fiale (*sic*), laden with cotton, figs, and other things, that she had been captured by a French privateer, and was now our prize.   At these words the joy of the sailors was such as you cannot conceive. When the master came aboard again we learnt that the two shots came from a brace of pistols which were handed to him by the captain of the *Frances* when she was boarded, and which he discharged for fear of accidents.

The French crew of eight men, all very ragged, was brought on board. As they manifested some unwillingness at first, Cannady thought fit to receive them with drawn cutlasses ; but they made no sort of resistance. With them came an English boy, son of the owner of the *Frances*, and from him we got an interesting account of her being taken. As his father had but a short time before lost another ship, the boy showed a joy at this recovery which was delightful to see, but he behaved very nicely about recommending the Frenchmen to us. They had treated him very well, he said, and were good sailors. It was settled that the prize master should be sent with three or four men, the master's mate at their head, to Plymouth. I took the opportunity of sending a few words home, and off she went. With a fair wind she was out of sight in an hour. As I was the only man in our ship who could speak a word of French, I was made interpreter in examining the prisoners. If the account they give is correct, our sailors, who are entitled to an eighth part of the salvage, will share 3,645*l.* 10*s.* 8*d.* I took an early opportunity, when Cannady talked of our luck and anticipated more, to assure him that the only good fortune I desired was a safe and quick passage to Constantinople, for fear he should think I was looking out for prize-money. I don't know what my share would be, if indeed I have any, but if I find I have, I shall consider how to dispose of it in a handsome way.

The poor Frenchmen were very miserable, and I, partly out of pity, and more because I wanted to practise speaking, rather made friends with them. They are very different from our men. They lounge about anyhow in a disorderly fashion, are much dirtier—in fact filthy, so that our sailors complain of them loudly in this respect—and are much livelier. I saw three of them sitting yesterday all of a heap reading ' Télémaque ' (fancy that!) with the utmost avidity, and when they see me drawing, they seem to crawl all over me to watch the operation. My special friend is one Esprit Augin, who appears to be superior to the rest and to speak better. We talk together every day till I am tired. In spite of his grief at being a prisoner—and he appeared to feel his position more than any of them—he began the very next day to talk to me of balls, masquerades, promenades, and so on with inexpressible delight, and I even thought at one moment that we should have had a *pas seul* on the deck. He sang me no end of songs. He was as vain as he was lively. I told him I should like to make a drawing of a youth named Jean Requette, a handsome, clever-looking boy of the party; at which he sighed deeply and said, ' Moi je ne suis pas joli.'

Amongst other things, Augin told us that he had great hopes of being set free again, for that there were two French privateer frigates off Ferrol; and when we came off that point on Sunday the 29th, and I heard the boatswain sing out ' Two sail ahead,' we made sure we had met them. All glasses were out in an instant, and sure enough there were two privateers.

Too proud to alter it, we held quietly on our course, and they came quickly up with us. We made the private signals to them, but as the sun was low and just behind them we could not make out the answer or what colours they flew.

Thereupon orders were given to clear for action. In a moment all was activity. The sailors stripped to their shirts. The guns were run out. Greville and I loaded the muskets and pistols. Every man had his place. Mine was at the stern in charge of the despatches, ready tied to a cannon shot, to sink them in case of necessity, and with orders to make the best use I could of the muskets. We were all ready by the time the first of the privateers came within speaking distance of us. There was a dead silence on both sides for a moment, a moment of intense suspense, then our commander spoke them, and the answer, to our delight, came in English. They were the *Iris* and *Matchless* privateers from

Guernsey on the look-out for the Isle de France men going into Bordeaux. A boat came aboard us, and I was not sorry that they should see our deck and that I knew how to take care of despatches. It is wonderful how the animation of preparations for fighting takes away from the natural fear. If I had had to look on without anything to do, I should have been in a dreadful fright.

After this false alarm we went on to Cadiz without any event, beyond meeting with occasional merchantmen, whom we always thought proper to board.

I could not go ashore at Cadiz, and I shall never cease to regret it; but the orders of the naval authorities were peremptory that the lugger should proceed immediately with her despatches to Malta.[1] We deposited our prisoners with the fleet."

The next place the *Black Joke* touched at was Gibraltar, where she delivered letters and despatches. She could only stay four or five hours, but Cockerell was able to go ashore. As it was a market day, the scene Gibraltar, and this was the first time he had ever been in a foreign country, it is not to be wondered at that he was intoxicated with delight. He gushes over it in the style of the very young traveller.

" I like watching the sailors. Many of them are

---

[1] The British fleet was at this time co-operating with the Spaniards in defending Cadiz against the French.

very fine fellows, and I have nearly filled my book
with drawings of them and the Frenchmen. Self-
consciousness had the most ludicrous effect upon them
when I was doing their portraits, and great rough
fellows who you might think would eat horseflesh would
simper with downcast eyes, like a coquettish miss.
Their ways of killing time are wonderful. Sometimes
you see one whittling a piece of hard wood for some
trifling purpose for hours and hours together. At
another time, if an unfortunate little bird comes on to
the vessel, they run about the rigging damning its
eyes till they are tired out. There are some great
singers amongst them, who treat us in the evenings.
Their taste is to sing about two hundred verses to the
same tune. I am told we have one highly accomplished, who can sing a song of three hundred. I
only hope we shall never hear him.

We arrived at Malta overnight and awaited despatches, which we have received this morning. Everywhere the authorities are so solicitous that no time
should be lost that we are sent on without mercy. I
am told the despatches we brought here were of consequence ; but, like all postmen, we know nothing of the
contents of the letters we bring. Only we see that all
rejoice and wish the commandant, General Oakes,[1] joy.
I also hear that the French are advancing on Sicily.

---

[1] Afterwards Sir Hildebrand Oakes, Bart., G.C.B. Served with distinction in India, Egypt, America, and elsewhere.

The harbour here is full of prizes. A frigate came in this morning full of shot holes. She had cut out a brig from Taranto in the face of two brigs, a schooner, and a frigate."

From Malta it took the *Black Joke* over a month to get to Constantinople. Most of the letters written home during the time were sent back by the *Black Joke* on her return voyage. It will be seen why they never reached their destination.

Meanwhile some notes were despatched by other means, and from them I extract the following :

"We took a pilot from Malta, a decayed Ragusan captain. Had I made but the first steps in Italian as I had in French, I might have profited by this opportunity as I did by the French prisoners ; for the man spoke no other language, and was to direct us through a dangerous sea by signs and grimace as the only means of communication between us.

At first we had a fair wind, but as we got nearer the Morea it became less favourable and blew us nearly up to Zante. Some ancient writer records the saying in his day, ' Let him who is to sail round Taenarus (Matapan) take a last farewell of his relations ;' and it is still dangerous, on account of the eddies of wind about Taygetus for one thing, and on account of the cruel Mainiote pirates for another. We passed it securely ; but the story of an English brig of war having been boarded and taken by them while the captain and crew were at dinner, and that not long ago, put us on our guard. We had nettings up at night, and a sharp look-out at all hours.

I shall never forget how we made our entrance into the Hellespont with sixteen sail of Greek and Turkish fruit-boats, all going up to Constantinople.

No yachting match could be so pretty as these boats, tacking and changing their figures, with their white sails, painted sides, and elegant forms, as compared with our northern sea boats. Our superior sailing, however, was soon confessed, and we went past them. As we did so, several goodnaturedly threw cucumbers and other fruits on board.

We cast anchor not far from the second castle near the northern side, and put ashore to water where we saw a spring. It was evening, and under the shade of a fine plane tree, by a pool lined and edged with marble, before a fountain of elegant architecture, sat on variegated carpets some majestic Turks. They were armed and richly dressed. Their composed, placid countenances seemed unmoved at our approach. One of them spoke and made me a sign to draw nearer. I did so, and with an air at once courteous and commanding he signed to me to sit near him and offered me a long pipe to smoke. After some pause he put questions, and smiled when I could not answer them. By their gestures and the word Inglis I saw they

were aware of our nationality. They looked approbation and admired the quality of my grey cloth coat.
After some minutes I rose and left them with a bow,
enchanted with their politeness, and fancying myself
in a scene of the 'Arabian Nights.'

Shortly after we were visited by our consul and
his son. We learnt later that they were Jews, but
their handsome appearance imposed completely on us,
and, in spite of the mixture of Jewish obsequiousness,
their Turkish dignity made us conceive a prodigious
opinion of them. The consul understood quickly
that I was a milordo, and taking from his pocket an
antique intaglio he begged my acceptance of it with
a manner I in my innocence thought I could not
refuse. I was anxious to show my sense of his
courtesy by the offer of a pound of best Dartford
powder, which, after some pressing, he accepted ; but
at the same time added, so far as I understood through
the interpreter, that he hoped I did not mean to
pay him for his intaglio. I was overcome with confusion, shocked at my own indelicacy in giving so
coarse an expression to my gratitude, and I would
have given worlds to have undone the whole affair.
Of course my embarrassment was perfectly needless.
A little experience of them taught me that this was
only the shallow *finesse* of the Orientals, and looking
back I have laughed to think of my ingenuous
greenness at that time.

The following day Captain Cannady and myself, with my despatches and baggage, the *Black Joke* not being allowed to approach the capital,[1] embarked in a Turkish rowboat with a reis and twelve men, to go up to Constantinople. Now for the first time I felt myself thoroughly divided from England.

The wind and current were against us, and we were forced to put ashore early in the evening of the first day. I pitched my tent on the shore opposite Abydos. It soon attracted the notice of an aga who appeared on a fine Arab horse, and sent a message to know who and what we were. We made a fire and stayed there all night sitting round it, and I felt as if I was at the theatre, passing my first night on foreign soil among strange bearded faces and curious costumes lit up by the flames. I refused a bed and slept on a rug, but next day I thought I should have dropped with faintness and fatigue.

I soon got accustomed to lying on hard ground, and, in after times, I have slept for many a three months running without even taking off my clothes except to bathe, or having any other bed than my pamplona or my pelisse. The second night we slept at Gallipoli, and altogether, owing to the strong wind, we were no less than five days getting to Constantinople.

---

[1] No ships of war were ever allowed up to Constantinople in those days, and, indeed, much later.

Our Turks were obliging and cheerful, but had very little air of discipline, and the work they did they seemed to do by courtesy. The reis was a grave, mild old man, who sang us Turkish songs.

We approached Constantinople as the sun rose, and as it shone on its glorious piles of mosques and minarets, golden points and crescents, painted houses, kiosks and gardens, our Turks pulled harder at their oars, shouting ' *Stamboul, guzel azem Stamboul!* ' The scene grew more and more brilliant as we drew nearer, till it became overwhelming as we entered the crowded port. Nothing but my despatches under my arm recalled me from a sense of being in a dream. In forty days, spent as it were, in the main, in the sameness of shipboard, I had jumped from sombre London to this fantastic paradise.

I left my boat and walked at once to the English palace with my despatches, which I then and there delivered."

CHAPTER II

CONSTANTINOPLE—CAPTURE OF THE *BLACK JOKE*—LIFE IN CON-
STANTINOPLE—ITS DANGERS—FRIENDS—AUDIENCE OF CAIMA-
CAM—TRIP UP THE BOSPHORUS.

" My first few days were spent in writing, executing
commissions, and fitting out my good Cannady, who
was to return with the answers to the despatches; all
as it turned out to no purpose, for off Algiers the poor
old *Black Joke* was taken by two French privateers,
one of ten, the other of eight guns. Becalmed off that
place, she was attacked on either side by these lighter
vessels, which, with oars and a superior number of men,
had an irresistible advantage. After being gallantly
defended by Cannady, she was taken with the loss of
several fine fellows, and her guns dismounted in the
discharging them, for she was a very old vessel. With
her were taken a number of little Turkish purses and
trifles, souvenirs to friends at home, and two fine
carpets I paid 30*l.* for, which were to have made a
figure at Westbourne [1]—I had made a present of the

---

[1] His father's home, Westbourne House, Paddington, a country
residence on the site of the present Westbourne Park.

same kind also to our commander—and all my letters home and sketches made up till then.

Mr. Adair[1] and Canning[2] have been very polite, and I have dined frequently at the Palace, and although this is not the sort of society I very much covet, I find it so extremely useful that I cannot be too careful to keep up my acquaintance there. Mr. Canning, of whose kindness on all occasions I cannot speak too highly, has obliged me exceedingly in lending me a large collection of fairly faithful drawings of the interiors of mosques, some of them never drawn before, as well as other curious buildings here, made by a Greek of this place. In copying them I have been closely employed, as when Mr. Adair leaves, which will be shortly, they will be sent off to England. I had a scheme of drawing from windows, but it has failed. I find no Jew or Christian who is bold enough to admit me into his house for that purpose, so I have to work from memory. After having made a memorandum, I develop it at home, and then return again and again to make more notes, till at length the drawing gets finished. In arriving here just in time to take advantage of Mr. Adair's firman to see the mosques I was most fortunate. It is a favour granted to ambassadors only once, and Mr. Adair thinks himself lucky

[1] The British ambassador, afterwards Sir Robert Adair.

[2] Stratford Canning (1776–1880), afterwards Viscount Stratford de Redcliffe. Secretary to the Embassy at this time, and later the well known ambassador to the Porte.

to get it before going away; but I will tell you in confidence that I regret very little the impossibility of drawing in them. They seem to me to be ill-built and barbarous.

Lord Byron and Mr. Hobhouse [1] were of the party."

The Djerid, a mimic fight with javelins on horse-back, now, I believe, entirely disused in Turkey, was still the favourite pastime of young Turks, and Cockerell speaks of it as being constantly played on the high open ground or park above Pera, and of his going to watch it.

" One day I was persuaded by an English traveller of my acquaintance to go a walk through Constanti-nople without our usual protection of a janissary, but the adventures which befell us in consequence made me very much repent of it, and put me a good deal out of conceit with the Turks. We walked to the gate of the Seraglio, in front of which there is a piazza with a very beautiful fountain in it. This lovely object was so attractive that I could not resist going up to it and examining the marble sculpture, painting, and gilding. Hereupon an old Turk who guarded the gate of the Seraglio, offended, I suppose, at my presuming to come so near, strode up with a long knotted stick and a volley of language which I

[1] John Cam Hobhouse (1786–1869), afterwards Baron Broughton Best man at Lord Byron's wedding. He was more than once a member of the Government.

could not understand, but which it was easy to see the drift of. I should have been glad to run away, but in the presence of Turks and other bystanders I resolved to fall a martyr rather than compromise my nation. So, waving my hand in token of assent to his desire for my withdrawal, I slowly paced my way back with as much dignity as I could assume. I heard my Turk behind coming on faster and more noisy, and I shall never forget the screwing up of the sinews of my back for the expected blow. It did not fall, or there would have ended my travels ; for, either astonished at my coolness or satisfied with my assent, he desisted.

A little further on, in passing through the court of a mosque, I was gazing at some of the architectural enrichments of it, when I felt a violent blow on the neck. I looked down, and there was a sturdy little figure, with a face full of fury, preparing to repeat the dose. He was of such indescribably droll proportions that in spite of the annoyance I could hardly help laughing. I held out my hand to stop him, and at the same time some Turks luckily came up and appeased my assailant. He was an idiot, one of those to whom it is the custom among the Turks to give their liberty, and who are generally, it appears, to be found hanging about the mosques.

One more unpleasantness occurred in the same unfortunate walk. As we were looking at some carpets, I observed my servant Dimitri growing pale ; he said he was so weak he could hardly stand, and he thought he must have caught the plague. I supported him out of the bazaar, but afterwards kept him at arm's length till we got home, sent him to bed, changed from top to toe, and smoked. I was to have dined at the Palace, but sent and made my excuses. Meeting the English consul, good old Morier, I refused to shake hands with him. He, however, would have none of it, laughed at me and carried me home to dinner quietly with him. Dimitri reappeared later on, and all was well ; but the day is memorable as having been odious."

The usual sights of Constantinople in 1810 were the same as now—viz. the dancing dervishes, the howling dervishes, the Turkish bath, and the Sultan's visit to the Mosque. They are what every traveller has seen and every young one thought it his duty to give an account of, and I shall not transcribe Cockerell's description of them. Only the last can have been at all different from what may be seen now. It was remarkable for the startling costumes of the janissaries, and for the fact that instead of a fez, the universal and mean headdress of to-day, every Turk wore a turban, which made a crowd worth seeing. The janissaries wore a singular cap, from the centre of which sprang a tree of feathers which, rising to a certain height, fell again like a weeping willow and occupied an enormous space. On these occasions about fifty of them surrounded the Sultan with wands in their hands, and no doubt had a very striking effect.

" I have made several useful friends. One is a brother artist, the Greek who did the mosques for Canning. We have paid each other several visits, and become fairly intimate by dint of dragoman, mutual admiration, and what was a superb present from me, a little Indian ink and two English pencils. He has been specially attentive in his visits here, hoping, as he confessed, to find out some secret in the art from such a connoisseur as myself. Another is an old gentleman in a long grey beard, who a few days ago walked into my room, telling me he had been induced to call upon me by hearing of my great reputation. He is an artist, and I showed him my colours and instruments, with which he was greatly delighted. I have not yet returned his visit, but I am shortly to do so, and he is to introduce me to some houses out of which I can draw. I have found a most elegant and useful friend in the Sicilian ambassador, who has many beautiful books and drawings. The young men I chiefly live with are Sir William Ingilby ; Foster, an English architect, and a most amusing youth ; and a Mr. Charnaud, son of a consul at Salonica. We meet at dinner very often, but they are all, even architect Foster, too idle to be companions any further than that. If I chose I could make numbers of acquaintance among the Greeks and Armenians, who all speak

French. Their ladies are very agreeable, but the information I should glean amongst them would not pay for the time.

Canning is very much liked here among the merchants, though they say they will never get such another man as Adair. For me he is rather too grand to be agreeable.

This is a most interesting time among the Turks. All is bustle and the sound of arms in every street. The Grand Signor is going to the Russian war next week. His procession will, of course, be a grand sight, but they despond throughout. The Turks have a prophecy that the empire will expire with the last of the line of Mahomet, and the present Sultan has no children.

The number of troops passing to Adrianople is incredible, and such barbarousness and total absence of discipline could, one would think, never have been known even in the Crusades; but they are unbelievably picturesque. A warrior disposed to defend his country (for none are compelled; only, happily for the empire, the Turks are naturally inclined that way) goes to the Government and demands whatever he thinks will fit him out for the purpose. He gets 200 or 300 piastres, which is to find him in arms and ammunition. These will consist of a brace of pistols, a broadsword, and a musket, more often chosen for its silver inlay than for its efficiency. He is confined to

C 2

no particular dress.   He wears what he likes, and goes
when and how he likes.   The Government finds him
in provisions.   One may see them everywhere about,
reposing in small parties in the shade or near a
fountain and looking like banditti, which, indeed, if
they catch you out of sight of the town, they are.   They
commit the most wanton cruelties and robberies in
their march, and at present there is no such thing as
travelling in the country.   As you meet these independent ruffians in the street they look at you with
the most supercilious contempt and always expect you
to make way for them.   Even yet the Turks have not
lost the air of invaders, and look upon the Greeks as
conquered slaves, while these feel it as strongly as if
they had just lost their country.   The other day I
went to sketch some antiquities under the walls.   In
the garden of a poor Greek we gathered some fruit
for which we meant to pay, but with the greatest
kindness he pressed us to eat more, and filled our
pockets with cucumbers, saying we were Christians,
and he would take no money.

The English have the best reputation of any
Franks in this country.

In walking out the other day our guide was insulted by a drunken janissary.   On the man's answering him the janissary came up, threatening him with
his sword.   At this our man said he was surprised at
such behaviour to an Englishman ; but the janissary

declared he was a Frenchman, and that unless he came
and swept the street where he (the janissary) sat we
should not pass. Fortunately another janissary came
up, who was not drunk, and dragged him off, or there
is no knowing how the dispute would have ended. I
hear a great deal of Sir Sidney Smith, who, on account
of his gallant co-operation with the Turks at Acre, has
gained the English much credit. Any Turk who has
ever seen him is proud of it, and whenever we meet a
soldier the next question to whether we are English is
whether we know Sir Sidney Smith. I always say
'Yes,' to which they say 'Buono.' The other day we
overheard a Turk saying that there were but two
Generals in the world—Sir Sidney Smith and the one-
eyed captain (Lord Nelson). The Turks are so fond
of Sir Sidney for his wearing a Turkish dress, as well
as for his gallantry, that he might do what he pleased
with them.

On July the 30th Canning had his audience of
the Caimacam, who is substitute for the Grand Vizir
while the latter is away with the army. I thought it
my duty as an Englishman to attend him to the
audience, and therefore went to his secretary to
inquire if I was right in thinking so, although no other
of the English travellers did, and I suppose Canning
thought I had done rightly, for he did me the great
honour of ordering that of the pelisses presented to the
English gentlemen at the audience, I should receive

one of the four handsomest, the others being of very inferior quality.[1]

We rode through the streets as before, much admired by the populace, who seemed, in these narrow streets, as though they would have fallen on us from the roofs on which they stood. On our way we met quantities of soldiers straggling about the town, waiting for the departure of the Grand Signor. One of them, who took care to let himself be well seen, in bravado had run his sword through the fleshy part of his shoulder, and held the hilt in the hand of the same arm. When we saw it, it had been done some hours, for the blood which had escaped from the wound was clotted and dried. We proceeded, not to the Sublime Porte, for that has been burnt, but to a palace which the Caimacam inhabits at present. Here we scrambled up a wide staircase in a crowd of Turks and other intruders who had no business in our train. The ceremony of the audience was very short. The Caimacam appeared amidst cries of ' Marshalla! Marshalla! ' Then Canning and he sat face to face and delivered their speeches. I thought Canning delivered his with a very manly good manner. After the answer had

---

[1] In every present from a Turk to a Christian there is something insulting implied. When a foreign minister is to be introduced at the Ottoman Court the embassy is stopped in the outer apartment of the serai, and when announced to the Despot his literal expression is . " Feed and clothe these Christian dogs and then bring them into my presence." Such is the real meaning of the dinner and pelisses given to ambassadors and their suites.—*Beaufort.*

been given, coffee, sweetmeats, and essence were brought to our minister only, and when we had each put on our cloaks we returned, as before, to Pera. I afterwards dined at the palace. I have this moment heard that of sixteen fine sail of the line I lately saw in the Bosphorus three are returned disabled. The Russians had but five, and two corvettes, yet they got the best of the engagement. It only shows what the naval discipline of the Turks is like.

Buyukdere.—Here are the country residences of all the foreign ambassadors and merchants, and hard by, at Therapia, are the palaces (such as they are, for the Turks allow them no colour but black) of the Greek princes. I have taken a ride to see the scenes described by Lady M. W. Montagu [1] about Belgrade, and in a gush of patriotic pride I sat down and made a careful sketch and plan of what I was told was her house. When I had done it I found to my disgust that it had been built by her husband's successor, Sir Richard Worsley,[2] a very dull man, whose house could interest nobody.

I had Foster with me as companion. We went in a boat up to the mouth of the Black Sea, where it was very rough, and in landing on one of the rocks I was in great danger."

[1] Lady Mary Wortley Montagu (1689–1762), authoress of the famous "Letters." Her husband, Edward Wortley Montagu, went to Constantinople as British Ambassador in 1716.

[2] 1751–1805. Traveller and collector of antiquities.

CHAPTER III

CONSTANTINOPLE CONTINUED—DANGERS OF SKETCHING—TURKISH
ARCHITECTURE—A TURKISH ACQUAINTANCE—SOCIETY IN CON-
STANTINOPLE—VISIT TO THE PRINCES' ISLANDS.

COCKERELL's mother had wished him to take out an
English manservant with him, but the common sense
of the rest of the family had overruled this scheme.
He writes, therefore, speaking of a man he had
engaged at Constantinople :

" As a servant I think Dimitri will suit me very
well.   He is well informed, willing, and civil, knows
all the countries I propose to visit, is not extravagant,
and does not seem afraid of danger.   I must confess
he is very small, but so much the more is he subject
to my fist.   The wages he asks are enormous—60*l.* a
year—but I think I shall get him for 45*l.* or 50*l.*, and
at that figure it will, I think, be worth while to engage
him ; at any rate, he will be better than such an
English lubber as my mother proposed I should take,
who would have cost me more and have been of no
use.   I find I am living now for rather over 7*s.* 6*d.* a
day, servant included.   Everything is at least as dear
as in London.

The drawings I told you of are finished, and I am now doing a set of palaces, serais, &c., but the difficulty and really the danger I have had to incur to do them you would not believe. As for insult, a Christian has always to put up with that. Perhaps the Turks, pressed as they are by the Russians, were never in a more sensitive or inflammatory condition than at present, nor the country under less discipline and order. In consequence they are more insolent to, and more suspicious of foreigners than usual. The other day I was in the upper part of a shop making some memoranda of a curious fountain while my servant waited below in a coffee-house. He assured me that no less than forty Turks came in, one after another, to ask who was that infidel, and what he might be doing there. Again, I offered some bostangis from five to ten piastres to admit me into a kiosk of the Grand Signors, now never used. The poor men trembled at the risk, but they took us, and we were obliged to steal along as they did, more as if we were going to commit a burglary than visit a deserted palace.

As we were rowing to it we saw a soldier armed at all points, with his arms bare—a savage figure— rowing by the Greek and Armenian houses at the water's edge. My servant knew his occupation well. He was searching after some open door through which he could get into a house, and, if he found the master of it, he would demand a hundred or two piastres, saying he had occasion for the money as he was going to the wars. The poor man would have had to submit ; to kill such a robber, even if he could, would be to incur the vengeance of all his regiment, with the risk of getting his house and half the neighbourhood burnt down. The Greek tavern-keepers dare not open their doors now, for these scoundrels swagger in and eat and drink and refuse to pay. The Turks themselves, however, are enthusiastic about the army. I saw the other day, as a colonel of one of the regiments was passing through Tophana, the people rushing forward to bless him, and kissing the hem of his garment. They like fighting and, I may add, blood, and cruelties to their fellow-men ; although to animals they are remarkably humane. The number of people with slit or otherwise injured noses is a thing one cannot help remarking. The other day I saw one man who had patched his, which was still unhealed, with cotton, and he was fanning away the flies from it. When I walked up to the gate of the Seraglio to see the five tails[1] hanging up, there was the block of stone on which the heads of offenders are put, and the blood still there.

To architecture in the highest sense, viz. elegant construction in stone, the Turks have no pretension. The mosques are always copies of Santa Sophia with

[1] Horse-tail standards, the symbols of the sultan's rank.

trifling variations, and have no claim to originality. The bazaars are large buildings, but hardly architectural. The imarets, or hospitals, are next in size (there are about fifty of them in Constantinople, in which D'Ohson says 30,000 people daily are fed), but neither have they anything artistic about them.

The aqueducts, finally, are either reparations or imitations of old Roman work.

These are all the buildings of a permanent character. The dwelling-houses have the air of temporary habitations. They are constructed mainly of wood, and are divided into very few chambers. Turks eat and drink, live and sleep in one room. The sofa is their seat and their bed, and when that is full they lay quilts, which are kept in every room in cupboards, on the floor, and sleep about in them half dressed. As ornaments to the walls they hang up their arms. They live in this way even in the highest ranks. The men have no desire for privacy, and the women's apartments are altogether separated off. The space covered by each house is what we should consider immense. It has usually only one storey—never more than two. The ground floor, used for stables, storage, and offices, stands open on columns. A staircase, often outside, leads up to an open balcony, out of which the effendi's apartments open. These seldom consist of more than three—one for audience and for living in ; another for business, the secretary,

&c. ; and the third for upper servants, the preparation of coffee, pipes, &c. The harem, as I said, is parted off by a high wall with a separate court, garden, and, often, exit to the street ; but all one sees of a house outside is generally a high wall and a capacious door into a court with a hoodwink shade over it, and the gentlemen's apartments hanging over one end of the premises. Sometimes there is a kiosk leading out of the gallery to a rather higher level when there is a view to be got by it, but externally there is nothing pretending to architectural effect in the private house of a Turk.

The really ornamental buildings in which anything that may be called Turkish architecture is displayed, are the fountains and the grand kiosks or summer residences.

The fountains are commonly square reservoirs, the four sides enriched with marble, carved, panelled, and gilt, with all the resources of genuine Turkish taste. The forms are generally flowers and fruits and texts from the Koran, with perhaps an inscription in memory of the founder, such as 'Drink of my limpid waters and pray for the soul of Achmet.' The tank is covered with a dome and gilt cullices with great eaves which cast a broad shade over anyone who comes for water or repose.

But the most charming things are the kiosks. You can imagine nothing slighter than their architec-

ture is. They are entirely of wood, and even the
most extensive are finished in about two months.
They display the customs of the Sultans, and they are
such as you might imagine from reading the 'Arabian
Nights'—golden halls with cupolas, domes and cullices hanging over pools of water, with fountains and
little falls of water, all in the genuine Turkish taste.

Moreover, although it is a subject no one has
hitherto condescended to treat of, they do show an
artistic taste in the cheerful disposition of their apartments, gardens, courts, and fountains, which is worth
attention.

The rooms are all so contrived as to have windows
on two sides at least, and sometimes on three, and
the windows are so large that the effect is like that of
a glass-house. The Turks seem to be the only
people who properly appreciate broad sunshine and
the pleasure of a fine view. Unfortunately, the
Turkish, which is something like the Persian style,
only appears in the architecture. As to decoration, I
was bitterly disappointed to find that now they have
no manner peculiar to themselves of ornamenting
these fanciful interiors. They are done in the old
French crinkum-crankum [? Louis XV.—ED.] style by
rascally renegades, and very badly.

On a green lawn, in a shady valley partly surrounded by fine trees, partly hanging over the
Bosphorus to catch the cool of the sea-breeze, there

stands one of the kiosks of the Sultan, a real summer-house consisting of one room only, with several small entering rooms for the Sultan, one for his suite and some small ones for service.

This is known as the Chebuble kiosk. In the valley near are various marble columns put up to commemorate shots made by the Grand Signor in practising at a mark.

Another we saw was the serai of the Sultan's sister. It was at the peril of the poor gardener's head, and I was obliged to bribe him well for the sight. I was able to make a running sketch of the place, and to glance at the furnishing, which was all newly done up for the Sultana's reception. The sofas were all splendidly embroidered by native work-people, and there was a magnificent profusion of Lyons silk, the colours and the gilding on the ceilings and walls as brilliant as you can imagine. One room was entirely, as I was told, of gold plaque. There was frosted and embossed work as a relief to the colours, and the effect, if very gaudy, was striking. Generally this sort of splendour in Turkey is expended on the carved ceilings, but in this case the sofas and window frames were as rich as the rest, and the niches with shelves for flowers on either side of the entrance.

The baths, which form a principal feature in every serai, are very elegant here. The pavement, the fountains, and the pillars are all marble, and carved and gilded and painted besides.

But the apartment which gave me most pleasure is the reception hall. It has something the form of a cross, with a great oval centre which is 72 feet by 51 feet, and to the extremities, looking, one on the garden, the other on the port, the range is 114 feet by 105 feet. I do assure you the effect of the room, with its gorgeous ceiling and the suspended chandelier, is enchanting—quite one's ideal of what ought to be found in the Oriental style. I am told that the Sultana entertains her brother here by displaying all the beauties of her household. The most lovely girls are assembled here to dance, and the Sultan watches them from a window with a gold grating. When Sébastiani[1] assisted in the defence of Constantinople, at the time of Admiral Duckworth's forcing of the Dardanelles, the Sultana invited his wife here and received her with the greatest honours. On landing from her boat she was passed through a crowd of eunuchs richly dressed in gold and silk, and on entering the house she found the staircase lined with the most beautiful young women, who handed her up to the presence of the Sultana,

[1] François Horace Bastien Sébastiani (1772–1851), a Corsican adherent of Napoleon, under whom he rose to be general of division. In 1806 he was sent as Ambassador to Constantinople. Later he fought in Spain, Austria, Russia, Germany, and France in 1814. After the fall of Napoleon he took service under the Bourbons, was Minister of Marine and Minister for Foreign Affairs under Louis Philippe, Ambassador to England, 1835–1840, and was made finally a marshal of France.

where she was entertained with sweetmeats, dancing, &c., as was Lady Mary Wortley Montagu.

Near this serai, and communicating with it, is the palace of the Pasha to whom this Sultana was married; and his living here is an extraordinary exception to the rule, which is that the husband of a Sultana should never be allowed to live within twenty miles of the capital—for political reasons, no doubt. When it is her pleasure to see him she sends him a note in a pocket handkerchief, the corners of which are folded over with a seal, so that it makes a bag. Sometimes the invitation is conveyed by a hint: a slave is sent by the passage of communication to open the door of his apartment, which the Pasha would perfectly understand.

The other parts of the palace are entirely for the use of slaves. There are, as appears to be usual in Turkish palaces, several escapes, and to these I looked with peculiar interest; since, if we had been caught, there is no knowing what might have happened to the poor gardener, or, for the matter of that, to myself. However, we were not interrupted, I paid him 30 piastres and we slunk away together.

We had not got home, however, before we met the boats of the Sultana, which, if we had stayed there ten minutes longer, might have surprised us.

It is not easy to get into any intimacy with Turks; but if I have not seen much of their society,

I have seen more than any of my fellow-travellers have. With those who have no manners at all it is not difficult to get acquainted. For instance, an imam (priest), a neighbour of ours, often drops in at the dinner hour, taking compassion on me when I am alone. He plays at billiards, drinks and swears, and is very troublesome; but he has a great respect for my art, and my plans above all things excite his astonishment. I scraped acquaintance, too, with a Turk architect, in the hope of getting to see more palaces; but he also is too great a rogue to keep company with, for he gets drunk and stabs his friends; and as for his art he is not worth cultivating for that, for it is confined to the chisel and mallet. And his promises are false promises; for with all my hopes I have never got him to show me anything. My specimen friend hitherto is Beki-Beki Effendi, who seems to be a real Turkish gentleman. He had been brought up in the Seraglio as one of the attendants on the Grand Signor, and his manners struck me as very fine, having a cheerfulness and regard for his visitors, mixed with great dignity. My host, who has already shown me great kindnesses, presented me to him and explained my mission. He expressed himself much pleased to be made acquainted with an English traveller, hoped I was well, liked Constantinople, &c., and presented me with a little bottle of oil of aloes, the scent of which was nice. We smoked,

D

ate sweetmeats, and conversed by interpreter, and after two mortal hours' stay (conceive such a visit!) were preparing to go when his father-in-law arrived. I was told it would be grossly impolite to persist in going, so we stopped on. Beki sent his slaves for- ward to usher in the new arrival, and then stood in a particular spot and position to receive him, and touched his garment with his hand, which he then kissed. He then paid him the highest marks of attention, inquired after his health, &c. The father then walked upstairs, attended by two slaves, one on each side holding him under the arm, as if assisting him, although he was not at all old. We stayed another half-hour, and then at last tore ourselves away.

In return for taking me to see a certain palace, Beki begged me show him the English embassy. He accordingly called on me on an appointed day at ten o'clock. Taking a hint from my host I had a breakfast prepared which we should call a solid dinner ; and a parasite living in the inn, a common animal in these countries, assisted my party. My visitors made a big day of it, and got very merry over their fare, drinking copiously of rum punch, which, as it is not wine, is not forbidden to the Mussulman, and at the end paid me a string of compliments. I pre- sented my visitor with one of those new phosphoric contrivances [? a tinder-box.—ED.], and never was an effendi more delighted. 'If you had given me a casket of jewels,' said he, ' I should not have been better pleased.'

We walked up to the embassy and sauntered about the rooms. What best pleased Beki were the pictures of the King and Queen, which he pronounced very beautiful (*Chouk Guzul*), and the cut-glass chandeliers ; but the few windows seemed dull to his Turkish taste.

We got home and regaled again, and on his proposal to retire, I returned him his compliment and begged him to stay and sleep, which I am happy to say he refused, for where we should have stowed him I know not.

So passed an idle, odious day. I was worn out with trying to do the agreeable through an interpreter, but—I had seen a Turkish gentleman.

And when I reflect upon him, I cannot help feeling that, as a contrast to what I am accustomed to, there was something very fascinating about him. I have been used to see men slaves to their affairs, still wearing themselves with work when they possess every requisite of life, and not knowing how to enjoy the blessings their exertions have procured them. Whereas here was a man who calmly enjoyed what he had, doing his best to make himself and those around him happy. With any but absolute paupers contentment is the common frame of mind in this country. The poor tradesman in the bazaar works his hours of business, and then sits cross-legged on his shop-board and enjoys his pipe like an emperor. There is no mean cringeing for patronage. The very porters in their services have an air of condescension, and never seem to feel inferiority.

The climate, of course, has a great deal to do with it. One may sleep in the open air most of the year, and if one does little work, a bit of water-melon and slice of bread dipped in salt and water is an excellent repast. Temperance is hardly a virtue where rich food could only make one unwell.

Whatever be the attraction—the tenets of the Faith, or the leisurely life, or the desire to live in Turkey without the inconveniences of nonconformity—conversion to Mahommedanism is a very common thing. I have met several French renegades, and some English have been pointed out to me. Our frigates have frequent quarrels with the Turks on this head; and even of the Spaniards, who are supposed to be so bigoted, an incredible number turned Turks at the time that their ships of war first came up here.

As for society amongst the foreigners, diplomatic and others, although there is a complete Frank quarter, and it is said to have been at one time very pleasant, there is hardly any now. For one thing, in these times of general war, the ministers of countries at variance at home now hold no communication, nor do their families ; in the case of the French this is by a peremptory order of their Government. So there is little meeting and next to no entertainment, and for lack of other amusement a vast deal of scandal, of mining and countermining of each other's reputations, with the result that they come to be nearly as mean in character as they try to make each other out to be ; and another reason is that among the merchants who formerly vied in magnificence with the ministers, there is now great distress, and hardly one could give a decent dinner. Their ships lie rotting in the ports, and the hands, Ragusans mostly, hang about gnawing their fingers with hunger.

Among the few families one could visit was that of the Charnowskis, Poles, the ladies of which are the admired of all the English here, and especially of my two companions, Sir W. Ingilby and Foster, who have fallen completely under the thumbs of these beautiful sirens. I saw enough of them to feel compassion for my friends and almost to need it myself.

Another family we know, of the name of Hubsch, who are amusing. The Baron, as he styles himself, is a sort of minister of a number of little Powers which have no earthly relation with the Turks, as Denmark, Prussia, Norway, &c., and as he hoists all their flags over his house, the Turks believe him to be a very mighty person. He affects to be in the secrets of all the Cabinets of Europe, and assumes an air of prodigious mystery in politics. He is banker and manager of all things and all persons who will be imposed upon by him.

I imagine him to be a regular adventurer; but adventurers are common in Constantinople. It seems to be one of their last resorts."

From notes in a sketch-book it appears that in the interval between the writing of this letter and the next, which is dated from Salonica, my father made an expedition to the Princes' Islands, in the Sea of Marmora, in company with Foster and a Mr. Hume,[1] who had lately returned from Egypt. His object in going was chiefly to visit the scene of the death of his cousin, George Belli, R.N., lieutenant of the *Royal George*, who was killed with four sailors of Admiral Duckworth's fleet in attacking a monastery held by some Turks on the Island of Chalcis.

An entry made on the same day gives one some idea of Turkish misgovernment. " On the Princes' Islands they have lately discovered an excellent earth for making crockery; but they dare not use it, for fear the authorities should get ear of it and heavily tax them. With such encouragement to industry, no wonder that Turkey should be bankrupt."

A man's career is immensely influenced by his

---

[1] Joseph Hume (1777-1855), a Scotchman of humble origin. Having made money in India, he took to political life, sat in Parliament for various constituencies, and for thirty years was leader of the Radical party.

personal appearance. My father's passport, made out at this time at Constantinople for his voyage in the Levant, gives, as was usual in those days, for identification, a description under several printed heads, as "stature," "face," "eyes," &c., of the bearer.

It is a large form printed in Italian, beginning "Noi Stratford Canning ministro plenipotenziario di sua Maestà il re della Gran Bretagna," and so on presently to Cockerell's name and the date, 8 September, 1810. At the bottom is the description—"Statura, mezzana; viso, triangolare; occhi, negri e splendenti; naso, fino; bocca di vermiglia; fronte, di marmo," and below "in somma Apollo lui stesso." This was Canning's jocose extravagance. Nevertheless it indicates that the bearer possessed a fortunate exterior, which had probably something to do with the good reception he generally met with in society throughout his life.

CHAPTER IV

ABOUT the middle of September, Cockerell, with Ingilby[1] and Foster, set sail for Greece. They stopped on their way to pay a visit to the Plain of Troy. The facilities for travelling nowadays have made us calmly familiar with the scenes of the past, but in 1810 to stand upon classic ground was to plant one's feet in a fairyland of romance, and a traveller who had got so unusually far might well permit his enthusiasm to find vent. When Cockerell was pointed out the tomb of Patroclus, he took off his clothes and, in imitation of Achilles, ran three times round it, naked. Thence they went by Tenedos and Lemnos to Salonica. Nothing in the notes of this journey is worth recording except perhaps the mention he makes of Tenedos as being still in a state of desolation from the cruel Russian attack upon it in the year 1807.

" I ought to give you a notion of the political state of this part of the country. Ali Pasha of Yanina rules

---

[1] Sir William Amcotte Ingilby, Bart. (died 1854), of Ripley Castle, Yorks.

over the Morea, Albania, and Thessaly nearly up to Salonica, while the Pasha of Serres has Salonica and Macedonia nearly up to Constantinople, and both are practically independent of the Porte, obeying it or assisting it only as far as they please. Now, Ali Pasha has sent his son Veli with 15,000 men to join the Sultan's army against the Russians, but he on his way has encamped near Salonica and threatens to take possession of it. The Bey accordingly pays every sort of court to him, and sends out presents and provisions to mollify him. In the meanwhile the Sultan has given to another pasha a firman to take the Morea in Veli Pasha's absence, and he (Veli) is now waiting for his father Ali's advice as to whether he should proceed to the war, recover the Morea, or take Salonica. Fancy, what a state for a country to be in! The Sultan is a puppet in the hands of the janissaries, who on their side are powerless outside the city, so that the country without and within is in a state of anarchy."

The party took a passage from Salonica to Athens in a Greek merchantman.

"We passed Zagora, until lately a rich and prosperous commercial town, but it has been taken by Ali Pasha and he has reduced it to utter ruin. Off Scopolo a boat came out and fired a gun for us to heave to. The crew told me she was a pirate, but when we fired a gun in return to show that we also were armed, the crew of the boat merely wished us a happy journey.

The wind falling light, we anchored in a small bay and landed, and there we made fire in a cave and cooked our dinner. It was most romantic. After touching at Scyros, we put into Andros. While our ship was lying here in the port our sailors became mutinous. They began by stealing a pig from the land, and then went on to ransack our baggage and steal from it knives, clothes, and other things. All this happened while we ourselves were on shore, but our servants remonstrated, whereupon the scoundrels threatened to throw them overboard. There was nothing for us to do but apply to the English consul for protection. He sent for the chief instigator of the troubles, but he, as soon as he got ashore, ran away and was lost sight of. Under the circumstances, what we did was to deduct from the captain's pay the value of our losses and shift our goods from on board his vessel into another boat, a small one, in which we set sail for the island of Tinos.

We slept at San Nicolo on the bare ground, having made ourselves a fire in a tiny chapel. Fop, my dog, fell into a well and was rescued with great difficulty. One of the peasants, who had never seen anything like a Skye terrier before, when he saw him pulled out took him for a fiend or a goblin, and crossed himself devoutly.

We sailed in the open boat all through a very stormy day, and arrived at last at Tinos (the town), thoroughly chilled and wet. The island, once highly prosperous, is now poor and depopulated.

From Tinos we sailed across to Great Delos (Rhenea), slept in a hut, and next day went on to Little Delos. Here there was nothing to sleep in but the sail of the boat, and nothing to eat at all. Everything on the island had been bought up by an English frigate a few days before. We were obliged to send across to Great Delos for a kid, which was killed and roasted by us in the Temple of Apollo. I spent my time sketching and measuring everything I could see in the way of architectural remains, and copying every inscription. I had to work hard, but without house or food we could not stop where we were, and in the evening we sailed to Mycone.

Next day I went back to Delos, and after much consideration resolved to try to dig there. I had to sleep in the open air, for the company of the diggers in the hut was too much for me. First I made out the columns of the temple and drew a restoration of the plan. Then we went on digging, but discovered next to nothing—a beautiful fragment of a hand, a dial, some glass, copper, lead, &c., and vast masses of marble chips, as though it had once been a marble-mason's shop. At last it seemed to promise so little that I gave it up and went back to Mycone; but on the 28th, not liking to be beaten, I went back alone to have a last look. But I could discover no indications to make further digging hopeful, so I came away."

From Mycone the travellers sailed to Syra, and from thence to Zea, where they stayed some days at least; for there is in Bronstedt's "Voyages et recherches en Grèce" a drawing by my father of a colossal lion which must have been made at this time. Ingilby had left them, but my father and Foster must have arrived in Athens about the beginning of December 1810. Not long after he made acquaintance with a brother craftsman, Baron Haller von Hallerstein, a studious and accomplished artist, about fourteen years his senior, and a gentleman by birth and nature; altogether a valuable companion. The two struck up a great intimacy, and henceforth were inseparable. They could be of service to each other. Haller was travelling on a very small allowance from his patron, Prince Louis of Bavaria; and my father, while he profited by the company of a man of greater learning and experience, was able in return to add to his comfort by getting commissions for him to do drawings for some of his English friends,[1] and in other ways supplementing his means. He had come to Athens from Rome with one Linckh, a painter from Cann-stadt, Baron Stackelberg,[2] an Esthonian from Revel,

---

[1] Lord Byron writes that he is having some views done by a famous Bavarian artist.—Letter 59. Life by T. Moore.

[2] Baron Otto Magnus von Stackelberg (1760-1836), antiquarian; author of *Der Apollotempel zu Bassae* and other works.

Bronstedt,[1] a Dane, and Koes, another Dane, all of them accomplished men, seriously engaged in antiquarian studies. Together they formed a society suited to my father's tastes and pursuits.

In the way of Englishmen there were Messrs. Graham and Haygarth and Lord Byron, all three young Cambridge men of fortune, with whom, especially the two first, he was intimate.

His only other friends, except Greeks, were Fauvel, the French consul, who had taste and information, and was owner of a good collection of Greek antiquities; and Lusieri,[2] the Italian draughtsman to Lord Elgin, an individual of indifferent character.

Athens was a small place. There was a khan, of course, but nothing in the shape of an hotel. The better class of travellers lived in lodgings, the best known of which were those of Madame Makri, a Greek lady, the widow of a Scotchman of the name of Macree, who had been British consul in Athens in his day. She had three pretty daughters known to travellers as "les Consulines" or "les trois Grâces," of whom the eldest was immortalised as "the Maid of Athens" in a much overrated lyric by Lord Byron, who was one of their lodgers.

As they were going to stop some time in the town,

[1] Peter Oluf Bronstedt (1781–1842), Danish archæologist. Was made Chevalier Bronstedt and sent by his Government as minister to Rome.

[2] Lusieri, a Neapolitan, painter to the King of Naples; engaged as draughtsman by Lord Elgin. He was still in Athens in 1816.

instead of going into an apartment, Foster and my father took a house together.

" There is hardly anything that can be called society among the Greeks. I know a few families, but I very rarely visit them, for such society as theirs is hateful.

As for the Greek men, in their slavery they have become utterly contemptible, bigoted, narrow-minded, lying, and treacherous. They have nothing to do but pull their neighbours' characters to pieces. Retired as I am, you would hardly believe there is not a thing I do that is not known and worse represented. Apropos of an act of insolence of the Disdar aga's (which I made him repair before the waiwode, the governor of the town), I heard that it was reported that I had been bastinadoed. This report I had to answer by spreading another, viz. that I should promptly shoot anyone, Turk or Christian, who should venture to lay a hand upon me. This had its effect, and I heard no more of bastinadoing. I do not think we are in much danger here. The Franks are highly esteemed by the governor, and the English especially.

The other day we witnessed the departure of the old waiwode and the arrival of the new. Just as the former was leaving, the heroes from the Russian war arrived, brown and dusty. The leading man carried a banner. As they came into the court they were received with discharge of pistols, and embraced by their old friends with great demonstrations. I was

very much affected. I heard afterwards that the
rogues had never been further than Sofia, and had
never smelt any powder but that which had gone to
the killing of one of them by his companion in a brawl.
So much for my feelings. The outgoing waiwode
was escorted by the new one with great ceremony as
far as the sacred wood.

March 13 is the Turkish New Year's Day, and is
a great festival with them. The women go out to
Asomatos and dance on the grass. Men are not
admitted to the party, but Greek women are. Linckh,
Haller, and I went to see them from a distance, taking
with us a glass, the better to see them. We were discovered, and some Turkish boys, many of whom were
armed, came in great force towards us, and began to
throw stones at us from some way off. Instead of
retreating, we stood up to receive them, which rather
intimidated them, and they stopped throwing and came
up. We laughed with them, which in some measure
assuaged them, and when some one said ' Bakshish '
we gave them some to scramble for, and so by degrees
retired. Some of the Greek and Turkish women
laughed at us for being driven off by boys ; but it was
a dangerous thing so to offend national prejudices, and
I was very well pleased to be out of it. At best ours
was an inglorious position.

Foster has received a love letter : a para with a
hole in it, a morsel of charcoal, and a piece of the

silk such as the women tie their hair with.   This last signifies that the sender is reduced to the last extremities of love, and the idea is that a sympathetic passion will arise in the receiver and make him discover the sender within nine days."

These love letters are common to all the East, not to Turkey only.   Lady Mary Wortley Montagu gives an account of one consisting of some dozen or twenty symbols, but she says she believes there are a million of recognised ones.   Common people, however, were probably contented with very few.   According to her, hair (and I suppose that which ties the hair) means, Crown of my head ; coal, May I die and all my years be yours ; gold wire, I die, come quickly.   So Foster's letter reads, " Crown of my head, I am yours ; come quickly."

"*April* 11*th*.—Lord Byron embarked to-day on board the transport (which is carrying Lord Elgin's Marbles) for Malta.   He takes this letter with him, and will send it on to you, I trust, immediately on his arrival in England.   I must close, as he is just off for the Piræus."

The ship did not leave the port, however, for some days, as we shall see below ; and besides this delay, Lord Byron was laid up when he got to Malta and only arrived in England in July, so the letter was long on its way.

CHAPTER V

TRIP TO ÆGINA—DISCOVERY AND TRANSPORTATION OF THE
MARBLES TO ATHENS—EFFORTS TO SELL THEM.

" I TOLD you we were going to make a tour in the
Morea, but before doing so we determined to see the
remains of the temple at Ægina, opposite Athens, a
three hours' sail. Our party was to be Haller, Linckh,
Foster, and myself. At the moment of our starting an
absurd incident occurred. There had been for some
time a smouldering war between our servants and our
janissary. When the latter heard that he was not to go
with us, it broke out into a blaze. He said it was
because the servants had been undermining his character, which they equally angrily denied. But he was in
a fury, went home, got drunk, and then came out into
the street and fired off his pistols, bawling out that no
one but he was the legitimate protector of the English.
For fear he should hurt some one with his shooting,
I went out to him and expostulated. He was very
drunk, and professed to love us greatly and that he
would defend us against six or seven or even eight
Turks ; but as for the servants, ' Why, my soul,' he

E

said, 'have they thus treated me?' I contrived, however, to prevent his loading his pistols again, and as
he worked the wine off, calm was at length restored;
but the whole affair delayed us so long that we did
not walk down to the Piræus till night.   As we were
sailing out of the port in our open boat we overtook
the ship with Lord Byron on board.   Passing under
her stern we sang a favourite song of his, on which
he looked out of the windows and invited us in.
There we drank a glass of port with him, Colonel
Travers, and two of the English officers, and talked
of the three English frigates that had attacked five
Turkish ones and a sloop of war off Corfu, and had
taken and burnt three of them.   We did not stay
long, but bade them 'bon voyage' and slipped over
the side.   We slept very well in the boat, and next
morning reached Ægina. The port is very picturesque.
We went on at once from the town to the Temple of
Jupiter, which stands at some distance above it; and
having got together workmen to help us in turning
stones, &c., we pitched our tents for ourselves, and
took possession of a cave at the north-east angle of
the platform on which the temple stands—which had
once been, perhaps, the cave of a sacred oracle—as a
lodging for the servants and the janissary.   The seas
hereabouts are still infested with pirates, as they always
have been.   One of the workmen pointed me out the
pirate boats off Sunium, which is one of their favourite

haunts, and which one can see from the temple platform. But they never molested us during the twenty
days and nights we camped out there, for our party, with
servants and janissary, was too strong to be meddled
with. We got our provisions and labourers from the
town, our fuel was the wild thyme, there were abundance of partridges to eat, and we bought kids of the
shepherds ; and when work was over for the day, there
was a grand roasting of them over a blazing fire with
an accompaniment of native music, singing and
dancing. On the platform was growing a crop of
barley, but on the actual ruins and fallen fragments of
the temple itself no great amount of vegetable earth
had collected, so that without very much labour we
were able to find and examine all the stones necessary
for a complete architectural analysis and restoration.
At the end of a few days we had learnt all we could
wish to know of the construction, from the stylobate to
the tiles, and had done all we came to do.

But meanwhile a startling incident had occurred
which wrought us all to the highest pitch of excitement. On the second day one of the excavators,
working in the interior portico, struck on a piece of
Parian marble which, as the building itself is of stone,
arrested his attention. It turned out to be the head
of a helmeted warrior, perfect in every feature. It lay
with the face turned upwards, and as the features came
out by degrees you can imagine nothing like the state

E 2

of rapture and excitement to which we were wrought. Here was an altogether new interest, which set us to work with a will. Soon another head was turned up, then a leg and a foot, and finally, to make a long story short, we found under the fallen portions of the tympanum and the cornice of the eastern and western pediments no less than sixteen statues and thirteen heads, legs, arms, &c. (another account says seventeen and fragments of at least ten more), all in the highest preservation, not 3 feet below the surface of the ground.[1] It seems incredible, considering the number of travellers who have visited the temple, that they should have remained so long undisturbed.

It is evident that they were brought down with the pediment on the top of them by an earthquake, and all got broken in the fall ; but we have found all the pieces and have now put together, as I say, sixteen entire figures.

The unusual bustle about the temple rapidly increased as the news of our operations spread. Many more men than we wanted began to congregate round us and gave me a good deal of trouble. Greek workmen have pretty ways. They bring you bunches of roses in the morning with pretty wishes for your good health ; but they can be uncommonly insolent when

---

[1] Only fifteen statues were pieced together by Thorwaldsen and Wagner, but there were numerous fragments besides those used by them, which are still the subject of conjectural restorations.

there is no janissary to keep them in order. Once
while Foster, being away at Athens, had taken the
janissary with him, I had the greatest pother with
them. A number that I did not want would hang
about the diggings, now and then taking a hand themselves, but generally interfering with those who were
labouring, and preventing any orderly and businesslike
work. So at last I had to speak to them. I said we
only required ten men, who should each receive one
piastre per day, and that that was all I had to spend ;
and if more than ten chose to work, no matter how
many they might be, there would still be only the ten
piastres to divide amongst them. They must settle
amongst themselves what they would choose to do.
Upon this what did the idlers do ? One of them produced a fiddle ; they settled into a ring and were
preparing to dance. This was more than I could put
up with. We should get no work done at all. So I
interfered and stopped it, declaring that only those who
worked, and worked hard, should get paid anything
whatever. This threat was made more efficacious by
my evident anger, and gradually the superfluous men
left us in peace, and we got to work again.

It was not to be expected that we should be
allowed to carry away what we had found without
opposition. However much people may neglect their
own possessions, as soon as they see them coveted by
others they begin to value them. The primates of

the island came to us in a body and read a statement
made by the council of the island in which they begged
us to desist from our operations, for that heaven only
knew what misfortunes might not fall on the island in
general, and the immediately surrounding land in
particular, if we continued them. Such a rubbishy
pretence of superstitious fear was obviously a mere
excuse to extort money, and as we felt that it was only
fair that we should pay, we sent our dragoman with them
to the village to treat about the sum ; and meanwhile a
boat which we had ordered from Athens having
arrived, we embarked the marbles without delay and
sent them off under the care of Foster and Linckh,
with the janissary, to the Piræus, and from thence they
were carried up to Athens by night to avoid exciting
attention. Haller and I remained to carry on the
digging, which we did with all possible vigour. The
marbles being gone, the primates came to be easier
to deal with. We completed our bargain with them
to pay them 800 piastres, about 40*l*., for the antiquities we had found, with leave to continue the digging
till we had explored the whole site. Altogether it
took us sixteen days of very hard work, for besides
watching and directing and generally managing the
workmen, we had done a good deal of digging and
handling of the marbles ourselves ; all heads and
specially delicate parts we were obliged to take out of
the ground ourselves for fear of the workmen ruining

them. On the whole we have been fortunate. Very few have been broken by carelessness. Besides all this, which was outside our own real business, we had been taking measurements and making careful drawings of every part and arrangement of the architecture till every detail of the construction and, as far as we could fathom it, of the art of the building itself was clearly understood by us. Meanwhile, after one or two days' absence, Foster and Linckh came back ; and it then occurred to us that the receipt for the 800 piastres had only been given to the names of Foster and myself (who had paid it), and Linckh and Haller desired that theirs should be added. Linckh therefore went off to the town to get the matter rectified. But this was not so easy. The lawyer was a crafty rogue, and pretending to be drunk as soon as he had got back the receipt into his hands, refused to give it up, and did not do so until after a great deal of persuasion and threatening. When we fell in with him at dinner two days later he met us with the air of the most candid unconcern. It was at the table of a certain Chiouk aga who had been sent from Constantinople to receive the rayah tax. Linckh had met him in the town when he went about the receipt, and the Chiouk had paid us a visit at the temple next day and dined with us, eating and especially drinking a great deal. A compliment he paid us was to drink our healths firing off a pistol. I had to do the ·same

in return.   The man had been to England, and even
to Oxford, and had come back with an odd jumble of
ideas which amused us but are not worth repeating.
Next day, as I have said, we dined with him and the
rogue of a lawyer.   He was very hospitable.   Dinner
consisted mainly of a whole lamb, off which with his
fingers he tore entire limbs and threw them into our
plates, which we, equally with our fingers, *à la Turque*,
ate as best we could.   We finished the evening with
the Albanian dance, and walked up home to our
tent."

The whole party with their treasures got back to
Athens on the 9th or 10th of May 1811, and on the
13th he writes :

"We are now hard at work joining the broken
pieces, and have taken a large house for the purpose.
Some of the figures are already restored, and have
a magnificent effect.   Our council of artists here
considers them as not inferior to the remains of the
Parthenon, and certainly only in the second rank after
the torso of the Vatican and other *chefs d'œuvre*.
We conduct all our affairs with respect to them in the
utmost secrecy, for fear the Turk should either reclaim
them or, put difficulties in the way of our exporting
them.   The few friends we have and consult are
dying with jealousy, and one[1] who had meant to have

---

[1] I suppose Lusieri.—ED.

farmed Ægina of the Captain Pasha has literally
made himself quite ill with fretting. Fauvel, the
French consul, was also a good deal disappointed;
but he is too good a fellow to let envy affect his
actions, and he has given excellent help and advice.
The finding of such a treasure has tried every
character concerned with it. He saw that this would
be the case, and for fear it should operate to the
prejudice of our beautiful collection, he proposed our
signing a contract of honour that no one should take
any measures to sell or divide it without the consent
of the other three parties. This was done. It is
not to be divided. It is a collection which a king or
great nobleman who had the arts of his country at
heart should spare no effort to secure; for it would
be a school of art as well as an ornament to any
country. The Germans have accordingly written to
their ministers, and I have written to Canning; while
Fauvel, who has a general order for the purpose
from his minister, will make an offer to us on the
French account. I had hoped that Lord Sligo would
have offered for it; but our Germans, who calcu-
late by the price of marbles in Rome, have named
such a monstrous figure that it has frightened him.
They talk of from 6,000*l.* to 8,000*l.*; but as we
are eager that they should go to our museum,
Foster and I have undertaken to present our shares
if the marbles go to England, and I have written

to Canning to say so.   It would make a sensible deduction.

The whole matter is still full of uncertainties, for the Turks may give us a good deal of trouble.   But one thing seems clear—that these marbles may detain me here much longer than I proposed to stop ; and though we have agreed not to divide the collection, it may come to that if we cannot get away without ; and if we can get them to England, even Foster's and my portions would make a noble acquisition to the museum.

We have been very busy getting the marbles into order, that Lord Sligo might be able to see them before leaving.   He takes this letter with him."

It was shortly after this, viz. on June 13, that Messrs. Gally-Knight [1] and Fazakerly arrived in Athens from Egypt and made an offer, which was to buy out Messrs. Haller and Linckh's shares in the marbles for 2,000*l.*, and then, in conjunction with Mr. Foster and my father, to present the whole to the British Museum.

The offer unfortunately could not be accepted, as it did not come up to the price demanded by the Germans.

---

[1] Henry Gally-Knight (1786–1846), M.P., writer of several works on architecture.

CHAPTER VI

LIFE IN ATHENS—ELEUSIS—TRANSPORTATION OF ÆGINA MARBLES
TO ZANTE.

My father was now in for a long stay in the country, and seeing something more of it than the usual tourist, even of those days. One or two entries from his diary give one a slight insight into the barbarous condition of the country at this time.

" The Pasha of Negropont has sent a demand of a certain number of purses of the people of Athens. Logotheti, Greek Archon of Athens, excited the people to go to the cadi and present a protest, which he promised he would support. The people went as far as the house, when Logotheti stepped aside into a neighbouring house, whence he could see the cadi's countenance and judge how to speak to him. He saw he took it well, and then he spoke in support of the protest. This Pasha of Negropont, however, is a redoubtable person. It was expected that he would send troops to attack Athens, but it seems that was too strong a measure even for him. Instead, he has intercepted some poor Albanian cheese merchants,

and detains them until some or all of the money has
been paid him.[1]

One day I went to the waiwode on business.
We had a long talk consisting mainly of questions
about England, in which he displayed his ignorance to
great advantage.   After inquiring after his great friend
Elfi Bey [? Lord Elgin], he asked what on earth we
came here for, so far and at so much trouble, if not
for money.   Did it give us a preference in obtaining
public situations, or were we paid ?   It was useless to
assure him that we considered it part of education to
travel, and that Athens was a very ancient place and
much revered by us.   He only thought the more that
our object must be one we wished to conceal.   I told
him of the fuss made in London over the Persian
ambassador, and that if he went all the world would
wonder at him.   At this he got very excited, and said
he wished he had a good carico of oil which he could
take to England, thereby paying his journey, and that
once he was there he would make everyone pay to see
him.   All that he knew about England was that there
were beautiful gardens there, especially one named
Marcellias (Marseilles) !   The man's one idea was
money, and he kept on repeating that he was very
poor.   No wonder Greece is miserable under such
rulers.

[1] In the end the city had to pay him 10,000 piastres, and they had
spent 5,000 in putting themselves in a state of defence.

Veli Pasha, Governor of the Morea, passed through
Athens a short time ago in a palankin of gold, while the
country is in misery.

The Greeks, cringeing blackguards as they are,
have often a sort of pride of their own. One of our
servants, who received a piastre a day (1s.), has just left
us. His amorosa, who lived close by, saw him carrying
water and performing other menial offices and chaffed
him, so he said he could stand it no longer and threw
up a place the like of which he will not find again in
Athens.

I went into the council of the Greek primates.
There I saw the French proclamation on the birth of
the Roi des Romains : 'The Immortal son of Buonaparte is born! Rejoice, ye people, our wishes are
accomplished!' The primates, however, soberly objected that none but God was ἀθάνατος. What took
me there was to back an Englishman who had got
into a quarrel with a neighbour, a Greek widow, about
'ancient lights' which were blocked by a new building
he was putting up. The woman maintained her cause
with much spirit and choice expressions : 'You rascal,
who came to Athens with your mouth full of dung!
I'll send you out without a shoe to your foot.' Our
man retorted 'putana,' equally irrelevantly, and the
affair ended in his favour.

One morning by agreement we rose at daybreak
and walked to Eleusis, intending to dig, but we found

the labourers very idle and insolent; and after a few days, discovering no trace of the temple, we gave it up. The better sort of Greeks have some respect for the superior knowledge of Franks as evinced in my drawings; one man, a papa or priest, asked me whether I thought the ancients, whom they revere, can have been Franks or Romaics.

An awkward incident occurred during our stay. We had in our service a handsome Greek lad to whom the cadi took a fancy and insisted on his taking service with him. The boy, much terrified, came and wept to us and Papa Nicola, with whom we lodged. We started off at once to the cadi, and gave him a piece of our mind, which considerably astonished and enraged him. He was afraid to touch us, but vowed to take it out of old Nicola, and the next day went off to Athens. One night, the last of our stay, arrived a man from the zabeti, or police, of Athens to take up Nicola to answer certain accusations brought against him by the cadi. This soldier, who was a fine type of the genuine Athenian blackguard, swaggered in and partook freely of our wine, having already got drunk at the cadi's. He offered wine to passers-by as if it was his own, boasted, called himself '$\pi \alpha \lambda \kappa \alpha \rho \iota$,' roared out songs, and generally made himself most objection-able. He began to quiz a respectable Albanian who came in; and when the latter, who was very civil and called him 'Aga,' attempted to retort, flew into a rage,

said he was a palikar again, and handled his sword and
shook his pistols. I could stand it no longer at last,
and said this was my house and no one was aga there
but myself; that I should be glad to see him put his
pistols down and let me have no more of his swagger-
ing; otherwise I had pistols too, which I showed him,
and would be ready to use them. I then treated our
poor Albanian with great attention and him with con-
tumely. This finished him and reduced the brute to
absolute cringeing as far as his conduct to me went.
The wretched papa he bullied as before, and when he
got up to go he and all the rest were up in an instant;
one prepared his papouches, another supported him,
a third opened the door, and a fourth held a
lamp to light him out. But he had not yet finished
his evening. Soon I heard a noise of singing and
roaring from another house hard by, and received a
message from him to beg I would sup with him, for
now he had a table of his own and could invite me.
The table was provided by some wretched Greek he
was tyrannising over. Of course I did not go, but I
moralised over the state of the country. Next day he
carried off Nicola.

Another instance of the tyranny of these scoundrels
was told me as having occurred only a few days before.
A zabetis man had arrived and pretended to have lost
on the way a purse containing 80 piastres. All the
inhabitants were sent to search for it, and if they did

not find it he said it must be repaid by the town—and it was.

Among the people we met at Eleusis was a Greek merchant, a great beau from Hydra, at this time the most prosperous place in Greece ; but away from his own town he had to cringe to the Turks like everyone else.   On our way back to Athens we overtook him carrying an umbrella to shade his face, and with an Albanian boy behind him.   When he saw our janissary Mahomet the umbrella was immediately lowered.

The population of Greece is so small now[1] that large spaces are left uncultivated and rights to land are very undefined.   In the neighbourhood of towns there is always a considerable amount of cultivated ground, but although the cultivator of each patch hopes to reap it, there is nothing but fear of him to prevent another's doing it, so far as I can see.   A field is ploughed and sown by an undefined set of people, and an equally or even less defined set may reap it.   And in point of fact people do go and cut corn where they please or dare.   We met a lot of Athenians on our way back, going to cut corn at Thebes."

By the middle of July the Æginetan Marbles had been thoroughly overhauled and pieced together, and

[1] According to De Pouqueville, 548,940, in 1814; it is now over 2,000,000.

it was pressing that something should be done about them. The schemes of selling them to Lord Sligo and Messrs. Knight and Fazakerly had fallen through, and it had come to be seen that the only fair way for all parties was to sell them by public auction. To do this they must first be got out of the country, and various schemes for effecting it were considered and abandoned.

As the proprietors meanwhile were in daily fear of their being pounced upon by the Turkish authorities, they agreed at length to put the whole matter into the hands of one Gropius, a common acquaintance. He was half a German, but born and bred amongst Orientals, and being conversant with their ways and languages, and a sharp fellow besides, they felt he was more likely than themselves, unassisted, to carry the business through successfully. They accordingly appointed him their agent, and settled that the collection should be got to Zante, as the nearest place of security.

Eight days were spent in packing, and on July 30 the first batch, on horses and mules, was sent off at night to a spot indicated on the Gulf of Corinth, near a town and castle [? Livadostro.—ED.].

Cockerell followed two days afterwards with the rest, and sleeping two nights at Condoura, on the third day reached the rendezvous. There they found the first batch all laid out on the beach, and congratulated

F

themselves on having got so far unmolested. Gropius
went into the town to hire a vessel while the rest
sketched and rested. The weather was furiously hot,
and Cockerell, who was very fond of the water, went
out for a long swim in the bay, but some fishermen he
came up with frightened him back by telling him that
they had seen sharks about. Gropius returned in the
evening with a boat, and all set to work to get the
packages aboard. It took them nearly the whole night
to do it. When finally he had seen them all stowed,
Cockerell, tired out, lay down to sleep. When he
woke they were already gliding out of the bay.

They sailed along prosperously, and had long
passed Corinth and Sicyon when, as evening came on,
they heard the sound of firing ahead.

"Our first idea was pirates, and when we presently
came up with a large ship, which summoned us to
come to, we were rather anxious. Our felucca was
sent aboard. She turned out to be a Zantiote merchantman, and had been attacked by four boats which
had put out from the shore to examine the cargo in
the name of Ali Pasha. She had refused to submit
to overhauling, and when asked what her cargo consisted of had replied 'Bullets.' When the captain
understood we had four milordi on board, he begged
pardon for detaining us, and let us go on. Next day
we made Patras, where we went ashore to see Strani,
the consul, and get from him passports and letters for

Zante. In the town we fell in with Bronstedt and the rest of that party, who were, of course, much interested and astonished to hear all our news and present business, and when we set sail in the evening gave us a grand salute of pistols as we went out of port. We had a spanking breeze.

A storm was brewing behind Calydon, and when at length it came upon us it burst the sail of a boat near us. We were a lot of boats sailing together, but when the rest saw this accident they took in their sails. Our skipper, however, insisted on carrying on, so we soon parted company with the others; and after a fair wind all night we arrived in the morning at Zante."

CHAPTER VII

ZANTE — COLONEL CHURCH — LEAVES ZANTE TO MAKE TOUR OF
THE MOREA — OLYMPIA — BASSÆ — DISCOVERY OF BAS-RELIEFS
—FORCED TO DESIST FROM EXCAVATIONS.

" HITHERTO we had had an anxious time, but once they
were landed we felt at ease about the marbles. Henceforth the business is in Gropius' hands. The auction
has been announced in English and continental papers
to take place in Zante on November 1, 1812. It took
us some time to install them, and altogether we passed
an odious fortnight on the island. The Zantiotes, as
they have been more under Western influence—for
Zante belonged to Venice for about three centuries—
are detestable. They are much less ignorant than the
rest of the Greeks, but their half-knowledge only makes
them the more hateful. Until the island was taken in
hand by the English, murder was of constant occur-
rence, and so long as a small sum of money was paid
to the proveditor no notice was taken of it. For
accomplishing it without bloodshed they had a special
method of their own. It was to fill a long narrow bag
with sand, with which, with a blow on the back
scientifically delivered, there could be given, without

fuss or noise, a shock certain sooner or later to prove fatal. Socially they have all the faults of the West as well as those of the East without the virtues of either. But their crowning defect in my eyes is that they have not the picturesque costumes or appearance of the mainland Greeks.

The most interesting thing in Zante for the moment is Major Church's[1] Greek contingent. He has enrolled and disciplined a number of refugee Greeks, part patriots, part criminals, and generally both, and has taken an immense deal of pains with them. He flatters them by calling them Hellenes, shows them the heads of their heroes and philosophers painted on every wall in his house, and endeavours generally to rouse their enthusiasm. He himself adopts the Albanian costume, to which he has added a helmet which he fancies is like that of the ancient Greeks, although it is certainly very unlike those of the heroes we brought into Zante. Altogether, with a great deal of good management and more fustian, he has contrived to attach to himself some thousand excellent troops which under his command would really be capable of doing great things.

[2] At last, on the evening of the 18th of August, we considered ourselves fortunate in being able to get

---

[1] Afterwards Sir Richard Church, and commander-in-chief of the Greek forces up to his death in 1872.

[2] An epitome of the following appears in Hughes's *Travels in Sicily, Greece, and Albania*, p. 190.

away, and we started to make the tour of the Morea. Gropius, Haller, Foster, Linckh, and I left Zante in a small boat and arrived next morning at Pyrgi, the port of Pyrgo, from which it is distant two hours and a half. We obtained horses at a monastery not far from where we landed, and rode through a low marshy country, well cultivated, chiefly in corn and melon grounds, and fairly well peopled up to the town.

Pyrgo itself lies just above the marshes which border the Alpheus, and, as it happened to our subsequent cost, there was a good deal of water out at this moment. We ordered horses, and while they were being brought in we entered the house of an old Greek, a primate of the place. I had been so disgusted with the thinly veneered civilisation of the Zantiotes and bored with the affectations of our garrison officers there, that I was congratulating myself on having got back to the frank barbarism of the Morea, when my admiration for it received a check. The old Greek in whose house we were waiting seemed anxious to be rid of us, and, the better to do so, assured me that Meraca, or Olympia, was only 2½ hours distant, equal at the ordinary rate of Turkish travelling, which is 3 miles an hour, to 7½ miles. The horses were so long in coming, on account of their being out among the marshes and the men having to go up to their knees to get them, that Haller and

I got impatient and resolved to go on foot as the distance was so little. It turned out, however, to be 7 hours instead of 2½, and at nightfall we arrived dead-beat at a marsh, through which in a pitch darkness, I may thank my stars, although invisible, for having struggled safely. We wandered about, lost our way, waded in pools to our knees, and finally took 8 hours instead of 2½ to get to our destination.

It was two o'clock in the morning when we got to Meraca, utterly tired out, and with our lodging still to seek. We were directed to a tower in which lived an Albanian aga. The entrance was at the top of a staircase running up the side of the house and ending in a drawbridge which led to the door on the first floor. Once inside we went up two other flights of stairs to a room in which we found two Albanians, by whom we were kindly received. When they heard how tired we were they offered us some rasky. Besides that there was some miserable bread, but no coffee or meat to refresh us. We had to lie down and go to sleep without.

There are few visible remains of the once famous Olympia,[1] and not a trace of stadium or theatre that I could make out. The general opinion is that the Alpheus has silted up and buried many of the build-ings to a depth of 8 or 10 feet, and our small

---

[1] Olympia was thoroughly excavated by the Germans in 1875–76, when the Hermes of Praxiteles and the Victory of Pæonios were discovered.

researches point in the same direction. We dug in the temple, but what we could do amounted to next to nothing. To do it completely would be a work for a king. I had had some difficulty with the Greek labourers at Ægina, but the Turks here were much worse. In the first place, instead of one piastre apiece per day they asked $2\frac{1}{2}$, and in the next they had no proper tools. The earth was as hard as brick, and when with extreme difficulty it had been broken up they had no proper shovels ; and when the earth, which they piled along the trench as they dug it out, ran into the hole again, they scooped it out with their hands. The thing was too ludicrous. Worst of all, as soon as we turned our backs for a moment they either did nothing or went away. This happened when we left them to cross the river and try for a better view of the place. We got over in a caique, which the aga himself, from the village across the water, punted over to us ; but the view over there was disappointing, and we came back to find, as I say, our workmen all idling. The long and short of our excavations was that we measured the columns of the temple to be 7 feet in diameter, and we found some attached columns and other fragments of marble from the interior, the whole of which I suppose was of marble, that of the pavement being of various colours. Such stone as is used is of a rough kind, made up entirely of small shells and covered with a very white and fine plaster.

And that is about all the information we got for a largish outlay.

From Meraca we rode through romantic scenery to Andritzena, a charming village in a very beautiful and romantic situation ; and next morning we settled to go on to the Temple of Bassæ—the stylæ or columns, the natives call it. But before we started the primates of Andritzena came in, and after turning over our things and examining and asking the price of our arms, they began to try and frighten us with tremendous stories of a certain Barulli, captain of a company of klephts or robbers who haunted the neighbourhood of the stylæ. They begged us to come back the same evening, and to take a guard with us. As for the first, we flatly refused ; and for the second, we reflected that our guards must be Greeks, while the klephts might be Turks, and if so the former would never stand against them, so it was as well for us to take the risk alone. We did, however, take one of their suggestions, and that was to take with us two men of the country who would know who was who, and act as guides and go-betweens ; for they assured us that it is not only the professional klephts who rob, but that all the inhabitants of the villages thereabouts are dilettante brigands on occasion.

Our janissary Mahomet also did not at all fancy the notion of living up in the mountain, and added what he could to dissuade us. However, we turned a

deaf ear to all objections and set out.   Our way
lay over some high ground, and rising almost all the
way, for 2½ hours.

It is impossible to give an idea of the romantic
beauty of the situation of the temple.   It stands on a
high ridge looking over lofty barren mountains and
an extensive country below them.   The ground is
rocky, thinly patched with vegetation, and spotted
with splendid ilexes.   The view gives one Ithome,
the stronghold and last defence of the Messenians
against Sparta, to the south-west ; Arcadia, with its
many hills, to the east ; and to the south the range
of Taygetus, with still beyond them the sea.

Haller had engagements, which I had got him, to
make four drawings for English travellers.   I made
some on my own account, and there were measurements to be taken and a few stones moved for the
purpose, all of which took time.   We spent altogether ten days there, living on sheep and butter,
the only good butter I have tasted since leaving England, sold to us by the few Albanian shepherds who
lived near.   Of an evening we used to sit and smoke
by a fire, talking to the shepherds till we were ready
for sleep, when we turned into our tent, which,
though not exactly comfortable, protected us from
weather and from wolves.   For there are wolves—one
of them one night tore a sheep to pieces close to us.
We pitched our tent under the north front.   On the

next day after our arrival, the 25th, one of the
primates of Andritzena came begging us to desist
from digging or moving stones, for that it might bring
harm on the town. This was very much what happened at Ægina. He did not specify what harm,
but asked who we were. We in reply said that we had
firmans, that it was not civil, therefore, to ask who
we were, and that we were not going to carry away
the columns. When he heard of the firmans he said
he would do anything he could to help us. All the
same, he seemed to have given some orders to our
guide against digging ; for the shepherds we engaged
kept talking of the fear they were in, and at last
went away, one of them saying the work was dis-
tasteful to him. They were no great loss, for they
were so stupid that I was obliged to be always with
them and work too, in doing which I tore my hand
and got exceedingly fatigued. I was repaid by getting some important measurements.

In looking about I found two very beautiful bas-
reliefs under some stones, which I took care to conceal
again immediately."

This incident is described in greater detail by
Stackelberg in the preface to his book.[1] The interior of the temple—that is to say, the space inside
the columns—was a mass of fallen blocks of some

[1] *Der Apollotempel zu Bassae.*

depth. While Haller and Cockerell with the labourers
were scrambling about among the ruins to get their
measurements, a fox that had made its home deep
down amongst the stones, disturbed by the unusual
noise, got up and ran away.   It is not quite a pleasant
task to crawl down among such insecure and ponderous masses of stone with the possibility of finding
another fox at the bottom ; but Cockerell ventured in,
and on scraping away the accumulations where the
fox had its lair, he saw by the light which came down
a crack among the stones, a bas-relief.   I have heard
this story also from his own lips.   Stackelberg further
says that the particular relief was that numbered 530 in
the Phigaleian Marbles at the British Museum, and
naïvely adds, "indeed one may still trace on the marble
the injuries done by the fox's claws " He managed to
make a rough sketch of the slab and carefully covered
it over again.   From the position in which it lay it
was inferable that the whole frieze would probably
be found under the dilapidations.

"Early one morning some armed shepherds came
looking about for a lost sheep. They eventually found
it dead not far from our tent, and torn to pieces by a
wolf—as I mentioned before.   The day being Sunday
we saw some grand specimens of the Arcadian shepherds.   They stalk about with a gun over their
shoulders and a long pistol in the waist, looking very
savage and wild—and so they are : but, wild as they

may be, they still retain the names which poetry has
connected with all that is idyllic and peaceful.   Alexis
is one of the commonest.

As our labourers had left us, there was nothing for
it but to work ourselves.   We were doing so and had
just lit upon some beautiful caissons, when a man on
horseback, Greek or Turk (they dress so much alike
there is no distinguishing them), rode up accompanied
by four Albanians all armed.   He told us he was the
owner of the land, and, although he was very civil
about it, he forbade our digging any more.   We asked
him to eat with us, but being a fast day in the
Greek Church, he declined.   Finally, after writing to
Andritzena, he left us.

After so many objections being made to our excavations we felt it would be too dangerous to go
on at present, and promised ourselves to come again
next year in a stronger party and armed with more
peremptory and explicit authority to dig, and in the
meantime there was nothing to do but to get through
our drawings and studies as quickly as we could.

The uneasiness of our janissary Mahomet, since
our camping out began, gave us serious doubts of his
courage, and a plan was invented for testing it.   This
was to raise an alarm at night that we were attacked
by klephts.   Our Arcadian shepherds entered into
the joke with surprising alacrity and kept it up well.
Just after supper a cry was heard from the mountain

above that robbers were near.   In an instant we all sprang up, seized pistols and swords, and made a feint as though we would go up the hill.   Our janissary, thunderstruck, was following, when we proposed that he should go on alone.

But he would not do that.   In the first place he was ill; in the next place, Would it not be better to go to Andritzena?   He begged we might go to Andritzena."

CHAPTER VIII

ANDRITZENA—CARITZENA—MEGALOPOLIS—BENIGHTED—
KALAMATA.

" WE left the stylæ and went down to Andritzena by a
shorter road.   In going up, the drivers, to be able to
charge us more, had taken us round a longer way.
Andritzena is not only beautiful in its situation, the
people who live in it are charming.   Everyone seemed
to think it the proper thing to show some attention
to the strangers.   The girls—and some of them were
very pretty—brought us each as a present a fruit of
some kind, pears or figs, and did it in the prettiest
and most engaging manner ;   so that we had more
than we could carry home with us.   Disinterested
urbanity is so unusual a feature in Greek character
that we were surprised, and I must confess that it was
the only time such a thing ever occurred to us in
Greece.

The Turks tax these poor wretches unmercifully.
To begin with, they have to pay the Government one-
fourth of their produce.   Then there is the karatch or
poll tax, which seems to be rather variable in amount,
and the chrea or local tax levied for the local govern-

ment, which together make up about another fourth ;
so that the taxes amount to half the yearly produce.
Of course the people complain.   I can't tell you how
often I have been asked 'When will the English come
and deliver us from the Turks, who eat out our
souls ?'   'And why do they delay ?'   One Greek told
me he prayed daily that the Franks might come ;
and while I am on the subject I may as well mention
here, though it was said a few weeks later, when we
were near Corinth, by a shepherd, 'I pray to God I may
live to see the Morea filled with such Franks.'   They
like us better than they do the French, because they
have heard from Zante and elsewhere that we treat
our dependencies more honourably than they do.

We were five days at Andritzena.   Haller made
drawings of the village, and I finished up my memoranda of Phigaleia.   Besides that, as I thought we
ought not to leave the neighbourhood without making
a final effort to complete our explorations at the
stylæ, and that, the Pasha Veli being absent from
the Morea, we might perhaps get leave from the
Waiwode of Fanari, Foster and I rode over to see him.
We found him exceedingly courteous, perfectly a man
of the world ; and although his house and the two old
cushions in the corner of a dilapidated gallery on which
he was propped when he received us did not bespeak
great affluence, his manner was not that of a man to
whom one could offer a bribe.   He said he regretted

very much having had to write the letter we had received forbidding us to go on digging, but that it
was absolutely necessary that we should cease, and
there was an end of the matter. At the same time he
hoped there had been no expression in it to offend
us. ' Veli,' said he, ' is very peremptory about no
bouyuruldu or permission being given by anyone but
himself; for he insists on knowing all about travellers
who move about in his pashalik, and upon periodically
inspecting them and their firman and approving it.
The mere fact of my having allowed your party to
remain ten days at Phigaleia, no matter whether you
dug or not, was enough to ruin me; for these Albanians [that is, Ali Pasha and his sons] ask but few
questions [listen to no excuses].' So we had to go
back to Andritzena without having effected anything
beyond seeing an Albanian Turkish wedding on our
way. When we came upon them they were gorgeously
dressed, playing the djerid and brandishing their
swords. I never saw anything so picturesque. The
party were on their way to fetch the bride from Fanari.
They had an Albanian red and white banner, with a
silk handkerchief tied to the top of it, which was the
token sent by the bride to her lover as an invitation to
him to come and fetch her. After sunset she is taken
to his house on horseback, closely veiled.

Hearing of some columns in an old castle not far
off, as the account was a tolerably rational one, I

G

resolved, although I ought to have had experience enough of Greek lies to warn me, to go and see them. There was the hope of making some discovery of interest; for my informant insisted that no milords had ever been there before. So I girt myself with sword and pistol, and walked 2½ hours to a hill or mountain called Sultané. I only found a few miserable columns, a considerable fortress and cyclopean walls, and I made two sketches on the road. I was very tired when I got back. The Greek shoemaker, our landlord, came and supped with us, and got very maudlin over the wine.

We went next to Caritzena. The waiwode insisted on our putting up with him, and gave up a room to us, begging that we would order whatever best pleased us; that his servants would prepare anything, and we should purchase nothing. 'Our king at Stamboul is rich enough to receive our friends and allies, the English,' he said. We were preparing to go out and draw when a message came to say the waiwode would pay us a visit. Haller, however, would not stop for anybody. Foster had to ride back to a place where he had changed his coat and in so doing had dropped a ring he valued, and which, by the by, he managed to find. So Linckh and I, though I felt very unwell with a bilious attack, had to stop in and receive our visitor. He was very polite, and his manners really very fine. He told us he had been with the

ambassador at Vienna and at Berlin, and spoke a
few words of German, which enchanted Linckh. He
presently remarked that I seemed unwell, and I told
him that I was bilious, and had a pain in my head;
whereupon he took hold of my temples in his right
hand, while an old Turk who sat near doubled down his
little finger and repeated a charm, which he began in a
whisper and finished aloud, leaning forward and pro-
nouncing something like ' Osman Odoo—o—o.' Then
he asked me if I was better; because if I was not he
would double down his next finger and the next till he
came to the thumb, which he said was infallible. This
prospect seemed more than I could quite bear; so I
thought best to sacrifice my principles, and said ' Yes,
I was,' to get rid of the matter, but I was not.

Some Greeks came and joined in our conversation.
Really, if one had not some pity for their condition, one
could not suffer them, their manners are so odious.
Nevertheless, as they seem to have all the power here
and elect their own governor and give him an allowance,
the waiwode would not join me in criticising them.

The waiwode continued to be as civil as ever, but
I could not help thinking he looked anxiously for
presents, and we had none to give him. All I could
do was to offer him one of the common little brass
English boxes with a head of King George on it,
filled with bark. He took it with every expression of
delight, but I could see it was put on. We could only

G 2

thank him heartily, fee the servants handsomely, and bow ourselves out with the best grace we could assume. He especially coveted a miniature Foster wore of a lady, and this Foster promised to have copied for him and sent him from England; but he could not part with the original. He gave us strong letters of recommendation for Kalamata.

We left early next day. There was an awkward little episode of a box of instruments belonging to Foster, which he missed off a certain sofa. The Boluk bashi had admired them very much. Presently, when the inquiry was made, an officer of the Boluk bashi came in and searched near the sofa, and then suddenly went out. We did the same, and lo! there was the case. And the Boluk bashi looked very disconcerted as we bade him adieu.

We followed the course of the Gyrtinas. These are mountains which on all hands are celebrated among the modern Greeks for the exploits of the Colocotroni [1] and other captains who lived among the hills and maintained a sort of independence of the Turks ever since they have held the Morea. The peasants delight to sing the ballads composed on these heroes, and, exulting in their bravery, forget the horrible barbarities they committed. When Smirke was here the country must really have been in a fearful state of anarchy;

[1] One Colocotronis, a chief of klephts, attained great influence in the War of Independence.

and whatever we may say against him, it must be laid at any rate to the credit of Veli Pasha that he has cleared the Morea of banditti. The Colocotroni and the rest of them have had to fly the country and enlist in Church's contingent at Zante.

We spent some time at Megalopolis, and with Pausanias in our hands were able to identify remnants of almost everything he mentions, in especial the spring near the theatre, which only runs part of the year. At Lycosura the ruins are disappointingly modern, and there is not much of them ; nothing left of the ancient temple at all. The situation is very fine. Two and a half hours' journey up a stream through woods brought us to Dervine, the boundary of Messenia. Then we crossed the Plain of Messenia, admiring, even in the rain, the mountains, Ithome especially, and at dusk got to a village two hours short of Kalamata. Our agroati did not know the road on, and it was too late to get a guide ; but as they told us the road was quite straight we went on in the dark. At the end of an hour we had lost the track ; it was pitch black, raining still, and we on the edge of a river in a marsh. There I thought we should have stayed. For four hours we groped about, looking first for the lost path, and then for any path to any shelter. First we tried giving Haller's horse, who had been to Kalamata before, a loose rein and letting him lead the way. At first it promised well, for the horse went ahead willingly ; but the agroati took upon him to change his course, and then we were as lost as ever. We could hardly see each other. Then we sent off the agroati to try and reach a light we could see. He came back with awful accounts of bogs and ditches he had met in his path. Finally, after standing still for a time in the pelting rain, we resolved to reach the light ; and so we did, over hedge and ditch and through bogs, and Indian corn above our heads as we sat on horseback, and at length, wet through and wearied, reached a cottage in which were some Greeks. They, however, refused to lead us to any house ; for, said they, 'we know not what men ye are.' At last one good man took us into his house and gave us a room, and figs and brandy for supper. We were thankful for anything. He was a poor peasant with a pretty wife and a perfectly lovely daughter.

We got to Kalamata next day, meeting on the way numbers of Mainiotes coming to buy figs &c. in the Messenian plain, all armed. Our baggage had arrived very late overnight. We went to the so-called consul, an agent of the consul at Patras, and sent the letter of recommendation of the Waiwode of Caritzena to the Waiwode of Kalamata ; but he took no notice of it, and did nothing whatever for us, so we had to find a house for ourselves. We pitched upon a lofty Turkish tower commanding the city, with a very rotten floor which threatened at any moment to let us through

from the second storey to the base. The only way up
to our room was by a crazy ladder. The shutters
were riddled with bullets. Some time before there
had been a grand engagement between this tower and
the cupola of a neighbouring church, where some
Mainiotes in the service of one of their great captains,
a certain Benachi, had defended themselves. Kalamata seems to be a constant scene of fights between
the party of the Bey appointed by the Porte, or rather
the Capitan Pasha, and the party who want to appoint
a Bey of their own, and this is the way they fight, each
party from its own tower.

From our tower we made panoramic sketches of
the city, but were much interrupted by visitors.
Among them came a young Mainiote Albanian officer
from Church's contingent, who was here recruiting.
He was accompanied by two armed Mainiotes, and said
he had twenty more concealed about the town in case
of danger. He invited us to come with him into
Maina as far as Dolus, where his family lived, a proposal we eagerly closed with, and appointed the next
morning."

CHAPTER IX

TRIP TO MAINA—ITS RELATIVE PROSPERITY—RETURN TO KALAMATA. SECOND TRIP TO MAINA — MURGINOS — SPARTA—NAPOLI TO ATHENS.

" THE Mainiote border comes to within half a mile of Kalamata, and the neighbourhood of its ferocious population, who are as savage and even braver than the Turks, makes the latter much meeker here than in other parts of the country—that is, in a general way, for they can be very fierce still on occasions.   A ghastly thing happened during our stay.   We heard one evening the report of a pistol in the house of the Albanian guard which stood just under our windows. It seemed one of the brutes had shot his brother in a quarrel.   Here was a gruesome example under our eyes; and besides I was told all sorts of hideous stories of Mainiote and Albanian cruelties which made my blood run cold, and still spoils all my pleasure in thinking of this barbarous region.

Early in the morning we embarked on a Zantiote felucca, lent us for the occasion, and in an hour and a half reached the opposite coast of the bay, near the ruins of a village, of which we were told that it was destroyed and its inhabitants carried off for slaves by the Barbary pirates. Ever since this event the villages have been built farther from the coast. The village of Dolus, to which we were going, is an hour's walk from the shore.

Our friend's brother and a number of other men, all armed to the teeth, met us on the beach and saluted us, as soon as we were recognised, with a discharge of guns and pistols. Then we landed, and set off for the village. A difference in the appearance of the country struck me at once. Instead of the deserted languid air of other parts of Greece, here was a vigorous prosperity. Not an inch of available ground but was tilled and planted with careful husbandry, poor and rocky as the soil was. The villages were neater and less poverty-stricken, and the population evidently much thicker than in the rest of Greece. The faces of the men were cheerful and open; the women handsomer, and their costume more becoming.

Liberty seemed to have changed the whole countenance and manner of the people to gaiety and happiness. Everyone saluted us as we passed along, and when we arrived at Dolus the mother of our entertainer came out with the greatest frankness to meet us. Others came, and with very engaging manners wished us many years, a rare civility in Greece. The boys crowded round, and said Englishmen were fine fellows, but why had we no arms? How could we defend ourselves? Then they shook their fists at the Turkish shore, saying those ruffians dared not come amongst Mainiotes.

Our host's family had cooked us some chickens. While we were sitting eating them a multitude of visitors, women especially, who had never seen Franks before, came in, gazed, and asked questions. There was a great deal of laughing and talking, but every man was heavily armed. After dinner we went out for a walk and visited some remarkably pretty villages. The name of one was Malta, the others I could not make out; all more in the interior. The churches were very pretty. Each had a tall steeple in the Gothic style with bells, which a boy, proud of his freedom and anxious to show it, running on, would ring as we came up; for, as you know, neither bells nor steeples are allowed by the Turks. We saw a new tower, the tower of the beyzesday, or captain of the Mainiotes, armed with two thirty-pounders which had been given him, and though not very solidly built, standing in a fine position. We were told that all these towers are provisioned for a siege, and one of those near Kalamata has food for five years—not that I believe it. All slept together, ten of us covering the whole floor of a tiny room.

We went back in the morning to Kalamata, leaving behind us our host. He had been warned by letter from Kalamata not to go back there, for reports had been circulated by the Turks that he was gone to Maina to raise recruits and he would probably be arrested if he landed.

We had been so interested with our glimpse of the free Greeks—the Greeks who had always been free from the days of Sparta, who had maintained their independence against Rome, Byzantium, the Franks, Venetians, and Turks—that we longed to see more of them ; and the reports we heard of a temple near Cape Matapan gave us hopes of a return for the expense of an excursion. We therefore agreed with a certain Captain Basili of Dolus, owner of a boat, that he should take us to Cyparissa and protect us into the interior. Meanwhile we went home to get our baggage &c. As we rowed along the shore a storm hung on Mount Elias, rolling in huge coils among the high perched villages, and the awful grandeur and air of savage romance it gave to the whole country whetted our appetites to the utmost.

When we landed at Kalamata, however, a dispute about payment for the present trip led us to refer to the consul for a settlement, and incidentally to our tell- ing him our plans. As soon as he heard them he objected vigorously. The man we had engaged was, he said, a notorious murderer ; it was well known that he had assassinated a certain Greek doctor for his money when he was bringing him from Coron, and he might do the same for us on the way to Cyparissa.

It would be better if we insisted on going into Maina to write to a certain Captain Murgino at Scardamula and put ourselves under his protection. As he was one of the heads of the Mainiote clans, and a man of power, he would be able to guarantee our safety.

As this advice was supported by a French gentleman of Cervu, a Monsieur Shauvere, who seemed to be reliable, we took it, and wrote that same evening to Murgino ; but the first engagement had to be got rid of, and that was not so easy. Whatever his intentions had been, the boatman from Dolus thought he had made a profitable engagement, for he demanded 50 piastres indemnity, first for expenses incurred and next for the slight. He threatened to attack us on the way if we ventured to engage another boat. Finally we agreed to refer the dispute for settlement to the Albanian Mainiote, our late host.

We received an answer from Murgino to say that we should be very welcome, and that he would send a guard to meet us four hours from his house.

We accordingly set off in the evening to go by land, and arrived at night at a village called Mandinié ; and there we had to sleep, for the road was too breakneck for us to go on in the dark. Our host was exceedingly hospitable, and gave one a good impression of the free Greeks.

Early in the morning we went on to Malta, and

met four of Murgino's men come to meet 'us. We also fell in with the young captain or chieftain of Mainiotes on his way to Kalamata. He had a guard of eight or ten men, all armed and handsomely dressed, their hair trailing down their backs like true descendants of the Spartans, who combed their long hair before going into battle.

As regarding the origin of the name Malta, it may be called to mind that the Venetians during their occupation mortgaged part of the Morea to the Knights of St. John, and this may have been one of their fortresses.

Having hired mules to carry our luggage, as the road is too bad for horses, we proceeded to Scardamula, a distance of $1\frac{1}{2}$ hour. There we were rejoined by my servant Dimitri, whom I had sent on to arrange the affair of Captain Basili, the Dolus boatman. He had found the man in a state of exasperation, refusing to accept any accommodation, saying it was an affair of honour, and vowing that we should pay in another way. The wife and mother of the Albanian officer, dreading his resentment, had hung terrified on his (Dimitri's) arm, assuring him that we should be assassinated on the road. He himself arrived hardly able to speak with terror and pale as paper.

We did all we could to inspire him with a little courage, both natural and Dutch. First we appealed to him as a man to show a good face, and for the second we gave him a good and ample dinner, and, relying on our guard and on ourselves, set out.

But before starting we begged our Albanian friend to come, if he could, next day to Scardamula, bringing Captain Basili with him, and the dispute should be referred to Captain Murgino for arbitration.

The path to Scardamula—for there was nothing in the shape of a road—was now so difficult that we had to get off; and, even so, it was to me perfectly wonderful how the mules ever got along. There was nothing but rock, and that all fissured and jagged limestone, but they climbed over it like goats.

The situation of Scardamula is infinitely striking. At the gate of his castle Captain Murgino waited to receive us—a fat, handsome old man.

At the first our rather strange appearance seemed to put him a little out of countenance, and he received us awkwardly although kindly; but after a time he appeared to regain confidence and became very cordial. 'Eat a good supper, *Ingles archi mas*' ('my little Englishman'), he said to me, and gave me the example. He talked freely on the political state of Maina. He owned and regretted that the Greeks had no leader, and said he trusted that would not long be wanting, and that shortly the great object of his desires would be realised; but what that object was he would not explain. It might be an invasion of the Morea by the English, seconded by a native insurrection which he would take a leading part in—or what not; but he was careful to give me no hint.[1] His son was absent at a council of the [Greek] chiefs at Marathonisi.

The next morning we walked about his lands, which were indescribably picturesque. His castle stands on a rock in the bed of a river, about a quarter of a mile from the bank. It consists of a courtyard and a church surrounded by various towers. There is a stone bench at his door, where he sits surrounded by his vassals and his relations, who all stand unless invited to sit. The village people bring him presents, tribute as it were, of fruits, fowls, &c. On a lofty rock close by is a watch-tower, where watch is kept night and day. The whole gave us a picture of feudal life new and hardly credible to a nineteenth-century Englishman.

Behind the tower the mountains rise precipitously, and culminate in the Pentedactylon—a prodigious mountain of the Taygetus range.

Murgino made us an estimate of his dependents. He has about 1,000 men, over whom he has absolute authority to call them out or to punish them as he thinks fit. A few days before we came he had had an obstreperous subject, who refused to obey orders,

[1] It probably was the insurrection, for when it occurred he took an important part in it. He was the opponent of the Mavro Michali faction, headed by Petro Bey.

executed. Moreover, he showed a well in which he said he put those from whom he desired to extort money. When times are hard and the olives fail he makes war upon his neighbours, and either robs or blackmails them. The old man assured me that one winter they brought back from 1,000 to 1,500 piastres, from 50*l.* to 80*l.*, a day.

Such was our host and his surroundings.

As I told you, our object was to examine some remains we had heard rumours of, especially of a Doric temple said to exist in the southern part of Maina, and, by all we could hear, in a tolerable state of preservation ; but when we saw the tremendous preparations made by our good captain we found the enterprise beyond all our calculations or means. He declared he could not ensure our safety without his own attendance with a guard of forty men at the least. At this we thought it best, however regrettable, to retire before the expenses we should incur should embarrass us in our return to Athens. So we only stayed two days with Murgino, and then returned to Kalamata.

As you may suppose, I was very sorry to lose an opportunity of perhaps making another discovery of importance, but even as it was I did not regret to have made the visit into Maina. In no part of Europe at any rate, if indeed of the world, could one find such singular scenes or come upon a state of society so exactly like that of our ancient barons. The character of Murgino himself was a study. He was very hardy, bold, vigorous in mind and body, used from a boy to battle with all kinds of reverses.

His father was driven out of his home by the Turks, who brought several frigates and regularly laid siege to Scardamula. He escaped, but he was afterwards taken and hanged at Tripolizza. Murgino himself escaped to Coron, where, however, he was discovered and put in chains. A friendly priest brought him a file, wherewith he effected his escape to the house of the English consul, and was by him protected. He then took service on board a French privateer, and wandered into various parts of the Levant. After some time he reappeared at Scardamula, took possession of his father's castle, and became one of the captains or leaders of the Mainiotes. Then the Turks returned and surrounded him a second time. With a few followers he cut his way through and escaped to Zante. Some months later he came back once more, to find a neighbour had seized his possessions. He collected friends and laid siege to him. His rival was, fortunately for him, killed by a stroke of lightning during the siege, and Murgino came into his own again. But he did not hold it long in peace. He was again attacked by the Turks in force. This time he shut himself in the castle with 62 Greeks, who swore to die rather than yield.

H

For forty days they held the place with muskets against artillery, till all his powder was spent and his towers in ruins. Then he sent a message to the enemy to say that if they would give him two cannon and some powder he would hold the castle a year. Having soothed his mind with this taunt, he prepared to escape to the mountains. First he sent his wife off by night, and then followed with the few survivors of his men, and contrived again to get to Zante. It is characteristic of the man that when he learnt that his son was hanged he called, as he told me, for another glass of rum, saying 'Che serve la melancolia ?' Among the ruffianly crew who loafed about the place he pointed me out one or two of the poor fellows who had remained hidden in the hills when he went to Zante. Some had lost a toe or a finger in the frost ; others had been maimed in the siege. One youth in particular he indicated, saying 'This fellow's father was a fine fellow ; he was crushed in the falling of one of the towers !' Every one had a history.

Somehow, before we parted, I had got to feel a sort of affection for this ruthless cateran. He had an uncommonly open frank manner, he was certainly clean, and he had an air of natural superiority which it was difficult to resist.

I should not have written so much about this if I had not thought it the most interesting part of the tour—

but it had not, I admit, much architectural instruction
to offer.

From Kalamata we went to Sparta, over a rugged
and picturesque road, along the brink of precipices
and over the Taygetus. Some time ago it was infested by banditti,[1] and so it still is on the borders of
Maina. We arrived late at a small village near
Mistra. The road, which passed among overhanging
rocks and a wild and fantastic scenery, the effect of
which was heightened by the moonlight, was so stony
and rugged that we were obliged to walk by far the
greater part of the way. Sometimes the shepherds on
precipices above us would call out, ' What men are
ye?' And we answered, ' Good men.' There was no
step of the road that had not its annals of murder or
robbery. One of our party, to cheer us, sang us the
great deeds of a certain Captain Zaccani, who had
been something between a highwayman and a patriot
not many years back, infesting this part of the
country.

Sparta, I need not tell you, was strong only in its
inhabitants. It stood, as no other Greek city did, in
a plain. There are no remains. Its present inhabitants, far from being independent, are the most op-
pressed, the meanest and the stupidest of the Greeks.
We stayed only three days for Haller, who had

---

[1] Here it was that Chevalier Bronstedt was stopped next year and
robbed : *vide infra.*

H 2

various drawings to make, and then rode from Mistra to Tripolizza in one day. Haller had had a fall from his horse on the way which had strained him a good deal, so we had to stop three days there also. It is the capital of the Morea, and has a caimacam, whom we went to call upon one evening. It chanced to be during the Ramazan. He was very civil and gave us a bouyuruldu, an order which provided us horses gratis to Athens. The details of the visit were very much the same as those of other official visits. We drank coffee and smoked large pipes surrounded by a crowd of chiouks. The large and well-lighted room was filled with Albanian soldiers lying and sitting in all positions on the floor, and we had to be careful in picking our way through them.

We did not stop longer at Argos or Tiryns than was necessary to verify Gell's description.

At Napoli di Romagna, where we were detained for want of horses, we narrowly escaped the bastinado.

Napoli is one of the chief fortresses of the Morea, and the custom on entering such places is to get off one's horse. Our servant, who knew nothing of this, was cruelly beaten by the guard. When we came up we were told of it by the grooms who looked after our luggage, and conjured by the Panagia and the Cross to dismount as we went in. We, however, thought it unbecoming our dignity, and rode boldly in. The guard, seeing so many hats, was awed and said nothing ; but we could see by the frowns of the by-standers that our presumption was disapproved, and when we complained to the pasha, the head of the janissaries, of the way our servant was mishandled, he took very little notice of us. Generally speaking the Turks in their fortresses are insufferably intolerant and insolent. Our treatment was no inducement to stay, and we made on for Athens as soon as we could. We visited the sacred grove at Epidaurus,[1] the ruins of Mycenæ,[2] and stayed one day in Corinth. But we were glad to get to Athens ; it was like home to us. For three weeks I had slept with my clothes on, without a bed, and with only one blanket to wrap myself in."

[1] The Hieron of Epidaurus excavated by the Archæological Society of Athens.

[2] Excavated by Schliemann in 1876.

CHAPTER X

ÆGINA MARBLES CALLED FOR BY BRITISH GOVERNMENT SHIPS—
LEAVES ATHENS FOR CRETE AND EGYPT WITH HON. FRANCIS
NORTH—CANEA—CONDITION OF CRETE—BY LAND—RETIMO—
KALIPO CHRISTO — CANDIA — AUDIENCE OF THE PASHA — HIS
BAND — THE ARCHBISHOP — THE MILITARY COMMANDANT —
TURKISH SOCIETY—LIFE IN CANDIA.

"WAITING for me in Athens I found letters from my
father detailing the measures he had taken in our
favour concerning the marbles. He had moved the
Prince Regent, who had given orders that 6,000*l.* and
a free entry should be offered for the collection, and
that a ship of war should be sent to fetch it. The
offer might be considered equal to 8,000*l.* The ship
might be expected at once.

Here was a bitter disappointment to be unable to
accept so splendid an offer, and a painful embarrassment as well ; for I had led the Government, quite
unintentionally, to suppose that they had only to send
for the marbles to secure them. In consequence of
which they were sending two great vessels at great
expense, whereas I should now have to tell the captain
not only that the marbles were no longer in Athens—
but that they could not be handed over at all."

At this moment the Honourable Mr. North,[1] an acquaintance already made in Constantinople, had turned up in Athens, and intended making an expedition to Egypt up the Nile as far as Thebes. He proposed to Cockerell and Foster to join him. Egypt had been part of the former's original scheme in planning his travels, and the opportunity of sharing expenses was not one to be lost. So it was agreed, and all preparations were made for the journey. They were to have started in the beginning of November, but were delayed by unfavourable winds.

" I was a month in Athens, for the most part unprofitably, as all time spent in expectation must be. Every day we packed up, to unpack again when the wind went contrary. Finally, on November 29th, the wished-for wind came, and at the same time an express from Captain Percival of the brig-of-war *Pauline* 25, come for the marbles, called us down to the Piræus to see the ship sent by the Prince Regent.

It was raining in torrents. Nevertheless we set out, with Haller and Linckh as well, to explain matters. I own my consternation was great when I saw the two big ships come on a bootless quest, for which I was in a way answerable. We had to tell Captain Percival not only that the marbles were now in Zante, but that even if they had been still here he could not have

---

[1] Chancellor of the University of Corfu, later Lord Guilford.

taken them, as they were now to be sold by auction ; and, finally, as there was danger oi Zante being at any time attacked by the French, to request him to remove them to Malta for greater security. At first Captain Percival was very indignant, not unnaturally ; but when he had done his duty in this respect he was very civil and asked us to dine. Ale and porter, which I had not seen for so long, seemed delicious, and I drank so much of it that when, with North, Haller, and Stackelberg, I went aboard our Greek ship to bed, I slept like a stone till the morning drum on the *Pauline* woke me. The wind was blowing fresh from the north. We drew up our anchor ; Haller and Stackelberg shook us by the hand and went ashore.

And now for Candia and Egypt. Good port as the Piræus is once you are inside, to get in and out of it is very awkward. The brig, of course, well handled, had no difficulty ; but we failed altogether at the first attempt, and at the next as near as possible got on to the rocks at the entrance. The *Pauline* laid to for us till we were out, and then sailed ahead much more quickly than we were able to follow. The day was bright, the wind was fair, and it was new and exhilarating to sail in such good company. At Ægina, where the temple stood up clear for us to see, the brig and the transport lay to, to land a pilot, and we went in front, but they soon caught us up again ; and when

they passed us, comparing their trimness and order
with our state, I saw why a Greek always speaks
with such awe of an English ship.   Between Hydra—
a black and barren rock—and the mainland a storm,
which we just escaped, swept along, and our captain
seeing it, and thinking dirty weather might come on,
steered towards Milo so as to be able to put in there
in case of danger, and we parted with our convoy.   Of
our party I was the only one who was not ill, and
appeared at dinner ; and as the air was close below
among my sick friends, I passed the night on deck in
a seaman's coat.   In the morning Candia was in sight,
and by midday we were in Canea—only twenty-eight
hours.

As we drew near, the town, with its many minarets,
all white and stretching along a flat, with dark mountains, peak above peak, in very fine forms behind it,
had a most striking effect.   From a great distance one
could distinguish the large arched arsenals built by the
Venetians for their galleys.   The port is difficult to
enter, and we nearly ran ashore here again by mis-
taking a breach in the wall which encloses the port
for the entrance to it.   It is a gap which has once
been mended by the Turks, but it was so ill done that
it fell in again immediately ; and now it has been a
ruin for some time and seems likely to remain one.
We dropped our anchor ill too, so that the stem of our
ship ran foul of some rocks, but no harm was done.

We landed, dressed *à la Turque*, and I felt some 'mauvaise honte' in replying to the salutation of Turks who took us for their fellows, so I was not sorry to take shelter in the house of our consul, Sr. Capo Grosso, a native of Spalatro, with a pretty Tartar wife from the Crimea. It appears that besides himself there are very few Franks living here—only two families descended from the Venetians, and two other Catholic families, all kept in a perpetual tremor by the Turks, who are worse in Crete than anywhere. There are quarrels and murders every day between them and the Greeks. There never was such a state as the country is in. The military power consists of a local militia of janissaries and none other, so that their captains are able to terrorise the pasha into doing anything they please. But the militia, again, is composed of various regiments, and they are at variance with each other. So that you have both anarchy and civil war. Fancy, how nice!

The Venetians long possessed the island, and the fortifications and public buildings, which are really very noble, as well as every other decent thing in the place, are of their production. Indeed, in walking through the city, judging by the look of the buildings, one might imagine oneself in a Frank country, except that they are all left to go to rack and ruin. The sea walls are so neglected that the port is almost destroyed.

It is, as I said, a fortified town, and the Turks are absurdly jealous of any stranger and possible spy. One cannot stir out without being closely watched, and they shoot at anything which incurs the slightest suspicion—a Frankish hat, for instance. In consequence it was impossible to do any sketching, however much I might wish to.

The weather looked thoroughly bad. It poured all day, with a north wind which forbade all thoughts of sailing.

To make the best use of our time, it was proposed that we should make an expedition to see Ida and the famous Labyrinth ; but as Mr. North is no mountain climber he settled to wait in the ship for a fair wind to carry him to Candia, where whichever of us should arrive first was to await the other.

There was some delay in starting, because the rascally Turk from whom we first tried to job our horses came to a dispute with his agroates about the pay they were to get. Though he was to get ten piastres per horse, he would only give them five. As they could not agree, the negotiation fell through and it was rather late before we got others.

We were Douglas,[1] Foster, and myself, the consul's dragoman and two janissaries. Outside the ramparts, which are certainly strong, one comes on a fine plain

---

[1] The Hon. Frederick S. N. Douglas, author of an essay entitled *On Points of Resemblance between Ancient and Modern Greeks.*

dotted with white villas and thick with olives. One
owner whose house we passed, Hagi Imin Effendi,
makes as many as 60,000 barrels of oil per annum,
which at 60 piastres a barrel represents a vast
income. Having crossed the plain, one comes to
Suda Bay, an excellent harbour, a mile and a half or
two miles in length. The entrance is protected by
an island with a famous fortress upon it which resisted
the Turks for thirty-five years after the reduction of
the rest of Crete. It has 260 pieces of cannon now.
Soapmaking is one of the chief industries of Crete.
Along Suda Bay were numbers of salt-pans for winning
the salt wanted for the soapmaking. A Venetian
road, once good, now in a ruinous condition, led us
along a cliff flanked with watch-towers, and presently
turned inland. Before us was a beautiful hilly country
covered with olives, and in the distance Ida white with
snow. On our right the Sphakiote Mountains, high
and pointed, very like Maina to look at, and not
unlike it in respect of its population, though it has
not been quite so fortunate. The Sphakiotes maintained their independence till forty-three years ago,
but then they were reduced by the Turks, and have been
paying taxes ever since, and furnishing sailors for the
Turkish shipping. These sailors act as hostages for
the good behaviour of their relatives. All the same
they are a bold people never without arms, and
prompt in the use of them.

We slept that night at a wretched khan at
Neokorio in company with our horses and their
vagabond drivers, and fleas in infinite abundance.
Thomas, Douglas's English servant, made an ill-
timed joke here, which might have been awkward
among such savage people. The Turks at supper-
time pressed round him to see what was in our food-
bag, and he, to be rid of them, told them it was full of
pork. At this they expressed the greatest disgust,
pressed upon us to know if it was true, and refused to
eat anything that night. However, nothing more came
of it. Fleas and the manifold varieties of stinks drove
us to get through our night's rest as quickly as possible. We were up and away two hours before
daybreak, scrambling along a rough road. When
the sun rose the effect of it on the snow-covered
Sphakiote Hills was magnificent. Our way was
through a country rich in olives and full of beautiful
scenes. Well situated at the entrance to a valley
leading up from the sea, as a defence against piratical
descents, was a fortress with a πύργος or watch-tower,
built by the Venetians. It is of the fine workmanship
they always used, with well-arranged quarters for troops,
moat, &c., all very neat and well executed. There
we went down on to the sands and continued along
them for a length of time till we reached a small
river and the ruins of a splendid Venetian bridge.
Thence still along the seaside, but over rocks and

past watch-towers standing within gunshot of each
other, till we rose again on to a height from which we
gained a grand view of Retimo. We crossed a bridge,
a double arch of great depth, prodigiously effective,
and there I stopped to make a sketch before descend-
ing into the town, while the luggage went on. But
when we followed I was met by the dragoman before
I had dismounted. He looked very pale, and telling
me that my stopping by the road had been remarked
and commented upon, entreated me not to say what
I had been doing, but to give in fact a much more
natural reason. I had already, at Canea, been warned
of the danger of drawing the fortress ; so, my love of
truth notwithstanding, I was obliged for the dragoman's sake, he being responsible, to do as he asked.

We were received into the house of Achmet Aga,
the karahayah. He was not at home himself at the
time, but his nephews and relatives made us welcome.
As soon as he came in we were ushered into an upper
room into his presence. He was a remarkably handsome old man with a long white beard. He received
us with a proud, not to say cold, hospitality ; so much
so that when we thanked him for his polite offer of
his house, as he said it was ours, he looked the other
way.

As we drank coffee we made our apologies for our
dirty appearance, but he only said he feared we were
not comfortable and begged us to rest ourselves. His

manner was haughty not only to us but to the
wretched flatterers who came to pay him homage;
it was such that I was quite offended. His servants
treated him with the most abject respect, and even his
two nephews, men of thirty or thereabouts, sat at the
side without the divan, not venturing to approach
him. And yet, notwithstanding his manner, his treatment of us was hospitality and civility itself. He had
a son of sixteen or seventeen years dressed in a
Bosnian costume—one of the handsomest lads I ever
saw, like the youths one imagines in reading the
Arabian tales. He came by his father's order to sit
by me and entertain me. I asked him if he had ever
travelled, and whether he would come to Egypt with
me and see the world. He replied very politely that
to please me he would do so. The audience being
over, we went out and strolled down to the port. It
has lately been deepened by a Maltese engineer,
but is very small, and might hold fifteen or twenty
polaccas at the most. After seeing it we returned to
get ready for the dinner to which our host had invited
us. As usual in such houses one had to dress in the
midst of a crowd of servants, negroes, dervishes, and
hangers-on. We put on our best clothes and went
up. In the corner of the sofa or raised divan was
placed a large round tray on a small stool, and we sat
round it cross-legged. Over our knees was stretched
a long napkin from one to the other, and a small one

was thrown over each man's shoulder. We ate with our fingers, pinching off bits of meat from the same plate in the middle. Our janissary was invited to eat with us. The dinner was dressed in the harem. The servant tapped at the door communicating with it from the passage, and the dishes were handed in. There were many of them, and they were sent away by our host without any apparent notice of any disposition on our part to detain them. We had a stew of fowls, another of mutton, some strange made-dishes, a soup, a number of cakes, and I particularly remember some made of flour and cheese which were excellent. We greased our fingers handsomely and washed them as soon as we had done. For us there was wine, but Achmet would not drink any himself: not from virtue, he said, but because it did not agree with him. The handsome son waited without the divan and took orders from his father. Before dinner was over an old Turk came in with a fiddle and played or told long stories the whole evening. I was obliged to him, for it supplied the place of conversation, which did not seem to flourish. In the evening numbers of Turks came in to see the ' Inglesi,' and would have pressed forward, but until our dinner was done they were kept outside the sofa. Afterwards we formed into a sort of conversazione—very few words and much gravity. Finally the beautiful youth, the host's son, made beds for us of two quilts and a pillow on the sofa, and there we slept. I wonder what a young squire in England would say if his father told him to make beds for his guests

Next morning we were much pressed to stay both by our host and his son, but we had to resist, much as we had been pleased with our entertainment. So we distributed plentiful bakshish and rode away.

Our road lay along the shore, with fine views of Retimo and the Sphakiote Hills. Then over a high ridge to a khan at the foot of Ida. Here we had some refreshments and a dispute with the khangee, who tried to steal one of our spoons under cover of great professions of friendliness. After Avlopotamo the road became very dangerous. It ran by the side of awful precipices and over slippery rocks, and it was getting dark. Indeed, had it been lighter I don't suppose we should have ridden over it. In one place our janissary fell, and his horse's legs dangled over the precipice in a way to make one's blood run cold. No roads in Maina could be worse. The light of a fire beckoned us from afar to the monastery of Kalipo Christo, but we found the gate closed and the papades not to be seen. They were frightened and had hidden themselves. The fact is, the Turks in the country here are so brutal and lawless that if they once get into a monastery of this kind they eat and drink all they can get, never think of paying, and perhaps rob

I

or murder some of the monks.   There were several little boys hanging about to peep at us, one of whom our janissary caught, and by drawing his sword and threatening to imbrue it in his blood he terrified him into fetching the monks out of their concealment. Once in, the papades were very communicative. They told us that their convent was not freehold, and that it belonged to a Turk of Canea, who exacted an exorbitant rent.   The ruinous condition of the villages which we observed as we came along was due, they said, to the earthquake of February 14, 1810.   It came, as they always do, with a west wind, and as many as two thousand lives were lost.   A blackguardly Tartar came and sat with us, with whom we presently quarrelled, and finally, when his behaviour grew intolerable, we had to kick him out.

We left early, but our Tartar must have been ashamed of himself, for we saw nothing of him ; he had gone on.   The road wound up and up among barren rocks for about five hours, till we reached the ridge and a stupendous view of Candia, Ida, and the sea.   In three hours more we reached Candia, and took up our quarters in the house of a Jew.   There, in the course of the evening, we received a visit from the dragoman of the pasha, a very stupid Greek, who tried to be very, very grand, and later from the master of the pasha's household, Chiouk Emene, a most urbane Turk.   He was very particularly proud of his watch, and produced it, compared it with ours, and begged me to say his was the best.

We had to wait till the pasha should be ready to receive us at one o'clock. Then he sent to us, and we walked off through the streets to his palace, locally known as the porte. The entrance was surrounded with a crowd of janissaries. When we had passed them we were ushered into the room of the secretary, whom we found sitting in one corner of his sofa, surrounded with agas in so much state that I mistook him for the pasha himself. We were there but a few minutes, but long enough to see that he must be a man of talent. We afterwards learnt that he was and had many accomplishments. He could write, ride, and play the djerid better than anyone. The djerid he could cast as high as a minaret. Presently we were led through a crowd of servants into the presence of the pasha. He was in the corner, sitting in great magnificence. His pelisse was worth 20,000 piastres. By his side was a diamond-hilted dagger and two snuff-boxes set in diamonds and pearls. Three chairs, covered with red brocade, were placed before him for us to sit on. Our two dragomans stood on either side of us, and, at each word spoken and answered to the pasha, moved their heads and their hands from their mouth to their head. The conversation was as follows. We were asked whence we came, and when we had replied, the friendship between the Porte and England was referred to, and the pasha desired the Jew—our host—to treat us, being Englishmen, with all possible attention. The mention of authority led the pasha to tell us that he commanded in Retimo and Canea, as well as in Candia. He next begged to know if we brought any news ; whether there had been any fighting in the west of Europe ; and whether Buonaparte had put into execution his threat of invading England. To this we replied that he knew better than to try.

Sweetmeats were then handed round, and rose-water and other essences sprinkled out of narrow-necked bottles on to our hands and wiped with a beautifully embroidered napkin. After about half an hour we rose, and the pasha having said ‘ You are welcome : I am glad of your arrival,’ we withdrew. Our departure was marked by the usual battle among the chiouks for bakshish.

Our treatment by the pasha had had a great effect throughout the city, so that when we walked through it we were everywhere stared at as foreign grandees, just as the Persian ambassador was in London. As we passed people invited us into their houses, and a boy from a cafané threw down hot water before us, a thing we understood to be an altogether exceptional compliment, and which had of course to be exceptionally rewarded. It was now about two hours after midday, and at that hour it seems the band of the pasha always plays to the public. We saw it sitting on the

top of a house, and stopped in a shop over the way to
hear it discoursing what appeared to me to be the
most excruciating discords. When it was over two
chiouks came forward, crying, ' Pray first for the
grand signor, and then for our pasha.' We turned
home, and found that the Emene aga had just been,
bringing the compliments of the pasha and a present
consisting of six loaves of sugar, three packets of wax
candles, twenty in a packet, and three pots of honey.
We expressed our lively gratitude in all the best Greek
we could command.

In the evening the pasha sent us his band to
entertain us. It consisted of six performers, mostly
Persians. Their instruments were a dulcimer, a
violin of three strings held in the right hand, the bow
in the left, a Persian pipe which had some really
beautiful tones, melancholy, soft, and sentimental, a
guitar with a very long handle, a panpipe with twenty-
one pipes, and a double drum, which was beaten by
the man who did the singing. I could not observe
that they had guidance in their playing, except such as
the ear gave them ; but by dint of practice they
managed to keep their instruments together, and the
result was, I thought, rather tender and pleasing. As
for our poor dragoman, who had heard no music since
he had left Constantinople, he was quite overcome and
dissolved in tears.

We paid a visit to the archbishop. He seemed

to have as many religious attendants as the pasha had secular ones, but he received us in a very unaffected way at his door and showed us over his church.   His answers to our questions showed him to have very little learning.   Pausanias he had never even heard of. Thence we went on to pay a visit to the captain of 'fourteen,' the chief of the five regiments here, the military commandant in fact.   He has under him from 25,000 to 30,000 troops, second only for insubordination and lack of discipline to those at Canea, where they are in chronic open rebellion.   We found him in his room, a fat vulgar man with a good many handsome arms about him ; among them a shield which he told me is still in use.   Ali, our janissary, showed me afterwards how it is handled, and anything more barbarous or inexpert I never saw.

Being such rare birds, and received with so much form and cordiality by the pasha, all the notabilities were anxious to see us.   Many Turkish agas and others signified their wish to visit us, and our poor house, alas ! alas ! was full of them from morning to night.   Some were polite, but most of them merely curious to view us.   Few questions were asked, and those few not in the least intelligent.   In fact, we have been acting the part of embassy, and we could not do otherwise.   Received and stared at and made much of as we were, we were obliged to try and do credit to our country.   Besides there was nothing else to do ;

we were practically under surveillance. No drawings could be made, nor studies of Mount Ida or the beautiful country. I was always fuming over the waste of time, but there was no help for it.

As soon as the novelty is worn off, Turks and Turkish manners become very uninteresting. Their outward bearing is very dignified, but their society is inexpressibly dull. Those few who had travelled ever so little, even so far as Malta, could be distinguished at once. A little glimpse of the world had sufficed to remove their ridiculous Turkish *superbia* and make them respect their neighbours."

CHAPTER XI

EXPEDITION TO THE LABYRINTH—DELLI YANI—THE INTERIOR—
THE RETURN TO CANDIA—LIFE THERE—REJOINS MR. NORTH—
BAD WEATHER — EXPEDITION TO EGYPT ABANDONED — SCIO —
LEAVES MR. NORTH TO GO TO SMYRNA—STORMS—DANGER AND
COLD—ARRIVES AT SMYRNA.

" On the second day we started on our expedition to
visit the Labyrinth. It was delightful to get away from
a place where we were little better than State prisoners,
unable to go out at all unless in form, and then obliged
to stay within the walls for fear of being taken for
spies if we went outside. When we had to pass
through them to get out I saw that the works are
really very strong, with a ditch which can be flooded,
and walls thirty feet high.

At night we reached Schallous, a small village, and
passed the night in the house of an old Greek. Both
he and his wife were terrified at first, as we were in
Turkish dress, and they had suffered terribly at the
hands of the Turks. He told me afterwards that his
son, after an absence of five years, had come home, and
the very first night some Turks had broken into the
house, eaten and drunk all they could lay hands on,
and finally murdered the poor youth.

Next day, by Hagiospiliotissa to the convent of
S. Georgio. Our janissaries here gave us a sample of
the tyranny of Turks by preparing for us and themselves a magnificent repast, and getting drunk and
insulting the papades. Three hours more of hilly
country, commanded at intervals by fortified towers
(kopia), brought us to the foot of Ida.

In ancient times, as well as now, towns of importance in these parts were generally found by the sea,
which was their source of wealth ; but the greatness of
Gortyna, though so far inland, was no doubt due to the
magnificent cornlands of the rich plain of Messara.
As I guess, the town stood on a pointed hill over-
looking it.

In a steep part of the hill looking towards the
plain is an inconspicuous hole in the rock, unmarked
by any architectural or structural feature. This is the
entrance to the Labyrinth.[1] We had brought a
quantity of string for a clue, which we rolled on two
long sticks, then lit torches and went in. At first one
enters a vestibule out of which lead several openings.
Two of the three, perhaps four, dark entrances are
blocked up, but one remains open. This we followed,
and for three mortal hours and more we groped about
among intricate passages and in spacious halls. The
windings bewildered us at once, and my compass being

---

[1] Recent excavations by Messrs Evans and Hogarth throw quite a
different light on the true nature of the Labyrinth.

broken I was quite ignorant as to where I was. The clearly intentional intricacy and apparently endless number of galleries impressed me with a sense of horror and fascination I cannot describe. At every ten steps one was arrested, and had to turn to right or left, sometimes to choose one of three or four roads. What if one should lose the clue !

A poor madman had insisted on accompanying us all the way from Candia. He used to call me St. Michael ; Douglas, St. George ; and Foster, Minos. We knew him as Delli Yani. Much against our will he persisted in following us into the cavern, and when we stopped, going off with a boy who had a lantern. Conceive our horror when we found suddenly that he had disappeared. There in that awful obscurity he might wander about till death relieved him. We sent back two men along the clue with torches to shout for him, and listened anxiously, but the Turks were quite unconcerned. God, they said, takes care of madmen. We went on, and sure enough after about an hour Delli Yani turned up with the boy, who was horribly frightened. We entered many chambers ; in some were Venetian names, such as Spinola ; in another, ' Hawkins 1794,' 'Fiott' and other Englishmen, and many names of Jews. All the *culs de sac* were infested with bats, which were very annoying, and rose in thousands when one of our party fired a pistol. In one place is a spring.

Here and there we saw some lichen, and there were occasional signs of metallic substances, but not enough to support the idea of its having been a mine. The stone is sandy, stratified, and easily cut, the air dry, and it appears to me that the most probable purpose of this wonderful excavation was as a secure storehouse for corn and valuables from the attacks of robbers in the days of Minos. The work was plainly all done with the chisel.

The passage is always eight or ten feet wide, and four, five, six, eight, or ten feet or more high. In many places it had fallen in. The peasants tell all sorts of stories about it. They told me that in one place there are reeds and a pool, and that the hole goes right through the mountain for three miles ; that a sow went in and came out seven years after with a litter of pigs ; and so on.

We slept at Hagios Deka, left it at dawn and rode close to the foot of Ida through a very rich country, and in spite of waiting an hour on the road, reached Candia in seven hours and a half. It was evident that for purposes of his own our janissary had taken us something like fifteen hours out of our way in coming, and we had a serious dispute with him in consequence. Our hurrying back was of no use. There was no prospect of our getting away.

Candia.—We have plenty of time on our hands and can only employ it in the worst possible way by the assistance of the agas, who in the name of dull-ness come and pass away their ennui in our company. To crown our bliss, imagine us sleeping, feeding, and sitting all in one room, without the possibility of finding a hole to hide our heads alone in.

What was to me perhaps the worst affliction of all, was that to entertain our guests we had to have music, wearing on unceasingly in melancholy monotony. Our situation, in fact, was getting to be very trying.

We had a visit from our friend Alilah Agas, who begged us to send for music, which was brought. Then he wished the girls of the house (Jewesses) to come up and dance, and had we not been there no doubt he would have compelled them to come. As it was, we discountenanced it, and he gave it up. But he is a Turk ; which is as good as to say utterly unprincipled. He told me himself that in raising recruits in Anatolia for the Bey of Tunis, he gave them three hundred piastres apiece, and set it down as six hundred. That dishonesty and bestiality go hand in hand with ignorance is well seen among the Turks. Moreover they lack the civilising influence of women in their society. As soon as their affected gravity is laid aside, they betray the vilest indecency of feeling. One cannot give instances, but the fact was painfully brought home to us.

At last, on the 24th December, a note came from Mr. North to say that he was at Dia, the island across the bay. We replied begging him to stay where he was, for that if he came to Candia he would certainly be delayed. At the same time we sent to the pasha, begging to have the gate of the port opened in case Mr. North came. The gate, however, was never opened. Happily he did not come, and the dragoman we had sent with our message had to sleep at a cafané outside the gate, and we lowered dinner down to him with a piece of string over the walls. For a wonder we were left alone for this evening, and Douglas and I walked about in our little περιβολή by moonlight, and thought of home and happy Christmas parties there and our dismal Christmas out here. Amongst other subjects we talked of the divine Mrs. Siddons. I trust you never omit my love and duty to her, and my request that she will not forget her devoted admirer during his wanderings. You have never told me whether she intends ever to go on the stage again.[1]

We went to pay a farewell visit to the pasha. We found him sitting in the same state as before—in full dress, with his diamond-hilted dagger in his girdle and several magnificently rich snuff-boxes on the couch beside him. Our conversation, made up of his questions and our answers, lasted half an hour. He said he had seen a drawing of the Labyrinth which I had done, and that it was very beautiful. What was the age of

---

[1] Mrs. Siddons (1755–1831) formally retired from the stage in 1812, but continued to appear occasionally until many years later

the Labyrinth ? the name of the king who made it ? the age of the world ? &c. &c. Our answers were taken down, and our names. Finally he said our visit was agreeable to him, and bade us cordially farewell.

Then walking down to the port we took two boats for ourselves and our baggage, and urging the boatmen to hurry, in our eagerness not to miss a chance of sailing that evening if the wind allowed it, we reached Dia in two hours ; and there was Mr. North very pleased to see us. We now watched the wind for a chance of getting out of port, but it shifted unsteadily from point to point, and there we remained twelve days. My occupations were to wander about over the desert island, draw, and read a great deal. It was dull, no doubt, but nothing to the active boredom of society in Candia. Mr. North had several excellent cases of books, and I fell upon Gibbon, and became entirely absorbed in it.

At last the wind changed, the captain set all hands to work, and we got out of port, but lay outside rolling the whole day in a dead calm. Towards evening the wind came strong from the south, and our captain, always afraid to beat against it, let it drive us with it to the north, so that in the night we passed Nio, and in the morning found ourselves among the Cyclades between Paro and Siphanto, into the latter of which the captain begged leave to put, for he said the weather looked dirty. The harbour of Siphanto, which is called Pharo, is rather exposed to the south, but is otherwise good. There is the usual chapel to the Panagia at the entrance.

I had caught such a violent cold and fever from sleeping on deck the night before that I was forced to go to bed and stop there for the next two days, so that I was prevented from going ashore and visiting the town with North and Foster. It lies about one hour off on the hill, the houses scattered and looking from a distance like the broken remains of a wall Above is a castle, apparently of the time of the Dukes of the Archipelago. Foster found nothing there of interest except numbers of pretty girls, some of whom were so pressing that he found it difficult to get away alone. The fact is the men of the island, being mostly sailors, are away at sea, and the ladies, being left in a majority, make the love which in other countries is made to them. The costume, a Venetian bodice and high bonnet, with very short petticoats, is pretty and peculiar. There are no Turks in the island, but some Turkish sailors lying in the port took offence at the fine clothes of North and Douglas, saying we were Romaics, and had no right to ridicule their Faith by wearing their sacred dress. They even threatened to give stronger proofs of their displeasure than by mere words.

However, next morning we were towed out of port ; but being becalmed all day outside, Mr. North, who had been stirred by the remonstrances of the Turks just mentioned, sent in a boat, and got a wig, a pair of shoes and breeches for his own wear.

Next day we were still lying becalmed among the Cyclades, but the next a light breeze sprang up and carried us northwards through the passage towards Scio ; for Mr. North, tired of our delays, having lost all confidence in our captain, and frightened at the violence of the winds, had finished by making up his mind to give up the voyage to Egypt ; and this caprice, by which all our time and immense expenses were wasted, necessarily involved us all. I must say I was bitterly disappointed. But luck was against us ; we could not afford to make the journey alone, and I had to make the best of it. It took us two days to get to Scio.

A steady wind carried us gently on from Mykoni, and we seemed to enter a large lake : on one side were the mountains of Anatolia ; on the other, the left, the Isle of Scio, richly cultivated and populous. The whole coast is covered with the so-called mastic villages. The mastic plant, which is cultivated mainly on the east side—the side we were looking at—of the island, is a high evergreen. It is gathered much as resin is from firs, and the annual crop is about 6,000 okes, all of which goes to Constantinople. Besides mastic, the island produces a vast quantity of fruit, which also goes to the capital. The population is very large, almost entirely Greek. Compared to the wretched Cretans, they are very independent, both men and women. The latter paint extravagantly and wear an ugly costume ; but I must say that on a *festa*, such as the day after our arrival, being the 13th of January and New Year's Day in Greece, the crowds of them dressed in their best, sitting on either side of the street, looked as brilliant as banks of flowers.

Before leaving we went to see the chief curiosity of the island—viz. Homer's School. It lies northwards, along the shore, about an hour's ride. You arrive first at a fall of a small stream into the sea, and a little above is a singular hanging rock, the top cut smooth into a circular floor about 20 feet across. In the centre an altar is left, on which are carved in bas-relief, on three sides, greyhounds, and on the fourth— the front—something resembling the head and breast of a sphinx. It looks south-east. The situation is exceedingly pretty, but why it should be called Homer's School I cannot conceive. It was more probably an altar to some deity whose shrine was near—possibly the deity of the beautiful spring below.

There is in Scio an agreeable polyglot society of merchants of all nations living together in harmony. One may find an English family where English is the only language not spoken, the men perhaps speaking a little badly, and the women going to church on Sunday and not understanding a word. As Mr.

K

North intends to remain here and Douglas is starting homewards by way of St. Petersburg, Foster and I took leave of them and sailed for Smyrna in the evening.

We were carried gently along between Scio and the mainland till we reached the north end of the passage. There we fell in with a storm The wind rose very strong ; all around us grew fearfully black, and close to us fell a waterspout. Hereupon the man at the helm sunk terrified on his knees and made a large cross in the air with his hand. But our old pilot ordered him to look to the helm, for that he would save us from the danger. Drawing out a knife with a black handle (a very important point, I understand), he with it made also a cross in the air, and then stuck it into the deck and pronounced the words : Ἐν ἀρχῇ ἦν ὁ λόγος, &c. (' In the beginning was the Word.') Whereupon, or very shortly after, the waterspout did disperse and our pious Greek took to himself all the credit for having saved us from a considerable danger. Our next fright was that we should hardly be able to clear Cape Boronu, the point of the Gulf of Smyrna, but we did just manage to do that also.

The wind changed about several times, till presently it came down in a heavy gale from the north and continued to increase, till all was confusion and terror on board. And indeed we were in a very awkward plight ; for our ship was a very bad sailer and we were on a lee shore with a wind she could make no head against. Besides, the rain and the hail prevented our seeing anything. The captain completely lost his head, trembled with fear, and began reproaching us for persuading him to leave Scio. The only man who kept his presence of mind was the pious old pilot. He knew of a port near by, where we might possibly gain shelter, and by his great skill we succeeded in arriving there ; but it was neck or nothing. The smallest mismanagement and we should have been dashed on the rocks. As it was, we as near as possible ran on to them, owing to the anchor being let down too late ; for the ship, in swinging round, drove towards them with appalling violence. The captain fell on his knees, and we all expected the ship to be dashed to pieces. She actually swung up to within three yards of the rocks, and there the anchor held us. We all drew a deep breath and thanked our stars. It had been a very near thing.

For days the wind was still against us, and piercingly cold. We stayed where we were. I was thankful to have Pope's 'Homer' with me as a consolation.

Our vessel is managed on the system in use at Hydra, Syra, Spezzia, &c., viz. that half the profits of a voyage go to the captain or proprietor, and the other half to the crew. Sometimes the members of the crew have also shares in the venture, and so are

doubly interested ; sometimes the captain is sole proprietor and supercargo.   The system ensures a brisk
co-operation, as everyone is interested in the success
of the venture.

On the 20th we were still in the same place, the
wind still blowing from the N.N.E.—a Greco Levante,
as it is called—and the cold as bitter as ever it is in
England.   Snow fell and froze on the deck.   The sea,
which was warmer than the air, gave off a mist which
rose from it in a thick steam.

One of the sailors told me of some antiquities
inland, and I tried to get to them ; but first of all it
was difficult to persuade the crew to turn out to put
me ashore.   They complained of the cold, and would
not leave the cabin, where they were crouching over
the fire.   Once on shore I found everything frozen—
ice rather thick—and when I got up to the town I
found the antiquities were about three hours off, and
nobody could give me any clear account of them ; so
I had to give it up and return to Pope's ' Homer ' and
the cabin.

We lay here in all eight days—till the 22nd—
shivering in a filthy cabin among the sailors, utterly
idle and half starved.   At last on that day we were
able to move to the island of Vourlac, where we added
two more days of wretchedness to our account ; and
then, when we had consumed every particle of food
except our salt fish, we found a boat to carry us to

Smyrna. The captain of the ship would not stir. The weather was still very rough, and the wretched coward waited another eight days before he ventured up.

No one who has not experienced it, can have an idea of the horrors of a storm in a Greek brig. The sailors, out of all discipline or order, run about all over the ship in the most frantic attitudes of dismay, with their bushy heads of hair flying in all directions, and scream contrary orders to each other. Then the boldest, even if he be but the cabin boy, takes the command, abuses the captain and encourages the rest by his orders and example. All is in confusion, and if one escapes shipwreck it is more by good luck than by good management."

CHAPTER XII

LIFE IN SMYRNA—TRIP TO TRIOS—FOSTER FALLS IN LOVE—
COCKERELL STARTS ALONE FOR TOWN OF SEVEN CHURCHES—
PERGAMO—KNIFNICH—SUMEH—COMMERCE ALL IN THE HANDS
OF GREEKS—KARASMAN OGLU—TURCOMANS—SARDIS—ALLAH
SHERI—CROSSES FROM VALLEY OF HERMUS TO THAT OF THE
MEANDER—HIERAPOLIS—DANGER OF THE COUNTRY—TURNS
WESTWARDS.

"AFTER our experiences of danger, discomfort, and cold at sea, Smyrna seemed to us a paradise of delightfulness. The consul received us very hospitably, and introduced us to various acquaintance and to the pleasures of the carnival which was going on. To you in England its diversions would have appeared vulgar and flat. To us it was the quintessence of gaiety to meet the masques, bad as they were, with their forced hilarity, passing noisily from one Frank house to another. On the last days of the carnival there were processions, than which nothing could be more ridiculous. There was a Bacchus on a barrel with various spouts about his body which, when turned, distributed wine to the populace; and about the car it rode on, piped and danced a number of wretches dressed in nankeen stained to a flesh-colour and hung with faded leaves and flowers. There followed on another car the 'Illness and Death of Bacchus.' He was in bed surrounded by a procession of weeping bacchanals, priests, doctors, glisters, and other remedial engines of gigantic dimensions. In sober daylight such a sight calls for its enjoyment for an amount of lightheartedness Englishmen do not at all moments possess—but we, under the circumstances, were very much amused.

We would have started at once on a tour of the Seven Churches if the road had been clear. For the moment, however, it is blocked by the presence of a pasha, who with four thousand troops is raiding and making war on his own account. His army is stationed just across our path, and I have been strongly advised to wait until the storm is passed over.

I am really not sorry to have such a good reason for remaining a little longer where I am. The weather is still very severe and quite unfit for travelling.

Our chief friend in Smyrna is a Mr. Thomas Burgon, married to a Smyrniote lady. With him we started on February 15 to make a little trip of four days to Boudron, the ancient Trios.

We went in an open boat up the gulf to Vourlac, that is to say, to the scala or port of it, which is on an island opposite to the site of the ancient Clazomenæ, and walked from there to the town, spent the night there, and next day rode to Boudron. Here was only a tiny cafané, and nothing but a bench to sleep on.

The following days were passed entirely among the ruins of temples and magnificent buildings, among which now only a few scattered husbandmen guide their ploughs.   If in Chandler's day — 1775 — the Temple of Bacchus was anything like what he describes, it must have been a good deal knocked about since, for it is very different now.   The country we passed through generally is exceedingly fertile, and, in consequence of the great demand for produce in and about Smyrna, very prosperous.

When I got back to Smyrna I was fortunate enough to make the acquaintance of Captain F. Beaufort, R.N.,[1] of H.M. frigate *Frederiksteen*.   He is an accomplished antiquarian, a taste he has been able to cultivate in these countries, as he has been employed for some time in charting the coasts hereabouts.

I have suffered not a little from the changeableness of my companions : Mr. North first, in giving up the whole voyage to Egypt when we were halfway there, because of the weather ; then Douglas, in suddenly at Scio taking it into his head to go home to England because he was disappointed of the voyage to Egypt ; and now, finally, Foster has fallen in love and refuses to make with me the tour of the Seven Churches, as he promised, because he cannot tear himself away from his lady love.

[1] Later Sir Francis Beaufort, chief hydrographer to the Navy.

The difficulty mentioned before about the raiding pasha has been settled. The moslem of this place have conciliated him with a gift of 20,000 piastres, and he is to retire to his own pashalik of Kauna. So I only await my horses and janissary to set off alone.

March 1st.—I started in a boat for the scala of Menimen, where the horses were waiting for me to take me to Menimen on the Hermus. As my janissary got drunk overnight, I had to wait next morning till seven before I could start, and in consequence did not get so far as I intended, and had to sleep in a small cafané, on the site, as I take it, of the ancient Cumé. We slept six in a small space, the divan, with a large fire, while the three or four horses were in the space beyond. Greeks steal when they get a chance, but Turks as a rule may be trusted ; and though Dimitri and I were so tired that we left my arms, silver cup and spoons, &c., lying about all night, nobody touched them. In the morning I walked over the site of Cumé. There were large remains of the wall nine or ten feet thick, and I found the torso of a white marble statue five feet six inches long, of a very beautiful style. The head, arms, and legs had been broken off by the aga of the place because he thought he should find gold inside. It is not far from here to Pergamo, but it took us unusually long because the water was out in all the low ground, and one had to keep to the causeways.

These are made mostly of stones taken from ruined cities, in which one saw bits of architraves, friezes, and so on.   Getting off the causeway in one place, I was very nearly bogged.

At Pergamo I lodged in the khan.   The first thing I did was to walk up to the castle.   It is in three stages, with remains of fortification of all ages, from the earliest to the Genoese, but the Roman are the most important.   On the second stage are two towers and a great wall built of Roman-Greek fragments of white marble.   Above are two larger towers with a gate and strong wall full of fragments.   On the southwest side a gap or dell in the hill is filled up with arches fifty feet high by twenty wide, and above them a range of smaller ones, the whole forming a solid foundation for an immense temple [1] of white marble in the best Roman-Greek style.   The whole work is prodigious and very noble.   There are still considerable remains of the temple, but they are rapidly disappearing, for the Turks cut them up into tombstones. The ancient town seems to have been built on the hill.   Everywhere on the sides of it are immense foundations.   The amphitheatre is an extraordinary building.   It stands in a narrow valley astride of a river.   The two sides of the valley make the two ends of the oval, and the middle stands upon arches under which the river runs.   I was detained at Pergamo two

---

[1] Since excavated at the cost of the Prussian Government

days by the weather. It poured all the first day, and
the second the water was out and the river too high
for me to get across.

I went to the baths to see the vase for which
Canning offered 10,000 piastres, and bought there a
beautiful stone for 40 piastres, and some bronze coins.

I took a guide to show me the way across the
river, for the water was out all over the valley, and
even on the causeway it was over our horses' knees,
and to get off it would have been dangerous. On the
way we met the son of a neighbouring aga with a
party of fifty armed followers. . We took them at
a distance for a company of derrys, or mountain
robbers. But when they came near us we saw they
were much too smart. The young man was merely
going to the Aga of Pergamo with the compliments
of his father on the recovery of his health. Seeing me
and my suite dressed *à la Turque,* he sent in passing a
man with his compliments to me to wish me a happy
journey.

The pleasant taste left by this graceful courtesy
was wiped out by the next incident, which was far
from agreeable. We came upon a camel-driver whose
camels had got bogged in the swamp and could not be
made to move backwards or forwards. Impatience
at his trouble had put the man so beside himself
that as we passed on he insulted our party. I did
not understand a word he said, or the cause of

offence, but our janissary was in a moment as furious as he. Both drew their pistols, and I had the greatest difficulty in containing my man. One or other would have been killed for no reason that I could comprehend. I managed to drag my man away, and we went on to Knifnich ; after which our horses, wearied with their wetting and plodding through the heavy mire, could go no further, and we halted for the night. I had a letter to a resident Armenian merchant who received me with genuine hospitality ; he introduced me to a relation of his, and the two vied in their honest gallantry. Each insisted on entertaining me. Finally my friend gave a party in my honour ; and in the evening, the Turkish part of the company having departed, the women, contrary to the usual Armenian custom, appeared. The music which had been sent for began to play the Greek circle, the Romaika, and we all danced it together. At the end I did what I had understood before was the height of gallantry in these countries : on passing the musicians, dancing with my fair one, I clapped a dollar into the hand of the musician to express my enjoyment. Better still, is with a bit of wax to stick your sequin on his forehead, but I had no wax even if I had wished to try it. After eating and dancing to our heart's content, beds were spread, and in courtesy the landlord remained in the room till I was undressed. Nothing, in fact, could be more cordial than their treatment of me.

The trade of Knifnich is in raw cotton.

Next day I got as far as Sumeh. The roads were so heavy that our baggage horse fell and I thought we should never get him up again. This comes of having started too early in the year. Close to Sumeh, in a dell, is the picturesque village of Tarcala, with an ancient castle above it. A friend, Constantine Stephano, took me to call on a Greek family there. I cannot go into details ; suffice it to say I found the people so really barbarous that I could not bear it and came out. Indeed, in simple savagery it would be impossible to surpass the natives of this country.

In the khan I found a number of Romaic Greeks. It was the last day of carnival and they were singing Moriote songs, making a noise and behaving themselves generally in a way they would not venture to do in Greece proper. The fact is, that Karasman Oglu, who governs all this part of the country from Pergamo north to Samos in the south and inland to Sart and Magnesia, is an extraordinarily good administrator for a Turk. He sees that the Greeks form the most industrious and the richest part of the population, and that it is to his interest to protect them. Trade is flourishing, and Greeks from other parts, such as those from the Morea who were so noisy in the khan, come and settle under him. I am bound to say that here, and everywhere else where

they come into power, they are insolent and insufferably vain.

On the other hand, the Turks hereabouts are a
mild and hospitable but apparently a dull race. They
are even more severely taxed than the Greeks. For
instance, it was they who had to pay to buy off the
raiding pasha I spoke of, and in places remote from
the seat of government they suffer great oppression
from the hands of their petty governors. Indeed at
times they have openly expressed to me their desire
that the French or the English would take possession
of their empire, for that they would be better off
in the hands of anybody than in those of their own
countrymen. And nothing would be easier than to
take possession of it. In all my tour I saw only one
fortress, and that a small one, quite incapable of re-
sisting a regular force. Moreover, it is not a cramped
country like the Morea, but perfectly open; and after
you leave the coast, which is really populous and well
cultivated, it is a desert. In nine hours' journey from
Akhissar to Sart, I came across only one village and
a few Turcomans.

These Turcomans are a nomadic people. They
live in tents, of which you find perhaps twenty
together, with their herds of cattle, horses, and camels
around them, and wander about following the pasture.
They consider themselves just as much part of the
inhabitants as the settled population, and are well

armed and dressed. As a rule, in these parts at any rate, they are inoffensive, but further up the country I am told they are organised into larger bands, call themselves dervishes or desperadoes, and if travellers do not keep together in large caravans, attack, rob, and even sell them for slaves. I was even given the sort of price I might be expected to fetch in that capacity, viz. from ten to twenty pounds.

From Sumeh to Kerikahatch, and thence over a low watershed into the valley of the Hermus and to Akhissar, where there is nothing worth seeing. I spent the evening with Greek and Armenian merchants, very rough company.

Went on towards Sardis. At a village on a small branch of the Hermus we came upon a large party of Turcoman women, who had come down from the mountains to wash. They made no attempt to avoid observation as the Turkish women do, and some of them were exceedingly beautiful. They had with them three men as guard, who showed no jealousy of us and very civilly told us our way. In the afternoon we arrived at the Hermus, and the view of the valley I shall never forget. It was a glorious country up the river, but the cultivation and the rich population were behind us, and in front was a continued desert. A ferry-boat running on a rope set us over the river, and an hour later we reached Achmet Li, a miserable village of mud cottages, and prepared to pass the night in the wretched cafané. Happily, when it got about that we were not Turks, the widow of a Greek papa gladly received us and lodged me well. The raiding pasha aforesaid had passed through and burned the aga's house, but done no other harm beyond eating up all the fowls in the place; there was not one to be got for love or money for my supper.

Next day we got early to Sart. The neighbourhood affords the most lovely views imaginable of distant hills. The site itself is peculiar. The hills are wholly of fat earth, no rock seen at all, and the weather has worn them into the most fantastic forms. Amidst them the castle, standing at the foot of Bousdagh, is astonishingly picturesque. But the whole is a very picture of desolation. Where the ancient Sardis stood are now ten or twelve miserable huts. Far off across the glorious landscape I could distinguish one solitary wretched village, and here and there a Turcoman's tent. A veritable desert, where the soil is rich as anyone could imagine.

Besides the fine situation there is only one other thing to notice, viz. the Ionic temple. I spent my first day in examining it and making a drawing of it. Only three of the five columns still standing in Chandler's time remain erect; the other two were blown up three years ago by a Greek who thought he might find gold in them. The whole temple is buried many feet deep. As I wished very much to see the base of the column, I got a Cretan—whom I found here professedly buying tobacco, but I suspect a fugitive from his home for some murder—to dig for me. I had to give it up after we had got down ten feet without reaching it. One ought to be here for a month, and then, as the earth is very soft, one could do the thing thoroughly. Nobody would interfere. I spent the evening with the Turcomans in a tent, sitting cross-legged on a mat, smoking. They had a bold free manner and a savage air, but they were not uncivil to me. My janissary got into a dispute with one because he had taken his place. He ordered him out, and the man would not go. As he and all his companions were well armed, a fight would not have been pleasant, and when the dispute quieted down I was not sorry.

The ruins of the comparatively modern town, especially those of a large church, seem to consist entirely of fragments of ancient temples, some of the bits being very fine. The castle has no remains of earlier date than that of the Lower Empire. The more ancient fortress may have been swept away by the torrents, which tear the soil into such strange forms, and the whole site be changed. At any rate I could not find a scrap of ancient wall anywhere, and the later ones are rapidly being undermined, and totter on the edge of the precipice.

Next day we rode eastwards along the side of

L

Bousdagh (Tmolus). In five hours we passed only two small villages and a number of Turcoman tents, but we met many caravans, the camels whimsically decked with feathers and shells, and the largest male with festoons of bells as well. I was told that the Turks were very fond of witnessing camel-fights, and that those which I saw most handsomely dressed out were the champions at that sport.

The houses hereabouts are all built of mud, and so full of mice that I could not sleep in the night and was in consequence late in starting. We continued along the great valley and came by midday to Allah Sheri (Philadelphia), the most forlorn city ever I saw. The squalid mud houses cover several small hills and contain a population of about a thousand families, mostly Turks. There are twenty-four churches, of which only five are in use, while the rest are kept sacred by occasional services. In the shape of antiquities there is nothing to be seen. The chief curiosity is the warm mineral spring, which smells like addled eggs and has a taste of ink. The people about use it a good deal for scorbutic complaints. Some travellers have spoken of having been shown a wall of bones here. I saw nothing of the sort.

Two hours' travelling next day brought us at last to the end of the immense plain of the Hermus, and we began to get among the mountains, going up the east side of a steep romantic dell, the west side of which was wonderfully rugged and wild. Beyond were mountains covered with snow : beneath us an immeasurable giddy depth. Except a few sheep, we saw no living thing for hours together. Once I heard some wild duck by the torrent below. At the end of six hours we reached Derwent, a village of, say, two hundred houses. A wretched lodging and, as there was no fowl to be got—and that is what one depends entirely upon—no supper ; and I had to be content with smoke, coffee, and Homer. In the evening came, as usual, a number of Turks to see the stranger. They enter, they salute with a ' Salaam aleikum,' and sit down perhaps for hours. Their conversation generally turns upon the stranger, with conjectures upon his object in coming. Later at night came in the son of our host. He had been searching for a strayed ox, and was afraid that the wolves had got it. He examined my firearms for a long while, and admired them very much. The Turks of this part of the country are large, handsome, very slow in their speech, and stupid and ignorant.

Starting next morning, we began by following the course of a river till we got on to a high level plain surrounded by formless hills—an ugly country. We met a few Turcomans, and once I saw some ploughing. At the end of seven hours' riding we reached the edge of the valley of the Meander and looked over a glorious view ; then downwards through Bulladan, a village of about five hundred houses and a number of mosques, to a village the name of which I never learnt, where we slept.

As one expects nothing of one's host but shelter, it was an unusual hospitality in ours to give us some of his bread. It was a strange compound, such as I had never seen before. To make it, the dough is mixed very thin and poured on a heated copper. The result looks like rags of coarse cloth and tastes like bad crumpets. We slept in a barn with the horses.

Next day we descended into the plain of the Meander and crossed the river by a bridge of four or five arches, the parapet of which is made of the steps of a theatre. Just there was a man administering a singular remedy to a mule which had fallen sick in the road. He had tied all four legs together and thrown him down. Then he had cut the throat of a sheep, and holding the mule's mouth open, let the sheep's blood flow into it. I was assured it was an excellent medicine. From the bridge onwards we crossed a flat till we reached the ridge, at the foot of which is Hierapolis. It had cost me certainly a whole day more than was necessary to get here, because Tabouk Kalise (the castle of the cemetery), its proper name, was spelt in Chandler, Pambouk (cotton); and when I inquired for Pambouk Kalise no one could make out what I meant, so that practically I lost my way

until I got into the valley of the Meander. Once
there, Hierapolis is a conspicuous object from a great
distance on account of the remarkable whiteness of
the rock on which it stands.

This is due to a petrification deposited by the
river, which rises, a full stream, in the city and flows
over the front of the cliff. It makes a fine cascade,
and the spray of it, carried by the wind, spreads a
white coating like ice over everything it reaches. As
it gradually forms, it takes rounded shapes overlapping
each other, something like conventional clouds. The
ruins of the ancient city stand on the top above the
cliff and half buried in a sea of this singular deposit.
The vast colonnades present the most extraordinary
appearance. The most magnificent are perhaps the
ruins of the gymnasium, and the best preserved the
theatre, which is all perfect except the proscenium ;
but perhaps what astonished me most was to find, on
going out of one of the gates, a number of tombs of
various forms and sizes as complete as on the day
they were built, two thousand years ago. The style
of them is very large and magnificent. Many of the
sarcophagi are eight or nine feet long by three or four
wide, and the rest in proportion. All bear inscriptions, but the rough quality of the stone prevented my
reading them. Under the sarcophagus, and forming
part of the monument, is generally a stone bench for
the friends of the deceased to sit upon and meditate.

There are some beautiful bas-reliefs in high preservation lying exposed in the theatre.   Altogether, for
preservation there can be nothing but Pompeii to
compare to this place.

I did not forget to inquire for the remarkable cave
in which no animal can live, which Chandler tried to
find.   My guide led me to one near the spring and
told me that on certain days birds flying over it fall
down, overcome by the fumes.   There, sure enough, I
did find four small birds with the bones of various other
animals.   If travellers had been frequent here I could
have supposed that someone had put the birds there
for sightseers to wonder at; but according to the old
aga I am the first traveller here since Chandler's time
in 1765, and it seemed impossible that it should have
been done on such short notice merely to make a fool
of me.

When evening came on, I walked down again to
Yemkeni where the janissary and horses were.   The
aga had prepared a meal for me, and ate it with me,
sometimes tearing bits of meat off and throwing them
into my plate.   As usual, all the Turks came in, in the
evening, to stare.

All next day it blew and poured, but I went up to
the ruins attended by the aga's man, and worked hard
all day long.   I had bought a live fowl to try Strabo's
experiment of putting him into the cave; but whether
it was not really the right cave, or whether the violent

wind and rain prevented the gas having effect, at any
rate the fowl was none the worse after being exposed to
it for half an hour, and we ate him with a good appetite in the evening. Over his bones the aga grew
talkative, and told me of the real cave which was in
the mountain, one hour distant. He said that inside the cave is a bridge, and beyond that a chamber
in which is a treasure guarded by a black man.
He added that he who should get the better of
that black man had need have studied and learnt
much. Many and many an adventurer, after the
treasure, had died horribly in the cavern. And so on,
with all the cock-and-bull stories universal among the
Turks. But when I asked him to give me a guide to
take me to the cave, he put every sort of difficulty
into the way. I should need ladders, and there were
none—horses, and there were none. In short it was
quite clear he meant to prevent my going, so I gave
it up. I did so the more willingly because I already
felt exceedingly uncomfortable. The people around
me were utter savages, and the country perfectly lawless. South of the river, in the direction of Denisli or
Laodicea, it was worse; and besides brigands, which
were said to abound between Denisli and Aidin
and would oblige my taking an expensive escort,
the agas themselves had a very bad reputation for
extortion. Moreover, my janissary was anxious, because in coming to Hierapolis we were already

outside the limits to which my travelling firman referred, and he wished to get back within them. So, all things considered, I decided to give up seeing Laodicea (I could make out the situation of it at a very great distance) and passed on to avoid the desert country and dangerous neighbourhood."

CHAPTER XIII

BACK INTO CIVILISATION—NASLI BAZAR—NYSA—GUZUL—HISSAR (MAGNESIA)—THE PLAGUE—AISALUCK (EPHESUS)—SCALA NUOVA —A STORM—SAMOS—PRIENE—CANNA—GERONTA—KNIDOS— RHODES—MR. NORTH AGAIN—SAILS FOR PATARA—CASTEL ROSSO —CACAVA—MYRA—THE SHRINE OF ST. NICOLAS—TROUBLES WITH NATIVES—A WATER SNAKE—FINICA—CAROSI—OLYMPUS —VOLCANIC FIRE—PHASELIS—FALLS IN WITH THE *FREDERIK-STEEN.*

" Two days' riding down the river brought us to Nasli Bazar, which is within the government of Karasman Oglu, and the fact was at once perceptible. Greeks were numerous and impudent, trade flourishing, and the bazaar full of all kinds of merchants. It is the great mart for the interior. I had to pass the night in a wretched khan. In the chamber adjoining mine was a slave merchant with two young negresses, one of whom had a child for sale, and also a fine young negro.

I followed the valley of the Meander to Sultan Hissar. On the way I went up a steep ascent to see the ruins of Nysa. They stand on an elevated plain over the river, and command a grand view and good air above the malarious bed of the Meander and its bordering marshes. There is first of all a large

agora, with traces of temples in or around it.
Further on, in the side of the mountain, is a very
considerable theatre, with the remains of the proscenium and apartments for actors &c. on all sides.
Seated in the theatre one had a glorious view of
the senate house and prison, with the amphitheatre
beyond, and the bridge which spans a gully in one
magnificent arch.   All these buildings are in a
grandiose style, very impressive, and made all the
more so by their absolute solitude.   In Nysa was but
one man, a shepherd, who had taken up his abode in
one of the arches of the theatre.

After a stay there of two hours we went on down
the valley.   We had now quite left the desert behind
us and come into civilisation, cultivation, and orderly
government.   Every two or three miles we passed a
cafané and a guard, with an air of order and discipline.
My janissary was full of admiration for Karasman
Oglu, and related to me stories illustrating his character.
I recollect two.   A Greek merchant going to Akhissar
was robbed by four Turks of 800 sequins.   The
poor man made his complaint to Karasman Oglu,
who at once gave him the money, as recognising his
responsibility for order, and that the merchant might
not stand out of his money while it was being recovered.   Then he despatched his police, who in a
few days brought in the four Turks, and they were
then and there hanged.   The Turks resent his pro-

tection of the Greeks and Christians, and call it partiality. Hearing of this, Karasman called together the chief Turks of Magnesia, and when he had given them coffee, he told them that he had summoned them as he wished to raise a sum of 30,000 piastres for government purposes, and they should be repaid in a few months with the interest due. The proposition being received with dead silence, he sent for four poor Greek primates of some small villages in the neighbourhood, and made them the same proposal in the presence of the Turks. They at once assented, and the money was brought in an hour. 'Now,' said he, 'you see why I prefer the Greeks. The first of you who complains again shall lose his head.'

When we got in the evening to Guzul Hissar I found the reports I had picked up on the road exaggerated in two main particulars. I had been told that the plague was raging in the town, and that there were English corn-merchants to whom I could apply for harbourage. There was a good deal of plague, no doubt, in the town, which is extensive, but hardly enough to deter one from entering it ; while the nearest thing to an English merchant was a Genoese merchant living in the house of a Sardinian doctor who enjoyed English protection. They made room for me, and were very kind and hospitable ; and it was a comfort to be in a Frank house, but outside it was rather nervous work. A house close to our lodging was infected by the plague, and as I was going down the street a Greek warned me to make room for him. ' I have nothing the matter with me,' said he, ' but a few days ago my brother died of the plague.' Need I say that I complied at once. The panic that grows in a plague-stricken city, and which one cannot help imbibing, has a strange effect on characters. The woman of the neighbouring house, which, as I said, was *impestata*, was seen going about out of doors by my host the doctor, and he was beside himself at the sight.

The importance of Guzul Hissar as a place of commerce arises from its standing on the track of the corn trade between the interior and Scala Nuova. I came upon caravans of one hundred to one hundred and fifty camels, bringing corn from Cæsarea. Some bring it from even as far as the borders of Persia. Once here, its value is doubled or trebled; but the greed of the agas and the roguery of the Greek merchants prevent much of the profit going to the growers. Signor Mora told me that the great trouble he found was the system of constant *douceurs* and bribery. It makes it impossible for a merchant to make his calculations.

I walked up to see the few remains of the city of Magnesia. Like all Greek cities, it stood above the plain. There is a theatre just discernible, a stadium below it, and a few remnants of a gymnasium.

One night in Guzul Hissar was enough for me, and next day I started for Scala Nuova ; and leaving the valley of the Meander on the left, kept by the mountain to the right, and came late to Aisaluck, the ancient Ephesus. Here I dismissed my janissary and horses, and, relieved of my expensive suite, spent a blissful, tranquil day alone. The castle is a vile Turkish fort. The great mosque, in which are some grand columns of granite, is fine, and, like the others— for there are many in the place—thoroughly well executed in the true Oriental taste. The degraded modern Turk is incapable of producing anything half so good.

The remains of Ephesus are very trifling, and what there are, are in a very poor style. I did not, any more than other travellers, find out the Temple of Diana,[1] though of course I have my own opinion as to the site. Aisaluck is now an almost deserted town. It has only about fifteen inhabited houses, and the mosques and forts are in ruinous condition, but their number and splendour show that it must once have been an important Turkish city. I called on the aga, and by way of a present gave him a little gunpowder, with which he was delighted. My lodging was in a miserable little cafané, anything but a palace of luxury.

[1] The Temple of Diana was discovered by Mr. J. T. Wood, who carried on excavations from 1863 to 1874 on behalf of the British Museum.

The fleas within, added to the jackals howling without, prevented my getting any rest.   But it was not
much worse than my other lodgings on this tour.
Luxuries have been few.   All I can say is I have
learnt not to miss them.   In my Turkish dress I pass
without observation or inconvenience.   In the evening,
after eating my meal, I smoke my pipe with the other
Turks, go to sleep and get up early.

I rode from Aisaluck to Scala Nuova, which is
only four hours off, and from thence I took a passage
for Samos on a Maltese brig of twelve hands and
six guns and set sail the following morning (March
25th) ; but when we had made half the passage,
which is by rights only about two hours, we met a
furious wind which obliged us to put back.   I went
ashore again, and as the wind rose to the force of a
hurricane I watched out of my window no less than
eighteen boats and vessels of various sizes blown
ashore and wrecked under my very eyes.   It was a
scene of incredible destruction.   The shore was strewn
with wreckage and cargoes which had been thrown
overboard—oranges, corn, barrels of all sorts of goods—
while the sailors, ruined, although thankful to have
escaped with their lives, sat round fires in some sheds
by the port, the pictures of dejection.

The wind detained me till the 28th, when
I crossed over in a boat to Bathi in Samos.   Here
I had to wait first for horses, and then on account of

the bad weather. I had to stay indoors, and indoors in a Greek house means anything but privacy. No matter where you sit, you hear everything that goes on in it. Application of any kind is out of the question. In this case, the consular court being at the other end of the house, I had to hear the cases proceeding in it. One in especial went on in detached chapters all the time I was there. A Zantiote had deserted his wife and children eighteen years ago in Mykoni. He had since lived and been married in Cyprus, while the deserted wife went to Smyrna and maintained herself and the children by hard work. She had done what she could to find her husband, in vain, till just as I arrived she discovered him in Samos. She haled him before the consul and demanded that he, being rich, should support her. Not till the whole assembly had joined the bench in calling him every name they could invent would he consent, but finally he signed an agreement to live with his wife in Samos and support the daughter. But this was but the beginning. Every day we had visits from both parties to complain that the conditions were not adhered to : he to say that the agreement to live with them did not involve supporting them ; they to say they must be supported, and meanwhile, as they were half starved, to take an opportunity of satisfying their appetites at the consulate.

I made acquaintance of a pleasant Russian,

Monsieur Marschall, and with him crossed the island to see the antiquities—first of the ancient city and then of the Temple of Juno, lying three-quarters of an hour to the eastward of it. There is only one column of it remaining, but that one very finely cut and of beautiful marble. A few years ago, I understand, there were still many standing ; but some were blown up for the sake of the metal rivets, and others knocked over by the Turkish men of war, who, as they were very white, used them as a target for gunnery practice. We returned to the village of Samos for the night, and lodged with the bishop, who was more hospitable than Greeks generally are. He was a man of some ingenuity and amusing, but very ignorant and superstitious.

We went by Bathi to Geronta and across the Bogas to Changlu on the mainland—rode to Kelibesh over the top of range of hills commanding the valley of the Meander—and the lake of Myus—and on to Sansun Kalesi (Priene), which I was very glad to see. It is an exceedingly fine site. Unfortunately it rained and blew so violently that I could not do much ; but if one could stay and dig in the temple, I dare say one might find a treasure of statues, for it remains exactly as it fell.

Two days after, we set out, riding along the foot of Mount Titanus, in frequent danger of being bogged in the low new-made ground of the Meander, which near the sea is covered with sedge and rushes inhabited by numberless waterfowl. The scenery was often very fine. We reached the corn warehouses at Canna after midday, and found there my Sardinian corn-merchant friend from Guzul Hissar. He was trying to make up a cargo, and at the moment was full of the wrongs suffered by merchants in this country. A caravan of fifteen camels he was expecting had been stopped by an aga, the corn they carried unloaded and left by the road, while the camels were sent away to carry cotton into the interior.

Here we hired a boat ; but, hearing firing in the Bogas, which we could only attribute to a pirate, we were not without some qualms at starting. With this in our heads, when we saw a large caique making directly towards us, we were naturally enough alarmed and made for the mouth of the Meander, and there remained till the bark came up and proved itself to be only a fishing caique. Setting forward again with a very strong wind, we reached the port of Geronta after dark. The boatman mistook the entrance and very nearly ran us on to a rock some distance from the shore, upon which he got into a fright and lost all presence of mind. The wind, as I said, being very high, the position was so serious that Marschall and I took the management of the bark, and giving the man a cuff sent him forward to look out for the port. In this fashion we found it and got in. Even then we

M

were not well off, for the place was perfectly solitary,
and we had no mind to remain all night in the boat.
It grew extremely dark, and it was an hour and a half
before we could find the village   On the way to it,
we passed the massive remains of the Temple of Apollo
Didymæus, and as they loomed through the darkness
they looked very grand—grander than I thought them
next morning by daylight.   The village of Geronta is
only about thirty years old and is inhabited entirely
by Albanian and Greek immigrants who seem fairly
prosperous.   The pasha, Elis Oglu, like his neighbour
Karasman Oglu, is a great patron of Greeks.   We set
sail at night, but had to put back, after a hard night,
to a port close to Geronta and wait there three days
till the weather improved.

When at last we got away, in five hours we were
off Cape Ciron, which ends in a lofty hill by which is
Knidos.   At my request the captain went into the
port, and very glad I was to see the place, the
situation is so curious . but I found no inscription or
antiquities of any kind.   I slept in the boat, and we
started at midnight.   The wind was furious ; and as
the bark laboured and strained in the waves, Dimitri
groaned with fear.   It was indeed far from pleasant ;
but as the day came on the wind went down, till we
were absolutely becalmed off the little island of Symi,
and did not get into Rhodes till afternoon.

I was preparing to go to visit the consul, and had

walked a few yards in that direction when I saw another boat come into port, and in it, to my surprise, who but Mr. North. He was as astonished as myself. and as pleased. We went together to the consul's. There we had long conversation on the subject of the island, its inhabitants, products, &c.

The present governor of Rhodes is Hassan Bey, slave of a previous governor—a man of great simplicity of life. I found him sitting in the passage of his palace without attendants or pomp. Although he is about seventy years old and deaf, he received as a present, by the same boat as Mr. North came in, a female slave. He builds ships here for Government, and has one, a frigate, for his own behoof, which he uses himself for piratical purposes while with it he clears the neighbouring seas of all other pirates.

Two days after, I left Rhodes and sailed eastwards with a light breeze, till in the evening we were becalmed off the Seven Capes. In the morning I was awakened by strange voices on board. We had been boarded by Hydriotes inquiring for corn. Their ship had been lying off the coast for some days, boarding every boat that passed for corn. She was a large ship with a crew of sixty men, who seemed to spend all their time in merrily dancing and fiddling. We rowed into the port, which is a fine harbour, and when I had landed I found a boy to undertake to guide us to Patara. It took two hours to walk there, keeping all the way by the side of an aqueduct. We met a few savage-looking Turks armed, and a boy or two playing on wild simple reeds. The whole country was very wild and desolate, and the road a mere track.

The ruins are considerable, and, although none of them belong to the finest time, very interesting. They have an inexpressibly forlorn appearance, standing as they do half buried in the sand. The once extensive port is entirely silted up.

The theatre is half filled up. I found in it an inscription, from which I gathered that the auditorium is of later date than the proscenium.

Near the head of the port are two large mausolea, at least I suppose that is what they are ; and besides these there are the remains of fortifications of the Lower Empire and of several churches. I could not get over to examine the buildings on the opposite side of the port.

We started for Castel Rosso, but were becalmed. The boys played and danced, and we did not get in till the evening. The port, a poor one, is defended by a castle which is red, whence the name. The few savages we found on the beach received us with great suspicion, with arms in their hands, but sold us some provisions. In the morning I landed and looked about. Inside the walls there are many ruins of houses, all of the Lower Empire, while the walls themselves are of much earlier date in cyclopean masonry. Outside the old walls and in the modern town there are several ancient tombs that have been respected and are in good preservation. The ground is incredibly rugged and stony, almost as bad as Maina.

We sailed off at midday, and got to the small port of Cacava in the evening. There, among the modern houses, are a number of tombs, all of them respected and well preserved. As the cross is on most of them, the town must have flourished during the Lower Empire. I found and copied various inscriptions, some of them in a character I have not seen before. In the evening we crossed to Myra, and there I enjoyed a good bathe. Then when night had come on, we worked the oars against wind till we reached a port at the east end of Karadah, and when it was morning crossed to visit the shrine of St. Nicolas. The sea was so high we had to leave the caique and walk thither. St. Nicolas is a favourite saint of the Greeks, and his shrine is greatly revered. Our captain and crew were all dressed in their very best to make their cross, and had brought with them a bottle of oil as an offering. The road was wretched, and what made it worse was that in wading across a river which was over my knees I so wetted my shalvar that they were heavy to walk in. At the mouth of the river Zanthus we found many tombs, but none of which I could read the inscription.

The holy place consists of half of a ruined church of the Lower Empire, and by the side of it a small chapel in which is the tomb. The entrance to it is so low that we were obliged to go down on our hands and knees to get in. The Greeks knelt down, bowed their foreheads to the earth, made crosses and said prayers ; then, putting some parahs on a tray, took some small candles from a bundle beside it, and stuck them round the tomb. The ceremony being over, we took some earth from near the tomb to keep as a relic, and fell into conversation with the papa of the shrine, Nicola by name, native of Salonica. He told us that early in life in a severe illness he had vowed service to St. Nicolas for the rest of his life if he recovered : that, being restored to health, he had come here in fulfilment of his vow, but that he led but a miserable life, in constant apprehension of the Turks, who are very violent and fanatical hereabouts.

I went on with Dimitri and the captain to see some remains of which he told me, at no great distance, but the other Greeks were afraid to accompany me or even to show me the way. However, I found the ruins—a theatre in astonishing preservation, and some highly interesting tombs, and was quietly taking measurements of them when several Turks appeared. They seemed highly to disapprove of our operations,

While examining some statues I heard one of them exclaim : ' If the infidels are attracted here by these blasphemous figures the temptation shall soon cease, for when that dog is gone I will destroy them.' Then some of them went away and presently came back with a larger party. While I was above in the upper part of the building, they suddenly seized the arms of Dimitri and the captain, and ordered us to follow them to the aga, who lived at a distance of no less than six hours off. At this I remonstrated, saying that I was an Englishman, a friend ; but they answered that I lied, that we were giaour Russians, and were plotting to take possession of the place. They wanted to examine our things, but this I resisted. My firman unfortunately was left behind in the boat, and matters began to look ugly. The least encouragement from the elder members would have led the crowd of ruffians to take strong measures. I could perceive that, but I saw no exit from our dilemma. There was, fortunately, still one elder of the village to be consulted, and he was ill at home. The chief of our captors went off to consult him, and a quarter of an hour later returned a different man, his rage assuaged, and willing to accept the captain's assurance that I was an Englishman. He then returned me my arms and begged that I would go where I thought proper. Of course I was very much pleased at this *dénouemeut*, but I kept my countenance and pretended to be still very angry, at which the leader, who was now afraid of me, positively quailed for fear of my vengeance. We slept the night under protection of St. Nicolas.

Accompanied by the papas, we took a boat on the river and rowed down to the port at the mouth, and across the bay to the port where our bark lay. While I was swimming, following the boat, I was not a little frightened to meet a large snake which was making for the land. I got out of its way hastily and called to the boys in the caique, who killed it as it approached the shore. It was black, with some red spots on the belly, and measured five feet two inches in length. We heaved anchor at night, and in the morning reached the port of Finica.

The town itself is three-quarters of an hour from the sea. There are the remains of a theatre, the seats all gone, and a castle of the Lower Empire, built of the said seats I found various monuments, the inscriptions all in the same unknown character. At a mill hard by, I fell in with a number of merchants belonging to Sparta, in Asia Minor, six days from here. It is curious that they all talk Turkish, but write it in Greek characters. I found them very bigoted but civil. We slept in the open air, all in a row. As I had promised them some fish, they lent me a horse, and one of them accompanied me back to the port ; but unfortunately no fish had been caught in the night, so I had to make up for it with five okes of olives and a large botza of wine, on which my friends got excessively drunk.

We now got on board and tried to beat out of port, but it was not so easy. It is very narrow, and a southeast wind, such as we had at the moment, blows right into it. Once out, we crossed the bay and got into the small port of Carosi.

We had now to get round the cape. All along this coast an imbat or sea breeze springs up from the south regularly at midday. As we took care, by rowing hard southwards, to get round the point before twelve, we caught the breeze nicely, which carried us straight north to Porto Genovese by night.

This is a fine port, and the rocks above it are very grand. We caught and ate a fine supper of fish, and sat cross-legged on our little deck drinking wine with an enjoyment of this adventurous, unconventional life I can never forget. The night was cool, the moon shone bright upon us, and we crowned the evening with Moriote songs. It was past midnight before we got to bed.

It was a short distance to the foot of Olympus. When I met Captain F. Beaufort at Smyrna, he gave me an account of the volcanic fire which springs up out of a hole in the side of this mountain, and I wished to see it. It lies about an hour's walk up the hill. The flame was just like that of a furnace, and the mouth, about five feet wide, from which it issued, was all calcined.   Ten feet from it was another mouth, from which no fire but a strong sulphurous smell issued, and about fifty yards higher up the hill there was a spring.   Close by there were also the remains of a temple, showing that the spot had been held sacred in ancient times.   My guide told me that the fire would roast eggs well, but not if they were stolen— indeed it would not act upon stolen things at all. Greeks are very superstitious, and this is one of the favourite forms it takes with them.   I tried to confute him by cutting a scrap off his turban while his back was turned and showing him how it burned, but although he saw it consumed it did not shake his belief in the least.

I went downhill again to the ruins.   They consisted mostly of Venetian or Genoese work, but there was the door of a portico erected to Germanicus, a small theatre on the south side of the river, and some very rough tombs of Roman times, among which I drew until nightfall.

Next morning we had an enchanting sail to Phaselis. The breeze was slight and the dolphins played all round us, as though they enjoyed the fair weather.   Phaselis was once a favourite stronghold of pirates, and is just made for it.   It stands on a peninsula easily defended, and has or had—for all are now destroyed—three excellent harbours.   The town was defended by a strong wall, and was provided with numbers of cisterns, besides an aqueduct for bringing water from the mainland. Where the sea had undermined the cliffs, parts of the wall and sides of cisterns had fallen away into it. There were some tombs only just recently mutilated, which I thought worth making drawings of. In the evening we put out our net and caught some fish, but lost part of the net, owing to an octopus which clung to it and dragged it into its hole.

April 28*th.*—We weighed anchor early, but there was no wind as yet, and we had rowed for some hours when we became aware of a large sail coming up on a breeze. As I scanned her I had little doubt she would be the *Salsette* or the *Frederiksteen*; but my poor captain was very much frightened, and when he saw her send a boat to board a small vessel before us, he desired his sons to hide his money in the ballast. It was not long, however, before I made out with my glass the red cross, and then I was able to set his mind at rest. When our little caique came alongside, we must have been a shabby sight; but Captain Beaufort bade me heartily welcome and gave me so cordial a shake of the hand as I can never forget. He said he had hunted for me all along the coast, and pressed me to take a cruise with him, rather than go on travelling in this hazardous fashion in the caique. The offer was tantalising; but, as I was not sure if I should feel at my ease, I only promised to stay a few days to begin with."

Extract from Beaufort's " Karamania."—" At Avova we had the satisfaction of meeting Mr. Cockerell, who had been induced by our report to explore the antiquities of these desolate regions. He had hired a small Greek vessel, and had already coasted part of Lycia. Those who have experienced the filth and other miseries of such a mode of conveyance, and who know the dangers that await an unprotected European among these tribes of uncivilised Mahommedans, can alone appreciate the ardour which could lead to such an enterprise. I succeeded in persuading him to remove to His Majesty's ship, in which he might pursue his researches with less hazard and with some degree of comfort. The alarm felt by his crew on seeing the frigate had been excessive. Had she been a Turkish man-of-war, they were sure of being pillaged under the pretext of exacting a present, if a Barbary cruiser, the youngest men would have been forcibly seized for recruits, and the rest plundered ; and even if she had been a Greek merchant-ship, their security would still have been precarious; for when one of these large Greek polaccas meets even her own countrymen in small vessels and in unfrequented places she often compels them to assist in loading her, or arbitrarily takes their cargoes at her own prices."

CHAPTER XIV

" On the 1st of May we reached Adalia (or Satalia). It stands on a plain which breaks abruptly into the sea and looks very rich and Oriental from a distance. Considering the way Captain Beaufort had given protection to certain fugitive rebels last year, he was rather uncertain what sort of reception to expect. It turned out to be a very cordial one, for the old pasha having just died and his son not yet firmly set in place, he could not deal with the high hand as Turks like to do. He expressed himself as pleased at the captain's offer to salute the fortress, but begged the guns might not be more than eleven, probably because he had only eleven guns to answer with. It was clear, however, that the appearance of the vessel had excited no small apprehension in the town. No Turks came to look at her, as usually happens in a port, and we could see that the few miserable guns in the fort had been trained to bear upon us　At the same time a handsome present was sent to the ship, consisting of bullocks, goats, fowls, vegetables, and a very magnificent dress for the captain.　The dress was refused, but the eatables were accepted and a suitable return made.　This included English ale and porter, and a big barrel of gunpowder, which, slung on a pole carried by two seamen, looked imposing.　The captain and his boat's crew and guard of marines, all in their best, and my humble self then landed and went up to pay a visit of ceremony to the pasha.　Captain Beaufort in the course of the interview very kindly asked, on my behalf, leave for the captain of my caique—which had come on to Adalia with us—to load his boat with flour, a profitable cargo which would indemnify him for being discharged by me.　The export of flour is really contraband, but as there is an immense trade quite openly carried on in it by Greek ships, they need not have made such a great favour of it as they did.　However, they gave permission, and I was indignant that my late captain never came and thanked me.　During our stay we rode one day through the town and out into the country beyond, which is very rich and well cultivated.　There are two interesting gates to the town—one on the land side, of Roman architecture, very rich and much injured, and the other towards the sea, of Frankish work, with mutilated arms and inscriptions on it.

We set sail on the 7th, without doubt to the great relief of the people of Adalia, and cast anchor again at Lara. Here there are considerable ruins, but none of them very interesting. Our next stoppage was at Eshi Satalia, the ancient Sidé, where we remained four days. The Roman theatre is of vast dimensions and in good preservation, and it is noticeable that, as is evident from marks of crosses on the stones, it had been repaired in Christian times, which shows that theatres were still used after the conversion of the inhabitants to Christianity. The proscenium was in ruins, as usual, and some of its sculptures lay in the arena. In comparatively modern times it had been utilised to form part of the city wall, but the theatre itself was in wonderful preservation. Sidé is now absolutely desolate, probably because the aqueduct which supplied the ancient city is broken, and there is no water whatever on the site. This accounts for the theatre being so well preserved.

I spent all my time among these lonely ruins to very good purpose, drawing and studying. The architecture is some of it even absurd : for instance, the triumphal façade at the entrance ; but the sculpture is all far superior to the architecture. Although not in the very best style, it is exceedingly good, and cut with astonishing freedom and boldness. As I said, the site of Sidé, and even the neighbourhood, is absolutely deserted. Nevertheless, news of our being on the coast had got about, and a Turkish dignitary came down from the interior, ostensibly to offer us civilities, but in reality to watch our proceedings. He was invited on board, but refused, saying, with a great assumption of dignity, that he had ridden an hour to the coast to visit the captain, and now the captain should come to him. The real fact was he was afraid. The captain accordingly came in the jolly-boat, the crew of which was in charge of a midshipman who charmed the Turk so much that he wanted to buy him, and made an offer of 2,000 piastres for him.

On the 16th we reached Alaia and anchored off the town. It stands on a steep rock projecting into the sea. The houses have a very Oriental look, with their flat roofs and balconies, rather like rabbit-hutches supported on long poles. Our reception was very cordial ; a salute was fired, and a present of bullocks &c. sent us. We landed to take a little turn into the town and found it filthy ; stinks of all kinds in all directions. Through narrow streets down which wound gutters, disgusting with horrors flung from upper windows, we threaded our way in apprehension of more. The ladies, however, were eager to see the Franks, and from the streets and from the ship we could descry them peeping at us in their balconies. I went with the captain to pay our visit to the council which governs in the absence of the pasha. We found it sitting in a miserable tumbledown room with walls not even plastered. We sat a few minutes, asked a few questions mainly about antiquities, and then retired to the ship to receive their return visit.

Next morning we set off to the eastwards to look for ruins of Sydra. The expedition was not a success. In the first place the surf was high and we had difficulty in landing ; then after a long walk we came upon several villages, but no considerable ruins, and what there were, only of late date and uninteresting, and we had to trudge back disappointed. In the course of our walk we came upon a small Turkish boy all alone. He screamed with fright to see our strange figures and ran away, bounding over stock and stone, and still screaming for help. He had never seen Franks before.

The following day we, the captain and officers in uniform and myself in my best, landed to walk in the town. We were first detained a long time at the gate on small excuses, and then when we started were told by the guide that if we proceeded there was danger of a disturbance. The captain told him to go on all the same, but as he refused we turned back to the port.

Then we learnt that the evening before there had been a general meeting of the Turks to protest against our being allowed to go about the town. We went aboard again ; and from the ship an officer was sent to

N

the council with a severe remonstrance against our treatment, and the present of bullocks was re-landed on the beach.   This attitude of ours brought them at once to their knees ; the humblest apologies were sent with assurances that the offenders were being punished, and a request that Captain Beaufort would come ashore and see the castle as he desired.   The captain replied that an officer of his rank could not expose himself to the possibility of a repetition of such affronts as he had submitted to that morning, but that the beyzesday (myself) with some of his officers would go, as they allowed it   We accordingly went ; but as the authority of governors in these countries is at no time very great, we went in the fullest ex- pectation of a disturbance and of being forced to turn back.   The council seems, however, to have kept its promise, for nothing of the sort occurred.   We were entirely unmolested.   On the other hand, there was nothing whatever to see.   It was a most fatiguing walk up the hill.   The town is defended by three walls, one inside the other, never well built and now ruinous, although well whitewashed to conceal their condition, and in the whole place only four cannon, all of them old.   On the top of all is the citadel, itself ruinous and full of the ruins of several Christian monasteries and churches converted into mosques, some water tanks and a fountain.   Over a gate is an inscription to say that Aladin was conqueror of this city. There are remains of a fine ancient Greek wall. This was all we saw for our trouble and risk.

The council again sent apologies and invitations to Captain Beaufort, but he replied as before; only, to show he had no resentment, he sent his surgeon, while the anchor was being weighed, to see what he could do for a member of the council who was ill. I meanwhile, with a party of officers, went off in the gig to look at some ruins we had observed to the westward on the top of a hill. We had three miles to go in the boat and about two on foot inland. The hill is high and desperately steep. On the top is a town, deserted, with ancient Greek walls, a tower, the ruins of a temple, a number of pedestals and monuments, some with inscriptions which we copied, but none of them gave us the name of the place. We have made up our minds since, judging by Strabo's description, that it must have been Laertes. The city walls, the temple, and the tower are all of cut stone and the best Greek construction, while the walls of dwellings are of small stones and mortar. This town, being all of one sort of date, is a good example by which to judge of Greek habits of building. I suppose private houses were always built in this inferior style.

Our next stoppage was at Selinty, originally Selinus, and afterwards changed, on the death of Trajan within its walls, to Trajanopolis. It stands on a remarkable rock, the Cragus, absolutely precipitous

N 2

on one side and very steep on the other, with a river, sixty feet or so wide, at the bottom of the slope. It struck one as curious that with such a river there should be an aqueduct to carry water across it into the town. One could only suppose that the water of the river, like that of the cataracts near Adalia, was unwholesome because it contained a chalky sediment. To the top of the Cragus is a great climb. There we found a fortress without any inscriptions of any kind, but, to judge by the style, of no great age and no interest. The best thing was the view. Beneath us fell a sheer precipice right down into the sea, perhaps five hundred feet. As we looked over the top the eagles sprang out from the rocks far below us, so far that shots fired at them were quite ineffective. We found here a small theatre, much ruined, and the remains of a grand senate house, or perhaps a mausoleum to Trajan, also very much injured. The ship remained a day and a half. After passing a promontory we came opposite to a rocky ridge sloping rapidly to the sea, on which was a fortress, answering to Strabo's Antiochetta on the Cragus. We put off in the gig, and had to land on a precipitous rock in a high surf, which I did not like at all; but as we had been brought, it had to be done. We found a place that must have had some importance. There were fragments of polished granite columns, a modern castle, several Greek chapels, and ruins on all sides as well. The most promising were on the mountain above us and on a small peninsula jutting out from the site of the town. My companions made for the small peninsula, where they found some tombs like those at Selinty, and other matters of no great moment. I, hoping for something more considerable, went up the mountain—and a very rough climb it was. I was, however, well paid for my exertions. I found there numbers of granite columns, marble blocks and pedestals, and the ruins of a vast and magnificent edifice which might have been a senate house or a gymnasium. The situation of it was truly sublime, and it must have had a glorious effect from the sea. I hoped to return and examine it more perfectly next day, but unfortunately Captain Beaufort thought it necessary to get on to Cape Anemurium by the 24th, in order to make an observation of Jupiter's satellite which would determine at once his longitude, and the wind was favourable. We went on therefore, to my great regret, and the same evening (23rd) anchored opposite a small castle on a low rock by the sea.

Next day, as we were allowed, we went all over the castle. It appears to be of Saracen origin, and according to an inscription to have been conquered by the Turk Aladin. A remarkable thing about it is that it has a keep like those one sees in England. It is all in ruins ; such guns as it has are lying about dismounted.

I suppose the people hereabouts are so frightened at us that they send the news about in all directions ; for the bey of the district, who lives at some distance inland, had heard of our arrival, and sent down his compliments. Captain Beaufort hastened to send a suitable reply to his courtesy by an officer with an invitation to come on board, where he would be received with all the honours of war. He did promise to come when he could.

All day long Captain Beaufort was preparing, on a small island close to the castle, the necessary arrangements for making his observation. It was perfectly successful, and we got back on board at one o'clock A.M.

25th May.—Having done what was wanted with regard to the verification of the longitude, we went back in a boat to Cape Anemurium to see the ancient town. On the point is a fortress and citadel. Outside of that a second wall includes a theatre and an odeum, the seats of which are all gone. There are no traces of dwellings within the walls, so that one must suppose the inhabitants to have lived in mud or timber houses, for outside the walls there is the most perfect necropolis I ever saw. Each tomb has two apartments, and all, except for their having been broken open, are as fresh as if just built.

The ship being still at Anemurium, the bey above mentioned came down to the beach attended by his retinue. As soon as we made him out, we pushed off to pay him the compliments of the captain. Nothing could be more picturesque than the scene when we reached the shore. At the foot of the precipice of Anemurium he was seated on a small carpet spread on the rock, surrounded by about a hundred dark, savage-looking men all heavily armed. They were clearly as pleased to look at us as we were to see the barbarians of the interior. The gloomy evening cast a grave air over the wild crags and the savage figures, while the sea broke in heavy waves at the foot of the rock on which Abdul Muim sat. The manner with which the bey received us was free and polite. He told us the history of the country about us, and of the castle in particular. He was very much pressed to come aboard, but he would not be tempted. Instead of that, he contented himself with inquiring the length of the ship and sat looking at her with a pocket telescope for several hours.

We crossed a bay, and lay off Cape Kisliman, a bluff and remarkable cape on which were ruins, but the people of the country seemed to object to our examining them.

Thence to Chelindreh, which, being the nearest point of communication with Cyprus for couriers from Constantinople and other travellers, boasts some twenty huts and their inhabitants. They are barbarous and savage to a degree, and were disposed to treat the crew of the captain's boat, who were looking for inscriptions among the tombs of the ancient city, very roughly.   One man even drew his yatagan, when the sudden appearance of the frigate frightened them into politeness.

June 1st.—To the captain, who is always earnestly employed, one day is like another.   Even Sundays are only distinguished by the officers' invitation to him and to myself to dine in the gun-room, and by the clean clothes of the men at muster ; but the other officers did not forget that to-day was an anniversary, and we all drank the health of Lord Howe.

Porto Cavaliero.—To the eastward of us lay Isola Provenzale, once without doubt a settlement of the Knights of Rhodes. While the captain examined Cape Cavaliero, I went, burning with expectation, to the island, not doubting but that I should come home with a load of inscriptions and arms for the Heralds ; but we found no sort of remains of the occupation of the Knights that one could identify. We landed near a quarry of soft stone, in the middle of which an upright rock is left standing, in which it appears that a hermit had made his cell.   There are crosses cut in the three sides, and several neat little receptacles for utensils. At the top of the hill are fortifications and two churches, themselves built of the materials of older Greek buildings.   Clefts in the rock had been carefully stopped and used as reservoirs.   The walls are

built with an inner and an outer face of squared stones
set in mortar, the interval being filled in with chips
and rubble without cement, and the whole making a
thickness of eight or nine feet. The north-west side
of the island is also covered with ruins, all of the same
Romaic work. One was of a church to which several
rooms were attached, and in one of them a considerable
tomb—probably of a saint of the Early Church. This
must at all times have been a valuable station, and
would be now. It has one of the best and most
defensible harbours on this coast, and is within easy
reach of supplies.

The captain had fared no better than ourselves
in his search for remains of the Knights at Porto
Cavaliero. Here we fell in with a Myconiote ship full
of hadjis on their return from a visit to the Holy
Sepulchre at Jerusalem. My Dimitri and Andrea
were pigs enough to get drunk there and quarrel with
the crew. They got the licking they deserved, but they
came and complained to me that they had been ill-used
and ourselves insulted, and gave me the trouble of
inquiring into it. I found, as I had suspected, that
what they had got they had brought upon themselves.
Our next move was to Seleucia or Selefkeh. We
landed as near as we could to the end of the line
of hills on which it stands, and then walked to it, nine
miles across the plain at the foot of them. The ancient
town is beautifully placed at the side of a river, the

Calicadnus.   It is partly on the plain and partly on
steps of rock which rise gradually from it up to a
large castle of late date, which has an Armenian inscription over the gate.   The aga received us with obvious
ill-humour, which perhaps was owing to his being
unwell, for he begged to see our doctor, and promised
to send horses for him and for us to the beach next
day.   We looked about among the ruins, which are
very extensive.   There is a theatre, a long line of
porticoes, and a temple once converted to a Christian
church, together with several late churches of the date
of the ruins on Provenzale.   We then went back to
the ship.

Next day, no horses for the doctor or ourselves
appearing upon the beach, we started walking, and
on our arrival at Selefkeh complained.   The aga
affected to blame his servants.   We expected at least
to return well mounted when the doctor had seen the
aga and we had seen the town, but only one sorry
hack was prepared for the doctor ; and, as he refused
to ride alone, we made our exit, walking in a huff, and
went so briskly that a miserable Turk whom the aga
had sent on a pony, while we had to walk, to bring
him back his medicine, could not keep up with us, and
was quite out of sight by the time we got to the beach.
So we went aboard, rather pleased at first to deprive
the ungracious aga of his medicine ; but upon reflection we wrote him a sharp laconic note and sent

his dose. This aga, it is true, was not a man of good character; he had deposed and murdered his predecessor, but as that is the usual mode of succession in this country, it need not necessarily involve discourtesy to strangers. But I must not, in justice to Turks, forget to mention what occurred on our way to the beach as a set-off to the incivility of the aga.

We had had nothing to eat all day, and we were not a little sharp-set when, finding some peasants (Turks) amongst the corn making their evening meal, with that confidence which hunger inspires we pounced upon their dishes and devoured all that appeared before us. The poor fellows were not in the least disconcerted, but begged us to eat, one of them saying as he pointed to the corn all round him, 'There is plenty of bread. It is ours.' They would take no money, and when we got up to go pressed us to stay. Our hearts were melted at their noble benevolence, and we had to agree that all Turks were not brutes.

On the whole, Seleucia is worth the trouble of a visit.

An immense reservoir, 150 by 75 feet by 30 feet deep, supplied by an aqueduct, impressed me as a very fine work. The theatre also, although totally ruined, is delightfully situated; and the temple, which had been converted into a church, is very interesting. The Calicadnus, although it is on an even bed, is a noble river, wide and rapid, and gives great beauty to the scene.   It is unhealthy to drink, which accounts for the existence of the great reservoir.

It is evident that the population of these countries has decreased, and still is decreasing.   It has not one-tenth of what it could easily support, and not one-hundredth of what it has supported in past times.

While we were away at Selefkeh a bombard French privateer came into the bay of Seleucia in pursuit of a Turkish boat, and would have fallen into our hands if the captain and pilot had been on board ; but the necessary delay before this could be done enabled the Frenchman to get to shallow water, and the *Frederiksteen* in pursuit ran into four fathoms, and in another five minutes would have been aground.   So the bombard escaped.[1]

Anchored off Lingua di Bagascia.—We arrived at a castle named Curco, with another on a rock outside the port, which has an Armenian inscription on it. The one on the mainland, which I take to be the ancient Coricus, is a place of great strength.   There is a moat thirty feet wide, cut in solid rock, to disconnect from the land, and double walls and towers.   There are many ruins of modern churches and monasteries and numberless sarcophagi of ancient and early Christian times, but the whole place, town and castles, is absolutely deserted.

---

[1] Captain Beaufort seems to have thought that she was a Mainiote pirate. His account of this episode is worth reading.

We were in the boat following the frigate as she proceeded along the coast, when, perceiving ruins on the coast, we disembarked, and found on a striking eminence a Corinthian temple of bad execution which had been converted into a church. Further on was a town, a theatre, and a vast colonnade with a number of important and very perfect tombs. We had, however, to retire to the boat, for the inhabitants were very threatening, and had we been fewer or shown any fear might have fared badly. As soon as we were off in the boat we had a good bathe.

At the Latmus.—Captain Beaufort sent two of his officers ashore to inspect the long aqueduct leading to Eleusa, which we could see from the ship, but the aga, who had at first consented to their going, withdrew his permission, and they had to give it up.

At Pompeiopolis, as we had understood that the Turks of this part of the country were particularly dangerous, I took with me two marines as a guard to visit the ruins. Seen from the sea they presented a truly startling grandeur. The plan of the city is noble in the extreme—one single colonnade passes right through it from the port to the gate leading out into the country, and forty of its columns are still standing. The remainder, making about two hundred, lie as they fell. The town was defended by a fine wall with towers to it, enclosing a theatre and the port. The style of the architecture, which looked so well from a distance, when one comes to see it close is very bad.

Pompeiopolis is quite deserted, but the Turks from the neighbouring villages came in, and, although their appearance was barbarous in the extreme, they were very civil. I imagine the 36 guns and 350 men of the *Frederiksteen* had to do with this, for I observed that the further we got from the ship the less polite we always found the Turks to be.

We made sail in the evening and anchored off Mersine, at the beginning of the great plain of Tarsous, and put ashore to reconnoitre and pay a visit to the aga with a view to getting horses to go to Tarsous. The aga was very civil and promised we should have the horses we asked for.

In the morning the horses were ready ; but now the aga, for whatever reason, discouraged our going to Tarsous, and told us that since seeing us yesterday evening he had received news of an outbreak there, that a neighbouring pasha had attacked the town and all was uproar and arms. On reflection his account struck us as so improbable that we decided at any rate to start, and go on according to the information we should pick up on the road. We set out, a large party.

The country was a flat, covered with corn and in it many reapers, male and female, the latter going un-covered and quite unembarrassed by strangers. Their

language and costume were Arab, quite unlike anything I had seen before, and there were quantities of
camels about.

The ride took us four hours. From the inquiries
we made from time to time it was clear that the aga's
tale had been a downright lie.

Tarsous lies on the plain about two miles and a
half from the mountains. At the entrance to it is a
hillock about a quarter of a mile long, which commands
the town ; it was included in the ancient walls, which
were then strengthened by a moat into which the
river was turned. It is now dry, and the present town
has nothing but a slight wall round it. We passed
over the old moat and through an ancient gate of
Roman work. It had three arches, but only one of
them is standing, and the wall it formed the passage
through and every other antiquity in the town has
been destroyed and used up for building materials.
Nothing could exceed the surprise of the inhabitants
at our appearance. They had never seen Europeans,
and they crowded about us in such numbers that
we could with difficulty move. We went to visit
the aga and were detained, sitting among the servants an hour and a half before we could obtain an
audience. The aga, they said, was engaged. At last
we remonstrated and got up to go ; when, to our
surprise and indignation, we saw the aga sitting in a
room by himself smoking his pipe and quite unoccupied.

We would have passed the door had they not pressed us in, so angry were we. He was sitting on a sofa in a long white Arab cloak in a room that was neater and handsomer than it is usual to see in these countries. He made a slight motion on our coming in, but spoke not a word, nor did he deign to answer ' Yhary' when we conveyed to him the compliments of the captain. A Turk who sat by his side with our firman in his hands now addressed a Turk who was with us with an affectation of great indignation. He wanted to know what could be the meaning of four hundred men, when only eight men were mentioned in the firman—together with a number of other insolent questions, from which I gathered that he suspected us of being travelling merchants. Fortunately, as these remarks were not addressed to us, we were not bound to make any reply, for if we had we were by this time in such a state of impatience with their insolent barbarity that it would hardly have been a conciliatory one. As soon as we could get away, we mounted our horses again, and through a thick and insulting rabble went out of the town and homewards without delay. An old Turk of the aga's people, who had been one of the chief of our tormentors, saw us off for some distance. To him I had the satisfaction of giving a piece of my mind, and when we came within sight of the ship gave him an invitation on board that he might see how we treated strangers. The old rascal went home very much abashed and awestruck. We arrived on board late, and well wetted by coming through the violent surf.

The ship was two more days off the great plain of Tarsóus, moving slowly in a thick haze, and on the 16th arrived off Cape Karadash.

The captain proposed to me that I should go with Mr. Wingham to reconnoitre a great lake one could see from the ship. About one mile N.W. of the cape we turned up a deep channel like a river mouth, except that the current set inwards instead of outwards, and after about three-quarters of a mile entered an apparently boundless lake. It was very shallow, and before long we were aground, after which the men waded and towed the boat. In this fashion we went several miles till we had got a fair general notion of the size of the sheet of water. A deceptive atmospheric effect, due to the great evaporation, would hide the shore when very low, so that it presented the appearance of a sheet of water. Owing to this I had a bitter disappointment. Ahead of us we descried four beautiful deer, which, as we approached, fled to what appeared to me to be the isthmus of a peninsula. I cried to one of the boatmen, who had a musket, to run to the isthmus to cut them off, while I and two others made for the other side, hoping to get a shot at them. As we got nearer, the fancied water vanished, and the deer, a herd of ten beauties, ran up into the plain. They were

O

spotted like fallow deer, but with short horns turning back like those of a goat.   Coming back, we saw immense flocks, of perhaps ten thousand at once, of white stately birds about as big as swans [Flamingoes.—ED.], the tail beautiful with red feathers.   They stood in ranks like soldiers, and now and again flapped their wings all at once and shrieked.   There were numbers of large fish about, and the water was so shallow that their backs stood out of it.   All the same, when we tried to catch them they were too quick for us.   The only thing we did secure was a big turtle.

At Cape Mallo we went ashore and walked over the ruins.

Thence we moved down the coast, anchored eight miles west of Ayas Castle, and rowed on to it. There are the remains of the ancient town of Ægæ to be seen, and a modern Turkish castle.   When we entered the mouth of the port we noticed that some Turks standing on a tower which commanded it shouted and gesticulated to us in a threatening manner.   They were all armed.   I, however, set it down to fear on their part, and recommended our going on.   Unhappily, we did so; and I can never sufficiently regret the part I had in bringing on the catastrophe which will always make Ayas a painful recollection.   Nothing further occurred that evening ; we walked about, and when it grew dark went aboard again.

June 20th.—We went ashore, a strong party, and

scattered in various directions. The captain took his surveying instruments, a little to the westwards. Another party stripped to bathe and hunt turtles, of which there were many ; while two others and myself walked towards the castle. The jolly-boat, under command of a midshipman, young Olphert, was to meet us to the east of the castle. All at once Dimitri came running up to us to say that a Turk had robbed one of the party. His account was that while they were bathing, this Turk, attracted by the gilt buttons on the coat of a petty officer, and taking them for gold, had run off with it. We walked at once to the beach, where several Turks of the village were collected. They tried to conciliate us, saying it was a Turcoman from the mountains who had been the thief, and that the coat had already been restored. Just then up came Mr. Lane to tell us to get immediately to the boats, that the captain had been dangerously wounded and young Olphert shot dead. We did as he told us, and got back to the ship ; but my horror and surprise were succeeded by the most violent indignation, and there was nothing I hoped for so much as that orders would be given for a general attack on the village. As soon as I was on board I went to see Captain Beaufort. His wound, I was glad to find, was not so dangerous as was thought at first. The ball had entered the fleshy part of the thigh and had broken the bone at the hip. Still, it was a serious wound, and he was a good deal

shaken.   When he heard of poor Olphert's death he
burst into tears, and bitterly upbraided himself with
having been the cause of it.   It seems that when the
band of ruffians came to attack his boat and began to
point their guns, he, to frighten them, fired over their
heads.   Hereupon they all fell down in abject terror,
and the boats, pushing off, got nearly clear of the rocks.
One man, however, more resolute than the rest, rushed
forwards, and taking deliberate aim from behind
a rock, shot the captain : and had the rest of the
ruffians been like him, the whole boat's crew must have
been sacrificed.   As it was, the boat was out of range
before they recovered.   But having whetted their
appetite for blood, and furious at having been shot at,
they rushed off to where young Olphert was with his
boat and murdered him as he was pushing off.   The
condition Captain Beaufort was in was so serious, and
his concern lest Olphert's death should have been in
any sense his fault, so painful, that I took upon
myself to tell him a deliberate falsehood, for which I
trust God will forgive me.   I assured him positively
that Olphert had been already shot when the natives
came to attack his (the captain's) boat.   As he was
a long way from where Olphert was, he had no means
of knowing that it might not have been so, and he
was eventually persuaded and his mind very much
quieted.

At first we had hoped that we might be allowed to

seek our own redress, but the coolness and moderation of the captain were admirable. When one came to consider, it was not at all clear that the villagers had had any hand in it, and to destroy the village would not be to punish the offenders. It was sure to make all travelling dangerous, if not impossible, for the future, and finally it would be the act of war on the territories of a friendly Power, barbarous as that Power might be. It was therefore settled that we should apply for redress through the regular channel.

We crossed the bay to Scanderoon, which is a miserable town with a population half Turks and half Cypriote Greeks, and no resident official higher than an aga. We did what we could to frighten this person by representing the affair to him in its most serious light, at the same time calling his attention to the strict moderation of our conduct, and our respect for the authorities of the country.

Meanwhile a peremptory letter demanding reparation was despatched to the pasha himself, who lived some miles inland. He returned an immediate reply to the effect that Ayas was not within his pashalik, but in that of his neighbour the pasha of Adana, to whom he had at once written. Meanwhile he promised in his name that every reparation should be made. In our turn we informed him that a British squadron would be there in fifteen days to see that this was done.

In the cemetery attached to the old British factory and consulate we buried poor young Olphert. Ten marines (all the aga would allow ashore) fired a salute over him, and we set up over his grave a Greek tomb-stone brought from one of the cities on the coast.

Considering how many tokens of friendship Captain Beaufort had shown me, and that he was at the moment in a dangerous condition, with a risk of fever coming on ; and that, as he could not enjoy easy familiarity with his junior officers, my company might be pleasant to him, I thought I ought not to leave him and settled to go back with him to Malta. Two days after Olphert's funeral, on the 22nd June, we set sail.   On the 1st of July we fell in with the *Salsette*, Captain Hope, off Khelidonia, by appoint-ment.   She was to take Captain Beaufort's report to the admiral on the station, and to go on to Scanderoon afterwards to see that proper amends were made for the injury done us."

CHAPTER XV

MALTA—ATTACKED BY BILIOUS FEVER—SAILS TO PALERMO—SEGESTE
—LEAVES FOR GIRGENTI—IMMIGRANT ALBANIANS—SELINUNTO—
TRAVELLING WITH SICILIANS—GIRGENTI—RESTORES THE TEMPLE
OF THE GIANTS—LEAVES FOR SYRACUSE—OCCUPATIONS IN
SYRACUSE—SALE OF THE ÆGINA MARBLES—LEAVES FOR ZANTE.

" WE had nothing but west winds, very unfavourable
for us. Meltern, as this wind is called, follows the
rim of the coast of Asia Minor, being north in the
Archipelago, west along Karamania, and turning south
again down the coast of Syria. We were seldom out
of sight of land—first the mountains of Asia, then
Rhodes, Crete, the Morea, &c. Finally we reached
Malta on the 18th of July, being the twenty-seventh
day since we left Scanderoon, and the end of a month
of complete idleness. I spent most of the time in the
captain's cabin, showing him all the attention I could,
and profiting in return very much by his society and
his library.

To get to Malta was a refreshment to our spirits.
Numbers of visitors came at once under the stern to
salute Captain Beaufort, although until we had pratique
they could not come aboard. The plague is at present
in Smyrna, and quarantine for ships from thence usually

lasts thirty or forty days ; but as we could prove that we had had no communication with any infected town, we were let off in two days. Unfortunately, from the moment we arrived I began to feel unwell. All the time I was on the coast of Asia I had been taking violent exercise and perspiring profusely, while since we left I had been wholly confined ; and the consequence of the change was a violent bilious attack with fever. After stopping in bed three days I thought I would take a trip to Sant' Antonio with Gammon, the senior officer ; but I got back so thoroughly done up that I had to lie up again, and was ill for three weeks in Thorn's Hotel.[1] My chief remedies, prescribed by Doctors Stewart of the *Frederiksteen* and Allen of the Malta Hospital, were calomel in large quantities and bleeding.

Every day one or other of the officers of the *Frederiksteen*—Gammon, Seymour, Lane, or Dodd— came to sit with me.

When I was able to get about again, I found that Captain Beaufort had been moved to the house of Commissioner Larcom, where every possible care was taken of him. They were a most agreeable and hospitable family—the only one, indeed, in Malta. The officers—General Oakes, Colonel Phillips, &c.— were like all garrison officers. Mr. Chabot, the banker, honoured my drafts, and when I was going expressed

---

[1] Now the Hôtel de Provence.

Shabat (Jew)

his sorrow that I was off so soon, as he had hoped to have seen me at his house.

As soon as ever I was well enough I felt eager to get away from a society so odious to me as that of Malta, and having been introduced from two separate sources to Mr. Harvey, commander of H.M. brig *Haughty*, I got from him an excellent passage to Palermo. It took us from the 20th August to the 28th. Mr. Harvey himself was ill, and I saw little of him, but what I did delighted me. Like all sailors, he was very lovable, and so long as he remained in Palermo I went to him every day.

My first day I strolled over the town and delivered my letters to Mr. Gibbs and Mr. Fagan. The latter is an antiquarian and a great digger. He told me, I think, that he had dug up over two hundred statues in his time. I called on him several times afterwards, pleased with his conversation and hoping to learn something of Sicily from him, and found him exceedingly polite. A return of the fever I had in Malta confined me again for a few days, after which I managed to keep it at bay with plenty of port wine and bark. My chief friends in Palermo were General and Mrs. Campbell, Sir Robert Laurie, captain of a 74 lying here, Lord William Bentinck, generalissimo of the British army of occupation in Sicily, and Fagan.

After a fortnight in Palermo I started on a trip to Segeste. I could not but be very much struck by the

difference between the richness of Sicily, and the desolation of Greece under Turkish rule.   Mahomet II.
desired that on his tomb should be written that had he
lived he proposed in the ensuing summer to conquer
'the beautiful Italy and the island of Rhodes.'   Sicily
must have followed, and I pictured in my mind the
landscape as it would then have looked.   A few ruined
mosques would have supplied the place of the splendid
churches and monasteries, and a wretched khan and a
few low huts the rich towns of Sala and Partinico.

The temple of Segeste is the largest I have seen,
but it looks as if it had never been finished.   The
style of workmanship is good and exact, but as far
inferior to Athenian execution as its rough stone
is to Pentilican marble.   The turn of the capital is
very inferior in delicacy to Athenian examples, and
there is no handsome finish to the ceiling of the peri-
style, which was probably of plaster like Ægina.
The circular sinking cut in the plinth to receive the
column, leaving a space all round to give a play, it is
said, in case of earthquake, is certainly curious if that
was the purpose of it.   Nothing whatever remains of
the cella.

In the evening we returned to Alcamo and next day
breakfasted with Colonel Burke, who is in command of
a regiment of 1,400 fine men, all Piedmontese and
Italians, not Sicilians.   One finds Englishmen in command everywhere.   Returned to Palermo.

My fame had spread in my absence, and on my return I found my table covered with cards and invitations—the most conspicuous being from General Macfarlane and Lord Montgomery.

The palaces of the Sicilian nobles are exasperatingly pretentious and tasteless ; that of Palagonia is an unforgetable nightmare.

Though a paradise compared with Greece, I find Sicily seething with discontent ; and were it not for Lord W. Bentinck, to whom the people look up as the only honest man amongst the authorities, there would be an insurrection.

Ten days later I set out on horseback for Girgenti. On the second day I turned aside from Villa Fraté to visit one of the Greek villages so much talked of and so misrepresented. In Palermo I was told that the villagers are some of the ancient Greek settlers, who remain so unchanged that they still wear sandals and are almost pagans. In reality they are Albanians, who emigrated in the sixteenth century when the oppression of the Turks was specially severe in their country, and came in bands to various points of Sicily. Mezzojuso is one of their settlements, and has about 2,000 inhabitants. The situation, about two miles off the road from Villa Fraté to Alcara, is on the side of a mountain and very beautiful. I met some goodhumoured peasants who were ready to tell me all they knew. They talk Albanian amongst themselves, and they readily understood the few words of it which I and my servant could speak. The explanation of the report of their being almost pagans is that they retain the Greek ritual, although they have changed the altar to the Catholic form and acknowledge the supremacy of the Pope. Over the altar is a Greek inscription, which I read, to the surprise of those who attended me. The priests preserve the Greek costume, the bead cap, hair, &c. St. Nicolas, the Greek saint *par excellence*, is a conspicuous figure in the Church. What a pity I had not with me a little of the earth I took from the shrine of the saint at Myra in Asia Minor! It would have been an acceptable present to the priest. I saw none of the women, but I was told they wear a peculiar costume ; and at their communion, instead of the host, as in Roman Catholic churches, a piece of cloth is held up.

Started for the temples of Selinunto, accompanied by Don Ignazio, the son of my host, Don Gaetano. We took the road towards the sea, and passing through Siciliana and turning inland came in the evening to Cattolica. Here we added to our party a most enter-taining companion, Don Raffaelle Politi, a painter, not very excellent in his art, though one of the best in Sicily, but full of talents and of humour. He was staying at the time in the house of a certain marquis, for whom he had been painting two ceilings. We went to see him there, and found him with the marchese, sitting over a greasy table surrounded by a company of nasty fellows, such as in England one might see in a shopkeeper's parlour. No sort of civility or hospitality was shown us. On the other hand, a friend and equal of Don Raffaelle's received us very kindly. He and a company of tradesmen who had come over to a fair which was being held in Cattolica, and had of course brought their guitars with them, entertained us before supper in the locanda.

Next day we passed by the ancient city of Heraclia, of which, however, there are very trifling remains, to Sciacca, where in the market-place we saw dead meat—meat of animals that had died of disease owing to the great drought this year, which has killed a great many cattle—being sold to the poor at a cheap rate. Travelling with Sicilians I fell into their customs, and instead of looking out for an hotel I went with them into a café where we ate and drank. The cafetiere, to show his liberality, in pouring out lets the cup overflow until the saucer also is full, after which he brings spirits and cigars—all customs new to me. Arrived in a storm at Montefeice, wet through. My friends slept on a mattress, and I, who was accustomed to it, slept on the floor.

Nothing can be more solemn than the magnificent remains of the three temples of Selinus, but I had not many hours to study them. It is clear that earthquake was the cause of their destruction, and I guess from

the difference in preservation between the parts which
fell and were covered and protected, and the condition
of those which remain standing, that it may have
occurred about the eighth or ninth century.   We
went over twice from Montefeice, each time returning in the evening ; and when we got home, how
differently we spent our evenings from the ordinary
way Englishmen do !   Had they been my companions we should have cursed the fare and lodging,
and should have laid ourselves down grumbling to
pass a tedious and uncomfortable night.   Instead of
that, with these Sicilians, as soon as the demands of
hunger were satisfied, at the sound of a guitar in the
streets, we sallied out and joined the serenaders,
stopped under the windows of some fair one we did
not know, and Don Raffaelle, who is a perfect master
of the guitar and ravished the bystanders, played and
sang with much taste a number of exceedingly pretty
melodies.   If this was not enough for the evening, we
sat and told stories.

At Cattolica we arrived so late that every inch of
the locanda was occupied.   We did not care to disturb
our friend of the previous occasion, Don Giuseppe,
and the marchese's hospitality had been so grudgingly
offered that we were too proud to accept it, and so
we sought consolation by going about the streets with
a guitar till we were tired of it, and then taking horse
again ; but before going far we were so weary that we

got off under a tree, sat down, and waited for dawn to light us back to Girgenti.

After my return to Girgenti, I remained there till the 14th of November, applying myself with close attention and infinite pleasure to attempting to reconstruct the Temple of Jupiter Olympius. The examination of the stones and the continual exercise of ingenuity kept me very busy, and at the end the successful restoration of the temple gave me a pleasure which was only to be surpassed by that of originally conceiving the design.

My days went by in great peace and content. I lived with the family of Don Gaetano Sterlini, and when I got accustomed to them I learnt to like them. The bawling of the servants, the open doors, the dirt and disorder of a Sicilian household came after a time to be matters of course to me and passed unnoticed.

But there came an English fine gentleman, by the name of Cussins, to spend two days here, who was not so philosophical and made himself odious by protesting. When anyone came into or went out of the room, the doors, which never else turned on their hinges, must be shut; the windows, that perhaps lacked two or three panes, must be closed; the shutters bolted; he could not eat the food nor drink the wine. A creature so refined is as unpleasant an object to a barbarian as the latter is to him, and we prayed for his departure.

My fine friend was supercilious to me, but polite in a lofty fashion, and took a patronising interest in what I was doing. Would I give him some notes and a sketch? At first I said I would, but his manner disgusted me, so that I finally sent him only the notes. He wanted the sketch to flourish at Palermo.

In the last few days of my stay my fame got about. The Caffé dei Nobili, the bishop and all, heard with astonishment that I had unravelled the puzzle, and that all the morsels composing the giants were still existing and could be put together again. A dignitary of the Church, (Don?) Candion Panettieri, sent me a message to say that if I would mark the stones and give directions for the setting up of one of the giants, he would undertake the expense of doing it. I was tempted by this offer and the immediate notoriety it would give me, and agreed and completed my sketch as far as it could be carried and took it to him. It was copied immediately, and with my name appended as the author, sent to Palermo. Then I went over the fragments with Raffaelle Politi and marked the stones corresponding with the numbers in the design.

Don Gaetano could not contain his indignation at my suffering the results of so much labour to be launched into the world as it were semi-anonymously, instead of in a book duly written and published by myself, the author. From the moment I handed over my drawing to Politi to copy there was no peace between us. I could not help being gratified at the interest he took in my success, and my feeling for him was sharpened by the sentiment with which his fair daughter had inspired me, which was so strong that it made me feel the necessity of going away, and yet made me weep like a noodle when I did. But I had found my reward in the pleasure of solving the puzzle, and though I liked the notoriety, it was not worth giving oneself much trouble about.

I left Girgenti with Don Ignazio Sala, son-in-law of Sterlini, for Alicata, and the consul himself saw me as far as the River Agrigas. On our left were many sulphur works, which are so injurious to vegetation that there is a law in force that they shall not work from the time the corn begins to get up till after the harvest. From Palma the road lies along the sea-shore, and there at every mile and a half are watch-towers, or, failing these, straw huts for the coastguard to give warning of Barbary corsairs. Until lately this coast was infested by them. Their descents were small, and they carried off only a few men or cattle; but there was once a desperate action near Alicata, in which the inhabitants turned out, headed by the priest, and captured the whole party of twenty-five who had landed. The prisoners were sent by Palermo to Algiers to be exchanged.

P

Alicata to Serra Nuova.   Serra Nuova to Cartalagerone.   We had to cross a river on the way, the
banks of which were high and the river swollen by the
rain, and one mule with baggage and man rolled right
into it.

The night got very dark, and I really thought we
should have to stop on the bank all night or break our
necks, but by help of repeated invocations indifferently
to Maria Sanctissima and Santo Diavolone we got
across safely at last.

From Cartalagerone by Mineo to Lentini, and so
to Syracuse.   Although compared with the ancient
town it is tiny and confined entirely to the island of
Ortygia, the modern Syracuse has considerable fortifications.   We had to pass through four gates and two
dykes before we got inside.   At one gate the guard
wanted to take our arms, till I remonstrated on the
insult to the British nation, and they let me pass.
But, then, if they did not mean to enforce it, how
ridiculous ever to make such a regulation !

As soon as I was settled I despatched a letter
my friend Raffaelle Politi had given me to his father,
who came at once, offered me every civility, and
remained my fast friend throughout my stay."

Cockerell spent three months—December, January,
and February—in Syracuse.   For one thing his health
had been severely shaken by the grave illness he had
had in Malta, and he needed rest.   It seems to have

made a turning-point in his travels. Hitherto his letters
home had been full of joyous anticipations of getting
back to England, and with restless energy he had
endeavoured to cram the utmost into his time before
doing that, and settling into harness as an architect.
Seeing so many countries and going through so many
vicissitudes had, however, weakened the tie and he
could now make himself at home anywhere. For
another thing, a main object of his travels—perhaps
the main object—was a visit to Italy, as for practical
purposes Italian architecture was the best worth
studying. But the war with France continuing, Italy
remained closed indefinitely to a British subject. So
for several years there are no more references to
coming home. A last reason for stopping where he
was, was that the weather was detestable. It was the
terrible winter of the retreat from Moscow. "For
forty days," he says, "it never failed to rain, snow, or
hail."

His time was chiefly spent in preparing the drawings
for the plates of the great contemplated book on Ægina
and Phigaleia. Besides this, he seems to have drawn
in the museum, and to have read a good deal ; he learnt
the art of cutting cameos, and even executed some ; and
finally, fired by the performances of his friend Politi, he
spent two hours a day in learning to play the guitar.
He probably never carried this accomplishment very
far and abandoned it on leaving Sicily, for I never

recollect even hearing it alluded to. The time passed very quietly. He had some friends among the Sicilians, besides the Politis—Don Pietro Satallia, the Conte Bucchieri, and one English acquaintance, Lieutenant Winter, adjutant of the town and fort, who had a nice English wife and large family, with whom he spent occasional evenings. For the most part, however, he spent his evenings studying in his lodgings, and " on the whole," he says, " I can say of Syracuse what I wish I could say of all the places I ever stopped in : I do not repent of the time I spent there."

During the latter part of his stay, when the weather grew less severe, he was a good deal occupied in examining the walls of ancient Syracuse, and the fortress of Labdalum.

A letter received at about this time from Linckh records the death of the little Skye terrier Fop which my father had brought with him from England.

When he left Athens to go with Messrs. North, Douglas, and Foster to Crete, *en route* for Egypt, he left the dog behind in charge of a certain Nicolo, who seems to have gone with Bronstedt and Linckh not long after on the expedition they undertook to Zea in December 1811. . . . " Dans la lettre égarée je vous ai écrit le sort malheureux de votre pauvre Fope, qui a fini ses jours misérablement et en grande famine à Zea. Bronstedt et moi nous lui avons encore prolongé son triste destin pour quelques jours, car nous l'avons trouvé mourant dans un ravin entre la ville de Zea et le port. Vraiment ce Nicolo est un être infâme et malicieux. Vous savez que nous lui avons confisqué la bague du Platon qu'il a portée aussitôt que vous autres êtes partis d'Athènes pour Egypte. [He had stolen it, as he did later various articles from Hughes and Parker, *q.v.*] Comme nous avons quitté l'isle de Zea, il faisait une banque de pharaon pour piller les Zeotes."

He had kept in communication with his friends in Greece, and especially with Gropius, to whom he had written repeatedly on the subject of the sale of the Ægina Marbles, but it was not till March that he could have heard of the disastrous issue.

What had happened was this. It will be remembered that while the statues themselves had been conveyed for security to Malta, the sale of them had been advertised to take place in Zante on November 1, 1812.

When the day arrived only two bidders presented themselves in the sale room, one bearing an offer from the French Government, and Herr Wagner another from Prince Louis of Bavaria. The British Museum had sent out a Mr. Coombe with ample powers to buy for England, but he never turned up. He had reached Malta in good time, but having understood from Mr. McGill, who was *pro tem.* agent for Gropius, that the sale would take place where the marbles were, took it for granted that he knew all about it and there stayed, waiting for the auctioneer to come.

Meanwhile the sale came off at Zante. The French offer of 160,000 francs proved to be altogether too conditional to be accepted, and the sculptures were knocked down to Prince Louis for 10,000 sequins.

It was suggested afterwards that Gropius had been bribed by Wagner to keep the English parties in the dark, but it was never proved. What is clear is that if Gropius had kept his agent, McGill, properly informed as to the place of sale, Coombe would have been able to bid and the Ægina statues would be in the British Museum now.

Cockerell at once set out from Syracuse for Zante. But he found that when he joined there was really nothing to be done. He at first tried to upset the contract, but on reflection he found himself obliged in honour and in law to abide by the action of their agent. A new agreement was drawn up and signed, confirming the former and engaging to petition the British Government for leave to export the sculptures from Malta.

At home in England the deepest disappointment was felt by those who had interested themselves in the acquisition, and a protest was forwarded by Mr. S. P. Cockerell through Mr. Hamilton to the Government, petitioning that no permission to remove the marbles from Malta should be granted, and demanding a new sale on the ground of improper procedure in the first.

In the end, however, it was not found possible to contest the validity of the sale, and they were finally delivered to the Prince of Bavaria in 1814.

CHAPTER XVI

ATHENS—THE EXCAVATION OF MARBLES AT BASSÆ—BRONSTEDT'S
MISHAP—FATE OF THE CORINTHIAN CAPITAL OF BASSÆ—
SEVERE ILLNESS—STACKELBERG'S MISHAP—TRIP TO ALBANIA
WITH HUGHES AND PARKER—THEBES—LIVADIA—THE FIVE
EMISSARIES—STATE OF THE COUNTRY—MERCHANTS OF LIVADIA
—DELPHI—SALONA—GALAXIDI—PATRAS—PREVISA—NICOPOLIS
—ARTA—THE PLAGUE—JANINA.

THE fate of the Ægina Marbles being now practically
settled, Foster, who was engaged to make a marriage
very displeasing to his family, with a Levantine,
left for Smyrna, while Haller, Linckh, and Cockerell
went to Athens. The latter had not been in Greece
since November 1811. In the interval the expedition
to dig up the sculptures he had discovered at Bassæ
had been there and had successfully accomplished
their purpose, the party consisting of Haller, Foster,
Linckh, Stackelberg, Gropius, Bronstedt, and an English traveller, Mr. Leigh.[1] They had provided themselves with powers from Constantinople sufficient to
overcome the resistance of the local authorities, and
after many difficulties had succeeded in bringing away
the sculptures with one exception, to which I will
presently refer.

[1] Grandfather of the present Lord Leigh

The excavations were carried out in June, July, and August, while my father was absent at Malta and in Sicily. Nevertheless, as he had discovered their existence it was understood that he was to be a participator in any sculptures that should be disinterred.

The party of excavators established themselves there for nearly three months, building huts of boughs all round the temple, making almost a city, which they christened Francopolis. They had frequently from fifty to eighty men at work at a time, a band of Arcadian music to entertain them, and in the evening after work, while the lamb was roasting on a wooden spit, they danced. However, if Cockerell lost the pleasure, he escaped the fever from which they all suffered desperately—and no wonder, after living such a life in such a climate.

It was during this expedition that a misfortune befell Bronstedt which, although it had an element of absurdity in it, was very serious to the victim. While the work at Bassæ was proceeding he left his companions to take a trip into Maina. Before starting he wrote for himself a letter of introduction to Captain Murzinos purporting to be from my father, and would have presented it ; but, as ill-luck would have it, on the 20th of August, on the road between Sparta and Kalamata, he fell into the hands of a band of eight robbers. Understanding them to be Mainiotes, and supposing all Mainiotes to be friends, he tried to save his property by saying that he had a letter with him to Captain Murzinos ; but the robbers replied : " Oh, have you ? If we had Murzinos here we would play him twice the pranks we are playing you," and spared nothing. They decamped with his money, his watch, his rings, a collection of antique coins, all that he had in their eyes worth taking, to the tune, as he considered, of 800*l*. (11,000 piastres fortes d'Espagne), leaving him disconsolate in the dark to collect his scattered manu- scripts, which they had rejected with the contemptuous words : Καρτάσια εἶναι. Δὲν τὰ στοχάσομεν (" Papers ! we don't look at them.")   In the darkness and confusion after the departure of the robbers he managed to lose some of these as well.   The poor traveller returned quite forlorn to Phigaleia.   After this, Linckh writes in his delicious French : " Bronstedt parcourt la Morée en longue et à travers pour cherger ses hardes pertus par les voleurs.   Le drôle de corps a beaucoup d'espérance, parce que le consul Paul lui a recommendé fortement au nouveau Pascha dans une letter qui a etté enveloppée en vilours rouge."   Such a letter, bound in red velvet, was esteemed particularly urgent, but he obtained no redress whatever, nor ever saw again any of "ses hardes," except the ring which had been given him by his *fiancée*, Koes' sister.   This was re- covered for him by Stackelberg on a journey which he took through Maina, when he saw it exposed for sale in the house of one of the captains or chieftains of the country, together with the watch, purse, and several other articles which had been Bronstedt's; but the prices asked were too exorbitant for him to ransom any but this, which he knew the late owner had highly prized.

The piece of sculpture I have just mentioned, which the explorers of Phigaleia failed to bring away, was the capital of the single Corinthian column of the interior of the temple. It will be remembered by those who have read my father's work on the subject, that all the columns of the interior were of the Ionic order with one exception, which was Corinthian, and which stood in the centre of one end of the cella. The capital of this Corinthian column was of the very finest workmanship; and although the volutes had been broken off, much of it was still well preserved, and the party of excavators took it with them to the coast for embarcation with the rest. There are figures of it by Stackelberg in his book, and by Foster in a drawing in the Phigaleian Room of the British Museum. Veli Pasha, the Governor of the Morea, had sanctioned the explorations on the understanding that he should have half profits; but when he had seen the sculptures he was so disappointed that they were not gold or silver, and so little understood them, that he took the warriors under shields for tortoises, allowing that as such they were rather well done. It chanced that at this moment news reached him that he had been superseded in his command, and not ˌthinking much of them, and eager to get what he could, he accepted 400*l.* as his share of the spoil and sanctioned the exportation of the marbles. The local archons, however, put every impediment they could in the way by fomenting a strike among the porters which caused delays, and by giving information to the incoming pasha, who sent down troops to stop the embarcation. Everything had been loaded except the capital in question, which was more ponderous than the rest, and was still standing half in and half out of the water when the troops came up. The boat had to put off without it, and the travellers had the mortification of seeing it hacked to pieces by the Turks in their fury at having been foiled. The volute of one of the Ionic columns presented by my father to the British Museum is the only fragment of any of the interior capitals of the temple remaining. He brought it away with him on his, the first, visit.

To return to where I left my father before this digression. As I said, after the sale of the Ægina Marbles, Haller and he came to Athens, where, finding the summer very hot in the town, they went to live at Padischa or Sadischa, not far outside the town, and set earnestly to work upon the drawings for the book on Ægina and Phigaleia. All went on quietly till on the 22nd of August Cockerell was attacked by a malignant bilious fever, which brought

him to death's door : at least, either the illness or the
remedies did. The doctor, Abraham, the first in
Athens, thought it must be yellow fever, gave him up,
and fearing infection for himself, refused to attend him
,after the first few days. It was even whispered that
it might be the plague, for the enormous swelling of
the glands was not unlike it. But Haller would listen
to no counsels of despair, and refused to leave his
friend. The kind Madame Masson, too, the aunt of
the Misses Makri, came out from Athens, and the two
nursed him with ceaseless devotion. Haller never
left his bedside, night or day, for the first month. The
vice-consul, hearing that the sufferer was as good as
dead, came to take away his keys and put seals upon
his property, and was only prevented by Haller by
main force. The same faithful friend compelled the
doctor to do his duty. The first having deserted his
patient, a second was called in and kept attentive by
threats and persuasion. The methods of medicine
were inconceivably barbarous. Bleeding was the
great remedy in fever, and calomel the alternative.
When the patient had been brought by this treatment
so low that his heart was thought to have stopped,
live pigeons were cut in half and the reeking portions
applied to his breast to restore the vital heat. Medicine
failing, spells were believed in. Madame Masson,
though described as one of the first personages in
Athens, could neither read nor write, and was grossly

ignorant. She had a great faith in spells ; and Haller, fearing that in the feeble condition of the patient she might commit some folly, kept a strict watch upon her. One day, however, in his absence, when my father was suffering agonies from his glands, she took the opportunity to tie round his neck a charm of particular potency. It was a little bag containing some resin, some pitch, a lock of hair, and two papers, each inscribed with the figure of a pyramid and other symbols drawn with a pen. They even got so far as to speak of his burial, and it was settled that it should be in the Theseum, where one Tweddle, an Englishman, and other foreigners had been interred, and where Haller himself was laid not many years after.

The churches were kept lighted night and day for his benefit, and his nurse attributed his final recovery entirely to the intercession of Panagia Castriotissa, or "Our Lady of the Acropolis." At length, after long hovering between life and death, his robust constitution carried him through, and towards the end of September the doctor advised his being removed to Athens. He was carried thither in a litter and set down at Madame Masson's, where he was henceforth to live. Before this episode was fairly concluded or my father had progressed far in convalescence, a new cause of agitation arose. Notice was received that Baron Stackelberg was in the hands of pirates.

He had been for a tour in Asia Minor, and was on his way back between Constantinople and Athens, when in crossing the Gulf of Volo he was taken. His case was even more déplorable than Bronstedt's, for he not only lost whatever he had with him, and saw his drawings torn to pieces in sheer malice before his very eyes, but the miscreants claimed an enormous ransom, amounting to about 3,000*l.*, and sent a notice to his friends in Athens to the effect that the money must be forwarded promptly or portions of the prisoner would be sent as reminders. Meanwhile he had to live with the pirates, and his experiences were no laughing matter. The ruffians used to show him hideous instruments of torture to frighten him into paying a higher ransom. They made him sleep in the open air, which half killed him with fever ; and as they had nowhere to keep him when they went on their marauding expeditions, he had to go with them. On one occasion he saw a vessel run aground to avoid capture, and the sailors clamber up the rocks to escape. An old man who could not follow fast enough was brought in to be sold as a slave. The rest got away, and one of the pirates, in his fury at being eluded, in order to slake his thirst for blood seized on a wretched goat that was grazing by him and cut its throat. Several weeks of this sort of company and exposure left poor Stackelberg more dead than alive. His rescue, which was managed with great diplomacy and a splendid disregard for his own safety by Baron Haller, was finally effected at a cost of about 500*l*.

A Mr. Hughes, in company with Mr. Parker, whom he was "bearleading," arrived in Athens when my father was recovering; and about the last week of November, at their invitation, tempted by the opportunity of travelling with a Tartar and a buyulurdi—that is to say, in security and with as little discomfort as possible—he consented to join in a tour to Albania. I shall not give a detailed account of this voyage. It was over ground everyone has read about. It resulted in no discoveries and few adventures, and anyone who is curious about it will find it fully described in Hughes's book. General Davies, quartermaster-general to the British forces in the Mediterranean, was to form one of the party.

"We set out from Athens on November 29th, a large cavalcade. Two of my friends, though they had not yet learnt that to travel in these countries one must sacrifice a little personal comfort, were otherwise agreeable companions, gentlemanlike and good-humoured; but I early began to foresee trouble with the General. He was one of those people who think everyone who cannot speak English must be either an assassin or a rogue, and was more unreasonable, unjust, and unaccommodating than any Englishman I ever met, odious as many of them make themselves abroad. It rained heavily, but everyone tried to be gay except the general, who damned gloomily, right and left.

We went over an interesting country, but as it was all in the clouds we enjoyed the scenery neither of Parnes nor of Phylæ. Our way was beguiled by the singing of some of the party. The Tartar especially gave proofs of a good voice, a very desirable quality in a Greek companion. The recollection of the scenery of any part of Greece or Asia Minor is bound up with that of the cheerful roundelays of the guides as one rides through the mountains, or the soft melodious song of the Anatolian plains. It is the characteristic thing of Eastern travel. After about three hours in the clouds we got down into Bœotia and saw below us a splendid country of mountain, plain, and sea.

Our Tartar had gone on before us to Thebes, so that when we arrived at our conachi (lodging) it was all ready for us. It was as well, for the weather had given Hughes a return of his fever, and he had to lie in bed.

Parker and I rode next morning without the others to Platæa. It has an admirable situation, and its walls are in better preservation and more interesting and venerable than any I have seen yet.

We could find nothing interesting at Thebes, so as *Oh, my !!* soon as Hughes was better we all set out for Livadia. As we were passing through the hills that separate the respective plains of these two towns a pleasant

coincidence occurred.   We fell in with an English
traveller, a Mr. Yonge, who was a friend of Hughes,
and was bearing a letter of introduction to me.   After
greetings and compliments he gave us the latest
European news, viz. of the grand defeat of the
French at Leipsic.   Glorious news indeed!

Hughes being laid up again at Livadia and the
General impracticable, Parker and I made excursions
thence to the Cave of Trophonius, Orchomenus, and
Topolias, the point from which one visits the five
emissaries of the Lake Copais.   These last struck
me as perhaps the most astonishing work of antiquity
known to me.   Two are still running, but the first,
third, and fifth are quite dry.   At the entrances the
mountain has been cut to a face of thirty or forty feet
high at the mouth and not a tool-mark visible, so
they look like the work of nature.   I wanted to go to
the other side of the ridge to see the exits, but our
guide assured me that it was too dangerous, because
of the pirates who lie in the mountain in the daytime and would probably catch us.   Poor Stackelberg's misfortune was too recent a warning to be
neglected, so I gave it up.

All this country, broadly speaking, is quite uncultivated, and inhabited by immense herds attended by
whole families living in huts and wandering, according
to the pasture and season, in parties of perhaps twenty
with horses and mules.   They are not Turcomans,

such as I saw in Asia, but are called Vlaki and speak Greek. One can imagine nothing more picturesque than they are and the mountains they live in.

Our quarters during our three nights out had been of the roughest, and when Parker and I got back to Livadia our whole evening was spent in the bath, ridding ourselves of the fleas and dirt we had been living in

. Hughes was found to be better, and the General (thank goodness!) tired out and gone off to Salona. He was an odious individual—got drunk every day of our absence—and we were well rid of him. We had brought with us from Athens letters of introduction to the principal Greek merchants, primates of Livadia, Messrs. Logotheti. On the first day of our arrival they had come very civilly to call upon us. Now that we were back from our excursion we returned the visit. The Greeks appear to possess great wealth and influence here, whereas the Turks are but few in the place, and those there are speak Greek and to some extent have Greek manners. When we came into the Logothetis' house we found some actually arguing a point—a thing not to be thought of among Turks elsewhere : the affectation of pride among Orientals, so stupefying to themselves and so exasperating to others, would forbid it. When we came in they rose to go, leaving Signor Nicola to attend to his foreign guests. Our host gave us a striking instance of the devices used by well-to-do Greeks to conceal their wealth from the rapacious Government. He at once led us out of the room he had received us in at the head of the first landing, which was reserved for the reception of Turks and was very simple, into his own apartments, which were exceedingly splendid. There in one corner of the room was the beautiful Logothetina, wife of a Logotheti nephew, in bed. Her father went up to her when he came in and she kissed his hand. One might have thought her being in bed embarrassing, but not at all ; we all sat down and stopped with them for an hour. No one either said or did much, for those who talked had little to say, and many said nothing. When Logotheti went home we accompanied him, and very grand he was, with a large stick in his hand and five or six persons escorting him—quite in the splendid style of the ancient Greeks.

It so happened that in the morning while on a visit to the bey, or waiwode, we heard the reading of a firman bringing the news of the taking of Belgrade by the Turks. During the reading the primates all stood up, and when it was concluded all exclaimed : ' Thanks to God for this success ! May our Sultan live !' In the evening we went to dine with Logotheti There were a Corfiote doctor and several other Greeks. Our talk was of their hopes of emancipation, as it always is when one is in company with Greeks, with the inevitable references to Leonidas and the Hellenes.

Our hosts and the other Greeks struck me as heavier and more Bœotian in appearance than the Greeks I was accustomed to, but also more polished. The Corfiote, of course, was talkative and ignorant: they always are. We ate an immense quantity of turkeys—roast, boiled, hashed and again roasted—fowls and all sorts of poultry dressed in all sorts of ways, and we drank a great deal of bad wine in toasts to King George, success to the Greeks, &c.

As soon as Hughes could move we went on from Livadia by Chæronea to Castri,[1] the ancient Delphi. Until within the last few years the region we were now in was impassable owing to robbers, but Ali Pasha's tyranny has at any rate the merit of an excellent zabete or police, so that it is now fairly safe. The scenery among the mountains is splendid. Our visit to Castri was not a long one. Except the Castalian spring and the stadium, one could make out nothing of the ancient topography. The whole site is covered with walls running in every sort of direction, possibly to keep the earth from slipping down the hill.

In the evening we got to Crisso.

A buyulurdi such as we carried confers the most arbitrary rights; but it was not until the protocaro had been cudgelled by our Tartar that we were able

---

[1] By a convention with the Greek Government made in 1891, the French Government obtained power to buy out the inhabitants of Castri and remove the village in order to excavate the site. The ancient topography is now well ascertained.

to procure a lodging, a tolerably good one, in the house of the papa. I reflected how wretched is the position of the Greeks, and how ungenerous of us Englishmen to live at their expense and assist in the general oppression ; but I was too pleased to get a lodging for the night to act upon it.

From Crisso we went to Salona, and here it became necessary to settle upon our further route. When we came to look into it, it appeared that the plague is raging in every town on our way by Nepacto and Missalonghi through Ætolia. Moreover, the roads are rough and infested by robbers, the horses bad, and in fact the best way to get to Albania seemed to be to go by sea. This was settled upon accordingly, and we started to do it. From Salona to the port is a two hours' ride. Thence we set sail in a felucca. The sea was running very high, the wind was in our teeth, and though we got to Galaxidi at last, it was not without considerable peril. I have had a good many adventures, but I do not think I was ever in greater danger than during those four hours of sailing in that weather in the dark, and I thanked God heartily when I found myself ashore. The only lodging we could get was in the guard-house, a filthy magazine so alive with bugs that after a first failure I gave up all idea of going to sleep, and sat up with Parker smoking till morning. It was out of the question going to look for other quarters. The country is so infested with robbers, who think nothing even of penetrating into the town and carrying off a primate or so, that arriving late and knocking at doors we should have been taken for brigands and answered by pistol shots from the windows.

In the morning our buyulurdi stood us in good stead. With its help we were able to get some good fowls and a sheep, bread and rice. Then going to the shore we made a bargain to be taken to Previsa in a boat. The voyage was fairly prosperous. The second day we landed at Patras, and heard the news of the grand defeat of the French confirmed. We set out again at night and got becalmed, and with difficulty reached a small port, the Scrofé, beyond the flat at the mouth of the Achelous. Here was a scampavia from Santa Maura, and other boats, and we entered with some trepidation lest we should be taken for pirates and fired upon.

Here we were detained several days by stormy weather. Getting away we passed the mouth of the Achelous, and tried to find either of two excellent ports, Petala and Dragonise ; but as they were not marked in our bad charts we failed, and were finally obliged to put into a creek not far from Santa Maura, and lay there the greater part of the night, till the wind blew us off again to sea. At daylight we anchored in the shallow port of Santa Maura.

The weather again detained us some days, till we

with some difficulty got across to Previsa.   Here the
harbour is a fine one, but too shallow to admit large
vessels, and with an awkward bar.   The shore is all
desolation and misery, with one exception, the palace
of the vizier, which is splendid.   The foundations on
the side towards the sea are all of stones from Actium
and the neighbouring San Pietro, the ancient Nicopolis.

In Venetian days Previsa had no fortifications.
Now the pasha has made it quite a strong place, with
several forts and a deep ditch across the isthmus,
though the cannon, to be sure—which are old English
ones of all sorts and sizes—are in the worst possible
order, their carriages ill-designed, and now rotten as
well.   The population has fallen from 16,000, to 5,000
at the outside, mostly Turks.

We went of course to Nicopolis.   The ruins are
most interesting.   There are the theatre, the baths,
the odeum, and the walls of the city, all in fair preservation and most instructive : the latter especially, as an
example of ancient fortification.   An aqueduct, which
is immensely high, brought water from nine hours off.

We went from Previsa, in a scampa-via belonging
to the vizier, to Salona, the port for Arta.   It consists
of only two houses, the Customs house and the serai
of the vizier.   In the latter we got lodgings for the
night, and bespoke some returning caravan horses to
carry us to Arta.   The road, 25 feet wide, is one
which has been lately made for the vizier by a

wretched Cephaloniote engineer across otherwise impassable flats. It is not finished yet; 800 to 1,000 men are still at work upon it. There is no doubt that this road and the canal from Arta to Previsa, as well as the destruction of the Suliotes, who made this part of the world impassable to travellers without a large escort, are public benefits to be put to Ali Pasha's credit.

Arta is a flourishing place under the special eye of the vizier. The bazaar is considerable, and there is every sign of industry.

We left it about midday. The ice was thick on the pools and the road hard with frost. Passing the bridge, we got again on to the vizier's new road. The Cephaloniote superintendent, who was very desirous that we should express to the vizier great admiration for the work, was assiduous in doing the honours of it. After various stoppages, at last, at seven o'clock, nearly frozen, we reached the khan of Five Wells.

A rousing fire we made to warm ourselves by was no use, for it smoked so intolerably that it drove us out again to walk about in the cold till the room was clear. Our only distraction was a Tartar we fell in with who had lately been to Constantinople by land, and his account of the journey is enough to make one shudder.

He passed through no less than nineteen vilayets,

or towns, in which the plague was raging. At
Adrianople the smell of the dead was so great that
his companion fell ill. At the next place he asked at
the post if there was any pest. 'A great deal, God
be praised,' was the reply. At another town, in
answer to inquiries he was told 'half the town is
dead or fled, but God is great.'

What a miserable country !

Next day, riding along a paved way, we got to
Janina or Joannina, the capital of Ali Pasha.

The first *coup d'œil* of the great town and the
lake is certainly impressive, but not so much so as I had
expected. Once inside the town the thing that struck
me most was the splendid dress of all ranks and the
shabby appearance we Franks presented.

We made for the house of our minister, George
Foresti, with whom we dined, and there met Colonel
Church, just arrived from Durazzo."

CHAPTER XVII

ALI PASHA — PSALLIDA — EUPHROSYNE — MUKHTAR — STARTS FOR A
TRIP TO SULI—CASSIOPEIA—UNABLE TO FORD RIVER—TURNS
BACK TO JANINA—LEAVES TO RETURN TO ATHENS—CROSSES
THE PINDUS THROUGH THE SNOW—MALAKASH—A ROBBER—
METEORA—TURKISH RULE—THE MONASTERY—BY TRIKHALA,
PHERSALA, ZITUNI, THERMOPYLÆ AND LIVADIA TO ATHENS.

" NEXT day, as the vizier wished to see us, and we of
course to see him, Foresti took us to the palace he
was living in for the moment. He has no less than
eight in the town. This one is handsome, but the
plan is as usual ill-contrived, and there was much less
magnificence than I had expected.

We were first led into the upper apartments to
await his leisure, and found there a number of fine
youths, not very splendidly dressed. After half an
hour of waiting we were led into a low room, in the
corner of which sat this extraordinary man. He wel-
comed us politely and said he hoped we had had a
good journey and would like Janina, and desired
that if there was anything we lacked we would mention it, for that he regarded us as his children, and his
house and family were at our disposal. He next asked
if any of us spoke Greek; and hearing that I did,

asked me when I had learnt it, and how long I had remained in Athens. Then, observing that Hughes was near the fire, he ordered in a screen in the shape of a large vessel of water, saying that young men did not require fire, only old men ; and in saying this he laughed with so much *bonhomie,* his manner was so mild and paternal and so charming in its air of kindness and perfect openness, that I, remembering the blood-curdling stories told of him, could hardly believe my eyes. Finally, he said he hoped to improve our acquaintance, and begged us to stay on. We, however, bowed ourselves out.

The number and richness of the shops is surprising, and the bustle of business is such as I have not seen since leaving Constantinople. We understood that when the vizier first settled at Janina in '87—that is, twenty-seven years ago—there were but five or six shops in the place : now there are more than 2,000. The city has immensely increased, and we passed through several quarters of the town which are entirely new.

The fortresses on the promontory into the lake are of the vizier's building. He has always an establishment of 3,000 soldiers, 100 Tartars (the Sultan himself has but 200), a park of artillery presented him by the English, and German and other French artillerymen. We seem to have supplied him also with arms and ammunition in his wars with Suli and other parts of Epirus. Perhaps it is not much to our honour to have assisted a tyrant in dispossessing or exterminating the lawful owners of the soil, who only fought for their own liberty ; but one must remember that, picturesque as they were and desperately as they fought, they were nothing but robbers and freebooters and the scourge of the country.

. We passed the 6th of January with Psallida, who is master of a school in Janina. He is, for this country, a learned man. Besides Greek, he speaks Latin and very bad Italian, but as far as manners go he is a mere barbarian. From him I had an account of the Gardiki massacre.[1] I occupied a wet three days in drawing an interior view of a kiosk of the vizier's at the Beshkey Gardens at the north end of the town. Then I got a costume and drew the figures in. Psallida dined with us one day and entertained us with an account of the fair and frail Euphrosyne, who was a celebrity here. Her fate was made the subject of a ballad preserved in Leslie. The story is certainly an awful tragedy. She was of good family and married to a respectable man. Without possessing more education than is usual with Greek ladies she had, besides her great beauty, a natural wit which, with a good deal of love of admiration, soon

[1] The Gardiki massacre took place about 1799. In Ali's youth, his tower had been stormed by the people of Gardiki and his mother and sister outraged—at least, so he said He nursed his revenge for forty years, and then gratified it by massacring the whole population of the village.

attracted round her a host of admirers, and she became a reigning beauty. Mukhtar, the son of Ali, who is a dissolute fellow, was attracted by her, and, cutting out his competitors, became her acknowledged lover. His wife, whom he entirely neglected for his new passion, was a daughter of the Vizier of Berat, whose friendship Ali was at that time particularly anxious to cultivate ; and when she complained to her father-in-law of his son's conduct, he (Ali) determined to put a stop to it. At the head of his guard he burst at midnight into the room of Euphrosyne, and after calling her the seducer of his son and other names, he forced her to give up whatever presents he had made her, and had her led off to prison with her maid. Next day, in order to make a terrifying example to check the immorality of the town in general and his son in especial, he had nine other women of known bad character arrested, and they and Euphrosyne were led to the brink of the precipice over the lake on which the fortress stands. Her faithful maid refused to desert her, and she and Euphrosyne, linked in each other's arms, leapt together down the fatal rock, as did all the others.

Mukhtar has never forgotten his attachment or forgiven his father, or even seen his wife again, and from having been a gay and frank youth he has become gloomy and ferocious without being less dissolute than before. The court he keeps is a sad blackguard affair, a great contrast to the austere sobriety of his father's.

We called in the evening (January 14) to take leave of Ali Pasha. He was on that day in the Palace of the Fortress at the extremity of the rock over the lake. We passed through the long gallery described by Byron, and into a low anteroom, from which we entered a very handsome apartment, very warm with a large fire in it, and with crimson sofas trimmed with gold lace. There was Ali, to-day a truly Oriental figure. He had a velvet cap, a prodigious fine cloak ; he was smoking a long Persian pipe, and held a book in his hand. Foresti says he did this on purpose to show us he could read. Hanging beside him was a small gun magnificently set with diamonds, and a powder-horn, on his right hand also was a feather fan. To his left was a window looking into the courtyard, in which they were playing at the djerid, and in which nine horses stood tethered in their saddles and bridles, as though ready for instant use. I am told this is a piece of form or etiquette.

At first his reception seemed less cordial than before, whether by design or no, and he took very little notice of us. He showed us some leaden pieces of money, and a Spanish coin just found by some country people, and asked us what they were. Then he said he wished he had a coat of beaver such as he had seen on the Danube. He asked Parker whether he had a mother and brothers, and when he heard he was the only son he said it was a sin that he should leave his mother. Why did not he stay at home?

On January 15 we went to call on Mukhtar Pasha. We found him rough, open, and goodhumoured, without any of the inimitable grace of his father, which makes everything Ali says agreeable, however trivial the subject may be. Mukhtar's talk was flat. He was very fond of sport—were we? It was very hot in summer at Trikhala. He had killed so and so many birds; there were loose women at Dramishush; it was a small place, but he would send a man to see that we were properly accommodated; and so on—very civil and rather dull. He smoked a Persian pipe brought him by a beautiful boy very richly dressed, with his hair carefully combed, and another brought him coffee; while coffee and pipes were brought to us by particularly ugly ones. On the sofa beside him were laid out a number of snuff-boxes, mechanical singing birds, and things of that sort. The serai itself was handsome in point of expense, but in the miserable taste now in vogue in Constantinople. The decoration represented painted battle-pieces, sieges, fights between Turks and Cossacks, wild men, and abominations of that sort , while in the centre of the pediment is a pasha surrounded by his guard, and in front of them a couple of Greeks just hanged, as a suitable ornament for the palace of a despot.

On the 16th we set out early for an excursion to Cassiopeia and Suli, across the fine open field behind Janina, past the village of Kapshisda, over a low chain of hills south-west of Janina. Then, after a climb of over an hour, we entered a pass, and presently saw Dramishush in front, on the side of a high mountain. *Dodoni*

Cassiopeia is on a gentle height in the middle of a valley. The situation is beautiful, and the theatre the largest and best preserved I have seen in Greece.

Next morning we dismissed Mukhtar Pasha's man who had escorted us so far, and went on south-west-wards along the edge of the valley of Cassiopeia. As it grew narrower we climbed a ridge which overhung an awful depth, went over a high mountain, and reached Bareatis, a small village in a pass with a serai of Ali Pasha's, in which he lived for a length of time during the war of Suli. Three and a half hours further on we came to Terbisena, the first village of Suli. It had been pouring all day, and we were not only wet and cold when we arrived but the hovel we got as a lodging let in the water everywhere, and here, huddled in the driest corner we could find, we had to sleep and spend the next day.

On the 19th the weather was fine again, and we went on hoping to find the river fordable, but when we

R

got to the bank we found it rapid and deep. One of
our Turks, after a good deal of boasting, plunged in,
and in an instant sank, and the torrent was carrying
him and his horse floundering away. Another of his
brother Turks, seeing him carried down, called loudly
on Allah, and stroked his beard in great tribulation,
but without stirring a stump. In another minute the
man would have been drowned, but our servant
Antonetti, who was but a Christian, very pluckily ran
in and clawed him out. The poor boaster was already
senseless when we got him to land. We took him
back to Dervishina, and gradually brought him round,
when instead of thanking his stars for his narrow
escape, or Antonetti for the plucky part he had played,
he did nothing but lament the loss of his gun, ' Tofeki,'
which he had himself won, he said, and of his shawl
which had cost him 50 piastres. We promised to
make the latter good, and left him to rest.

The whole incident was in all senses a damper to
our ardour. When we considered that to pass this
river we must wait one day at least, and probably four
days to get across the one near Suli, the expenditure
of time seemed to us all, at least so I thought, greater
than we cared to devote to the expedition. So the
long and short of it was that we turned back and
slept at Bareatis. Next day we got back to Janina.
I made up my mind now that I was wasting time over
this trip, and wished to get back to Athens. But

before leaving I thought it my duty to call once more on Ali Pasha. A most agreeable old man he is. I was more than ever struck with the easy familiarity and perfect good humour of his manners. We found him in a low apartment with a fire in the middle, generally used for his Albanians and known as laapoda. Then we went to see Pouqueville,[1] the French resident. We found him with his brother, both of them the worst type of Frenchmen—vulgar, bragging, genuine children of the Revolution. Nothing worth remembering was said, but I did gather this from his tone—that the Empire in France is not likely to last.

On the 26th my friends, for a wonder, got up early, and we all set out in a boat for a small village where we were to find my horses. There we bid farewell and I mounted. It came on to rain, and I arrived, wet through, at the Three Khans to sleep.

Next day the rain became snow, but I set out nevertheless for Mezzovo. We had to ford the river several times, and for the last hour to Mezzovo were up to our middles in snow. The scenery was magnificent, and the country is well cultivated. Mezzovo is a Vlaki or Wallachian village; the people speak a sort of mixed Greek. They are exceedingly industrious and well-to-do.

Artistically I do not know that I have gained

[1] Author of a valuable account of Greece at this time

much, but I do not regret the time I have spent in Albania. The climate is more bracing than that of the rest of Greece, and has set me up after my illness. The scenery, though it cannot be at its best in winter, is most beautiful, and the inhabitants are a fine race—not handsome; but hardy and energetic. An Albanian has very few wants. A little bread of calambochi or Indian corn, an onion, and cheese is abundant fare to him. If he changes his linen five times in the year, that is the outside. A knife and a pistol in his girdle and his gun by his side, he sleeps quite well in the open air with his head on a stone and the lappel of his jacket over his face. In summer and winter he wears a fez. His boots are only goatskin sandals, which he makes himself. His activity in them over rocks is surprising.

As for Ali Pasha's government, one has to remember what a chaotic state the country was in before he made himself master of it. The accounts one gets from the elders make it clear what misery there was. No stranger could travel in it, nor could the inhabitants themselves get about. Every valley was at war with its neighbour, and all were professional brigands. All this Ali has reduced to order. There is law—for everyone admits his impartiality as compared with that of rulers in other parts of Turkey—and there is commerce. He has made roads, fortified the borders, put down brigandage, and raised Albania into a power of some importance in Europe.

That in arriving at this end he has often used means which civilised nations disapprove is no doubt true, but there has been in the first place gross exaggeration as to the crimes attributed to him : for instance, that he sees fifteen or twenty heads cut off every day before breakfast, whereas in point of fact there has not been such a thing as a public execution in the past year ; and then, in the second, one must make allowance for the ferocious manners amongst which he was brought up.

On the 29th of January, as the weather seemed favourable, we set out eagerly to cross Pindus. The snow was deep in places, but for the first hour and a half we had no great difficulty. It was the last half-hour before getting to the top that was worst. The road is desperately steep up a precipice, and the snow was above the horses' girths. Our chamalides, however, waded through it, often up to their middles, and, carrying the loads on their own shoulders, lifted the horses by their tails and heads alternately, I hardly know how. Although I constantly slipped down on the steep incline, I was so eager to see the view that I was the first at the top. Towards the interior it was glorious . the feet of Pindus rooting themselves far into the country, which, although mountainous, was free from snow ; conspicuous was Elymbo (Olympus), the top capped with snow, but the form of it is not beautiful. To the north were other snow-capped mountains. Behind us westward the air was so thick one could see nothing. The west side of the hills is covered with fir, while the east seems to have nothing but oak and birch—quantities of it, but all small trees. As we went down we noticed on the trunks of them the marks of the snow of the year before last, which must have been ten or twelve feet deep. Three and a half hours from our start we got to a khan, where we made a good fire and congratulated ourselves on having got over the hills so well and escaped the fatana—the wind the mountaineers dread.

Our next stage was to Malakash, a Vlaki town. It was astonishing the way our chamalides bore the fatigue of forcing our way through the snow, which was still five or six feet deep in places. They cut a way for the horses, which were constantly falling down and half smothering themselves in the drifts.

From there we followed the course of the river for six hours, and crossed it fifty times at least. On the way we passed a dervish, an Albanian. He was seated on a sort of balcony, very high up, and had a gun in his hand, which he pointed at me and called on me to stop and pay. The sight of the Tartar, however, brought him to reason. Without one a traveller is exposed to great insult from such ruffians.

As it was, a poor wretch who tried to pass himself off as one of our party was forced to stop and pay his quota.

In the afternoon we arrived at Meteora, the strange rocks of which we had seen from some distance up the river. We were given quarters in the house of a Cypriote Greek, from whom I learnt a good deal of the terrible exactions of Veli Pasha, in whose dominions we now were. Our host and his two sons, poor wretches with hardly a fez to their heads and mere sandals bound with a thong to their feet, came to welcome us. After the first compliments they fell into the tale of their woes. Their taxes were so heavy that unless the new year were abundantly fruitful the village must be bankrupt and become ' chiflik ' or forfeit. When a village is unable to pay its taxes, the vizier, as universal mortgagee, forecloses and the land becomes his private property and the villagers his slaves. This is becoming ' chiflik.'

While we were sitting and talking of these troubles a great noise was heard below. Two Albanians, being refused conachi, had broken in the door of a house and entered by force, and the soubashi was gone out to quell the riot. He very properly refused them any kind of reception and drove them out to the khan.

My hosts had roasted me a fowl, but my heart

was so full I could scarcely eat. How long will it please God to afflict these wretched people with such monstrous tyranny ? Besides the exactions of the Government, scoundrels such as these Albanians infest the villages, force their way in houses and eat and drink immoderately and pay nothing. To ease my mind, when the daughter of my host brought me some raisins to eat with my wine I gave her a dollar. She seemed hardly to believe her eyes at first, then took it and kissed my hand.

Next morning, January 31st, I ascended to the principal monastery of Meteora. After a tiring walk of half an hour, winding among the crags of this strange place, we came to the foot of the rock on which it is perched, and found that the ladder commonly used, which is made in joints five or six feet long, had been drawn up. We called to the papades who were aloft to let down the rope and net. After some hallooing, down it came, a circular net with the meshes round the circumference gathered on a hook. Michael and myself, with my drawing materials, got in and were drawn up by a windlass. To swing in mid-air trusting to a rope not so thick as my wrist and 124 feet long (I measured it) is anything but pleasant. I shall not forget my sensations as I looked out through the meshes of the net as we were spinning round in the ascent. There was a horrible void below—sheer precipices on each side, and then the slipping of the rope as it crossed on the windlass. Once up, we were pulled in at the entrance, the hook drawn out, and we were set at liberty. The company that received us were some wretched papades, as ignorant as possible. They could tell me next to nothing about their monastery, except that on the occasion of an invasion of the Turks, a bey of Trikhala, one Joseph Ducas, had retired hither and established it and seventeen others. The buildings of ten of them still exist, but only two or three are still inhabited. The church here is a very good one, and there is a chapel of Constantine. The view is magnificent. I gave a dollar to the young priest who took me round, desiring him to use it for any purpose of the church ; but I found, from what my peasant guide told me when we had got down, that the scamp had pocketed it for his own use, for that the chief papa had asked him as we were about to leave, if the stranger would not leave some parahs for the church. It was a lovely day, and beneath me, from the village, passed a procession of a bridegroom going to a neighbouring village to fetch his bride. His mother was on one side of his horse, another relative on the other ; before him a male relation carried a flag, and behind came all his friends and family in their best dresses with guns on their shoulders, making a gallant show. It was a pretty sight.

We left Kalabaki by Meteora, and reached Trikhala

about sunset.   The solitude of the town and the
vastness of the cemeteries gave one the creeps ; and
hearing that the plague was in the town at that
moment, I mounted again, and rode four hours further
to a khan and slept there.   *Pharsala*

Next day we rode to Phersala (twelve hours) ; but
the plague being there also, we proceeded a further
four hours to a khan under Thaumaco (sixteen hours'
riding).   From Meteora to Phersala is one uninter-
rupted plain which I thought would never end.   I
saw many villages, but much misery—especially in
Trikhala and Phersala.   ·

Next day we got to Zituni (six hours) about
noon.   I did not venture to stay on account of the
plague, and passed on to Molo, at which we arrived
in the evening, passing through the Straits of
Thermopylæ.

Molo is a village of only 200 houses, and yet forty
persons had died of the plague in it in the last three
days.   The terrified inhabitants had fled to the
mountains, and we found only two hangees (men
attached to the han) to receive us.   We meant to
have slept here, but the cats and dogs howled so
terribly (always a symptom of the plague) that I could
not sleep in comfort ; so as the moon shone bright,
we mounted and rode six hours further to a village
opposite Parnassus, passing in safety the fountain
famous for robbers who are almost always stationed

there. The scenery here is very fine and romantic. In six hours more, after crossing two little plains besides that of Chæronæa, we arrived at Livadia (February 3rd). What between the cold, the horror of the plague, and the fatigue, it had been an appalling journey.

CHAPTER XVIII

My father seems to have got back to Athens to his
old quarters at Madame Masson's with Haller and
Stackelberg, and there remained.   He kept a diary
only under the excitement of travel or novelty, and
as the sights and society of Athens were too familiar
to stir him, there is no precise record of how he
passed his time ; but he says in a letter that he intends
to spend his winter in completing the Ægina and
Phigaleian drawings.   After all, it was only two or
three months he had to be there.   The Phigaleian
Marbles were to be sold in Zante in May, and this
time he meant to be present.   The fiasco of the
Ægina Marbles in his absence was a warning of what
might happen again if the sale were not properly
looked after ; and as Gropius after his failure had been
dismissed from his functions as agent (although still
part proprietor) the necessary work had to be done by

the others—each one probably communicating with his own Government. He had taken care that his (the British) should be kept properly posted up. In consequence, everything went off without a hitch. In May he went to Zante. The marbles were sold to General Campbell,[1] commandant of the Ionian Islands, acting on behalf of H.R.H. the Prince Regent, and were already packed up for transport on the 12th of July.

During his stay in Zante my father made many elaborate drawings of the Phigaleian bas-reliefs, with a view to determining their relative positions for the book, and he now returned to Athens to go on with it. He arrived on the 11th of July. But his health was no longer able to bear an Athenian summer. In August he writes :

" A most tiresome fever has been worrying me for the past month, sometimes leaving me for a few days, at others rendering me incapable of doing anything. Few people, even natives, escape it, either in this or any other summer. Such is the fine climate of Greece, which poets would persuade you is a paradise, whereas really hyperborean England, with all her fogs, has still the best in the world. . . . .

I am summing up a few observations, wonderfully

---

[1] General Sir James Campbell, Bart. (1763-1819), Governor of the Ionian Islands till 1816.

savant and deep, on the temples we are preparing for publication, and the Grecian architecture in general. Between you and me, I verily flatter myself, we understand it practically better than anybody—as indeed we ought to. I arrived from Zante on the 11th July. While I was there I received a very fresh (!) letter from home of twenty-nine days.

I was rejoiced to find here my friends and old schoolfellows, Spencer Stanhope and his brother. Conceive our pleasure talking at Athens over Westminster stories and all our adventures since we left. He, poor fellow, has been a prisoner in France for two and a half years, having been taken in Spain owing to the treachery of a Gibraltar vessel, which took him into the port of Barcelona. He is now exploring and excavating (at his own expense) for the French Government as the condition for his freedom! A few days later he and I made a trip to Marathon. We proceeded to Rhamnos, and sleeping a night at a fountain near by, visited in the morning the Temple of Nemesis and stayed there the whole day. It had been well examined, and by this time will have been published by Gell [1] and Gandy. We then went on to a village near which we had the good fortune to find Tanagra, the situation of which had never yet been known. We could trace the whole circuit of the walls and a theatre.

---

[1] Sir William Gell (1777-1836), traveller, author of the *Itinerary of Greece, Pompeiana*, and other works. The Augustus Hare of his day.

Thence to Aulis, the walls of which are easily trace-
able ; then we crossed the bridge over the Euripos
into Eubœa.   The town of Negropont is a wretched
place, inhabited by nothing but Turks.   The fortress
is ruined and contemptible, and the cannon out of order, .
as usual, although it is by way of being one of the principal fortresses in these parts.   The more one sees of
the Turks the more one is astonished at their prolonged
rule in these countries.   We visited a bey in this place
who had a set of maps, and was considered one of the
most enlightened men in the town.   He produced them
immediately he saw us, and boasted of his extensive
knowledge on the subject, and the respect the by-
standers paid this philosopher was perfectly delightful.
The usual custom, before making a visit to these great
personages, is to send them an offering of two or three
pounds of sugar or coffee, and I thought he seemed
rather offended at our exempting ourselves, as Englishmen, from this tribute.   Next day we went along the
seashore, riding through delightful gardens and olive
groves, to Eretria, which has not been seen by modern
travellers.   It must have been a great city, little less
than three miles in circumference.   The whole extent
of the walls and theatres is still visible.

The greater part of Greece is naturally a rich and
productive country.   This needs no better proof than
the immense population to which the ruins still remaining bear testimony.   The ruins of towns of immense

extent and close to each other are found everywhere, and now it is a desert.   Neither plague, pestilence, nor famine is so destructive as tyranny.   We returned to Athens on the tenth day.

We hear that the plague is raging at Constantinople, Salonica, and Smyrna; whereas Athens, with the Morea and Greece in general, though surrounded on all sides by it, has escaped.

The festival of Ramazan is being celebrated.   The bazaar has been well sprinkled with water, and lights are hung before every shop.   The caffanee (coffee shops) are all open and lighted, as well as the balconies of the mosques.   All day, if any Turks are seen, they are walking about in their best, with long wands, but looking very cross, and not lightly to be accosted by a Greek.   At kinde (sunset) the imams call, and the faithful, having fasted from sunrise, not having smoked or even drunk a drop of water, sit down with holy zeal to the very best meal their funds can afford, for it is accounted a crime at this feast to deny themselves what the heart desires.   After this the mosque, gaily lighted, is filled with songs and prayer and thanksgiving.   Later on the streets are filled.   Each in his best enjoys whatever pleasures and amusements the town has to offer—*ombres chinoises*, long stories from the 'Arabian Nights,' music, chess-playing, &c.   Above all, the women now have liberty.   They go about in parties, unmasked, visiting, feasting, and amusing

themselves, and the whole place is a continual Vauxhall
from sunset to sunrise. At midnight the imam again
ascends to the minaret with a chorus, who sing a
solemn and beautiful hymn, far more impressive than
the finest bells in Christendom. The words begin—

Arise, arise, and pray, for ye know not the hour of death.

Towards the morning passes the dumbanum, a
huge drum which a man beats as he goes; while
another accompanies him in a sort of sing-song,
calling up each householder and bidding him eat his
pillau, for the morning is near. He winds up with
good wishes and kind terms, for which, at the end
of the Ramazan, he expects a present. My name
was brought in. What do you think of Cockarella to
rhyme with Canella?

From the minaret a beggar is crying for charity
and threatening to throw himself down unless he gets
it. He goes there at the same hour every day till he
has got what he wants.

The wife of the old disdar (commandant of the
castle) died a few days ago. She was one of the first
ladies of the place, and a respectable good woman.
Everyone was touched with the disdar's lamentation.
'She was the ship in which all my hopes were
embarked. She was the port in which I took shelter
from all the storms and troubles of the world; in her
my comforts and joys were confided; she was the

s

anchor in which I trusted.' Each morning he has visited her tomb, and, causing water to be brought, has poured it around that her remains may be refreshed. Three days after, as is the custom, the elders of his relations went to him, desiring that he should marry again. But he refused, looking, as he said, soon to follow his wife.

October 30.—I have been having continual relapses of this abominable fever ever since August. The worst was in the beginning of this month, and it has taken me till now to get over it. After having leeches on, I had removed one of the bandages too soon, and lost a greater quantity of blood than was intended.

It is impossible to describe the feebleness this fever leaves. I sometimes felt as if I was breathing out my soul, and had ceased to belong to this world at all. I lost all interest in my pursuits.

I should have been badly off indeed if it had not been for Madame Masson. She had been a second mother to me, and more attentive in this and in all my other illnesses than any attendants I could have hired. As soon as I was a little better she was so good as to accompany me to a monastery in the Sacred Way, some little distance from Athens, to which I had been advised to go for change of air. There was only one old woman there to take care of the keys, and in the big deserted place we were like two owls in a barn. I cannot say it was gay. I passed most of my time in sleeping, for that has been the chief effect of my weakness, and what little was left in reading. Occasionally we were favoured with a visit by some of our Athenian friends, who brought their provisions with them, as their custom is. The monastery stands in a beautiful dell or pass through the mountains. On one side is a beautiful view of the bay and mountains of Eleusis, and on the other, of the Plain of Athens, with the long forest of olive trees between us and the Acropolis, which dominates the plain and is backed by Hymettus. On the right is the Piræus, at no great distance. I could not enjoy this lovely scene. Alas! one can enjoy nothing with a low fever. And now, after a stay of a fortnight, we are just returned, and I am not much the better for it.

But one of the last days I was there I was tempted by my friend Linckh to ride to Piræus, to join in celebrating the anniversary of the victory of Salamis— the 25th October—by a fête on the island of Psytalia, where the thickest of the fight was waged. He had assembled a large party of Athenians, who, to tell the truth, were more intent on the feast than on the occasion of it. We embarked from Piræus in a large boat, accompanied by music—to wit, fiddles and tambourines—as is the Athenian fashion, and a great cargo of provisions which were to be prepared while the modern Athenians contemplated the interesting scene before us, and were to weep over the fall of

their country since those glorious days, &c. &c.   All
set out in the greatest glee.   Beyond the port, in the
open sea, some countenances began to change ; though
we had almost a calm, some began to feel the effects
of the ' gentle motion ' and hung their heads over the
side, while several pinched each other with fear and
anxiety at our distance from *terra firma.*   Gradually all
became silence.   Then some murmurs began to arise,
together with advice and recommendation to the
sailors to row gently and hold fast.   A council of war
sat, and agreed *nem. con.* that it would be best to return
to the nearest land.   A small bay was found and all
leapt ashore, crossing themselves and thanking their
stars for their deliverance.   A fire was lighted, the lamb
roasted in no time, a cloth laid on the ground, and all
set to.   The Greeks of old could not have attacked
the Persians with more ardour than these moderns
did the turkeys and lamb before us.   The bottle went
round apace, and all soon began to glorify themselves,
the demoiselles also playing their part ; and when at
length, and not until at length, the desire of eating
and drinking was accomplished, each one filched the
remaining sweets off the table as she found her
opportunity.   Music's soft enchantment then arose,
and the most active began a dance, truly ́bacchanalian,
while the rest lingered over the joys of the table.
Punch crowned the feast.   All was rapture ; moderation was no longer observed, and the day closed with

a pelting of each other with the bones of the slain, amidst dancing, singing, and roars of laughter or applause. I venture to assert most positively that not one thought was given to the scene before us, or the occasion, by any one member of the party except my friend Linckh and the διδάσκαλος, the schoolmaster of Athens, who, having brought tools for the purpose, carved on the rock an inscription which will one day be interesting to those who may chance to light upon it a thousand years hence—'Invitation [or repast] in memory of the immortal Salaminian combat.' Our party embarked not till after sunset; and though the sea was twice as high and the wind as contrary as it was coming, such are the powers of nectar and ambrosia that all conducted themselves with uncommon courage and resolution. Choruses, Dutch and Athenian, beguiled the way, and all was harmony except the music. So one might have hoped the day might have concluded, but no! the Greek fire, once lighted, is not so easily quenched. I, as an invalid, and exceedingly tired with so much pleasure, retired to my cell in a monastery where we were all to pass the night, and some of my friends kindly gave me a coverlet and a sort of bed, on which I threw myself; but not until long after midnight did the music or the dancing cease, or I or any sober person get a chance of sleep. We got away next day, but not without difficulty; for the Athenians are like our journeymen : when once they are out on the spree they must carry it on for a week.

We are now in Athens again, and I have just returned to my work-table covered with the dust of so many lost days. This waste of time is terrible. Altogether, out of twenty-four months spent in Athens, seven have been passed in illness. If ever I get away from this country in health and safety, how I shall thank my stars ! "

It was in these last days of his stay in Athens that he became possessed of a portion of the Panathenaic frieze of the Parthenon in the following strange manner. The disdar or commandant of the castle on the Acropolis was by now an old friend of Cockerell's, and had ended by becoming exceedingly attached to him. When he understood from the latter, who came to pay him a farewell visit, that he was leaving for good, he told him that he would make him a present. He said he knew that Cockerell was very fond of old sculptured stones, so if he liked to bring a cart to the base of the Acropolis at a certain hour at night (it could not be done in the daytime for fear of giving offence to the Greeks) he would give him something. Cockerell kept the appointment with the cart. As they drew near there was a shout from above to look out, and without further warning the block which forms the right-hand portion of Slab I. of the South Frieze now in the British Museum was

bowled down the cliff. Such a treatment of it had
not been anticipated, but it was too late for regrets.
The block was put on to the cart, taken down to the
Piræus, and shipped at once. Cockerell presented it
to the British Museum, and its mutilated appearance
bears eloquent testimony to its rough passage down
the precipices of the Acropolis.

" My fever continued to harass me until I took
a trip to Ægina, which I made for the purpose of
change of air, as well as of correcting and revising
our drawings of the Temple of Jupiter Panhellenius.
In both respects I have succeeded beyond my hopes.
I am now in perfect health, and have made some
improvements and additions to our observations
which will be of importance to our work. Taking
ladders from here, I have also succeeded in measuring the columns of a temple supposed to have
been that of Venus—I think Hecate—which are
of universally admired proportion, and so high that
hitherto no travellers have been able to manage
them. Only two columns still exist. They belong,
I found, to the posticum between the antæ. In
digging at their base to prove this, I came upon a
very beautiful foot in a sandal, life-size, of Parian
marble, of precisely the same school and style as those
of our Panhellenian discovery.[1] You may imagine

---

[1] This foot was presented to the Glyptothek at Munich.

I counted on nothing less than finding a collection as interesting and extensive as the other. I procured, with some difficulty, authority from the archons of the island, and struck a bargain by which they were to have one half of the produce of the excavation, which was to be made at my expense, and I the other, with a first refusal of purchasing their portion. I dug for three days without finding the smallest fragment, and, what was worse, satisfied myself that it had been dug over and re-dug a hundred times, the foundations of the temple having served time out of mind as a quarry for the Æginetans. The money spent was not very great, the time wasted was all to the good of my health, and I was able to make a curious observation on the foundations of the building. Greek temples are commonly on rock. This was not ; and the foundations were no less than 14 to 15 feet deep, the first three courses of well-cut stone, the last set in mortar on a wall of small stones in mortar, at the sides of which is a rubble-work of largish stones beaten down with sea sand and charcoal and bones of sacrifices. Underneath, again, are other courses of well-cut stones which form a solid mass under the whole temple.

I have also with great difficulty, since there are no carpenters in this country, ascertained what I spoke of before as a matter of conjecture—viz. the entasis or swelling of the Greek columns. A straight line stretched from the capital to the base showed the swelling at about a third of the height to be in the Temple of Minerva an inch, in that of Ægina half an inch, which is the same proportion in both. The ruined state of the columns of the Theseum makes it less easy to ascertain the exact swelling. Those of Minerva Polias and the Erechtheum are also swelled. I have no doubt that it was a general rule with the Greek architects, though it has hitherto escaped the eyes of Stuart and our most accurate observers."

Cockerell had long been anxious to get into Italy. There alone could he see and study an architecture in some measure applicable to modern needs, if he was ever to become a practical architect. For four years he had been studying abstract beauty, practising his hand in landscape painting, interesting himself in archæology, and generally, except for his vigour and perseverance, behaving as many a gentleman at large might have done whose place in the English world was already made for him. But he had a position to win, and in one of the most arduous of professions, for which all this unsettling life was not merely not preparing him but actually making him unfit.

Since his first startling success at Ægina he had been led on from one expedition to another, losing sight for months together, in the easy life and simple conditions which surrounded him, of the keen competition in the crush of London for which he ought to be girding himself. He had been forming a taste, but a

taste in the externals and details of building only. Of
composition and of planning he had seen as yet
no fine example and had learnt nothing. There was
nothing left for him to do in Greece. He had traversed it in all directions, seen every place of interest,
and whenever there appeared a prospect of finding
anything with the moderate means at his disposal, he
had tried digging.

Under Napoleon's continental system Italy of
course was closed to Englishmen, but to Bavarians it
was accessible, and Cockerell had often talked with
Haller of the possibility of smuggling himself as his
servant into the country under cover of his (Haller's)
passport. Fortunately this was never attempted.
Even if they had succeeded in passing the frontiers
under Governments where every foreigner was sub-
jected to continual espionage, the delusion would soon
have been discovered. It was a boy's scheme. He
had also tried to engage the good offices of Louis of
Bavaria to obtain him admission as an artist, but
nothing had come of it; and finally, when he heard
that Lady Hester Stanhope had got leave to travel in
Italy, he had applied to Lord Melville for a similar
indulgence. But with the abdication of Napoleon,
which took place in April 1814, the whole prospect
changed. France was at once thrown open to
Englishmen, and the rest of the Continent by
degrees. It is not easy to discover at what precise

date the kingdom of Naples and Rome became accessible, but it must have been during the summer. Western news took time to percolate into Greece, but as soon as he learnt that there was a possibility of penetrating into Italy, he had begun making preparations for doing so. And now that there was nothing left to detain him, he arranged to start with Linckh for Rome on the 15th of January, 1815. When the appointed day came, Madame Masson saw him off at the Piræus, and shed floods of tears. She was very fond of him. Two years after she writes : " Non si sa cosa è Carnovale dopo la vostra partenza."

A curious fact about the journey is that they brought away with them a German of Darmstadt of the name of Carl Rester, who appears to have been a fugitive slave, of whom more hereafter.

The party was joined by a Mr. Tupper. This young gentleman had been lodging at Madame Makri's, and had fallen in love, as it was the indispensable fashion for young Englishmen to do, with one or all of the charming daughters. He left them in tears, vowing to return, but it does not appear that he ever did.

The diary of this journey is kept in a sketch-book in pencil, and is not everywhere legible. The country was one well traversed by tourists and minutely described by Gell. There were no discoveries to be made or new impressions to be felt. They had no adventures. The weather was odious. The entries consist largely of the kind of information—estimates of population, accounts of products, and possibilities—which for the modern traveller is " found " by Murray or Baedeker, and would never figure in his diary.   At the mouth of the Alpheus he remarks how well suited the situation would be for a naval dockyard, close to vast forests of oak and fir—forests, all of which must have disappeared in the devastations of Mehemet Ali, for there are none there now.

The route taken was by Corinth, Argos, Tripolizza, Caritzena, Phigaleia, which they found buried in snow, Olympia, Patras, Ithaca, Corfu, Otranto, Lecce, Bari, and Foggia.   The Pass of Bovino, between Foggia and Naples, was considered exceedingly dangerous, on account of banditti, and perhaps the most interesting thing in the whole diary is the extravagant size of the escort considered necessary to see the travellers through it.   It consisted of no less than sixty men— thirty cavalry and thirty infantry.

But on the whole the diary of the journey, which was through interesting places and at an interesting moment, could hardly be duller.   It may be due to Cockerell's having been in poor health, or to Tupper's having been a stupid, unstimulating companion.

They arrived at Naples on the 14th of April, 1815.

CHAPTER XIX

NAPLES—POMPEII—ROME—THE GERMAN RESTER GOT RID OF—
SOCIAL SUCCESS IN ROME—LEAVES FOR FLORENCE—BARTHOLDY
AND THE NIOBE GROUP—LADY DILLON—THE WELLINGTON
PALACE—PISA—TOUR IN THE NORTH—MEETS STACKELBERG
AGAIN—RETURNS TO FLORENCE AND ROME—HOMEWARD BOUND
—CONCLUSION

WITH one exception there were no Englishmen, artists
or others, in Naples at that time, but a number of
Frenchmen, with some of whom Cockerell struck up a
great intimacy. In spite of national feeling, which was
running very high at the time, he got on very well with
them, but he says in a letter from Rome they were
dreadful time-servers in their political views. Of course
it was a difficult moment for Frenchmen. After Napoleon's abdication at Fontainebleau in April 1814, they
had had to accommodate themselves to a revival of the
ancient monarchy, which could not be very satisfactory
to anyone, and now Napoleon was back again in France.
Between two such alternatives no wonder that their
judgment oscillated ; but to Cockerell—patriotic, enthusiastic, and troubled by no awkward dilemmas—
their vacillation was unintelligible.

The one Englishman was Gell (afterwards Sir

William), who speaks of a stay they made together at Pompeii as the pleasantest time he had spent in his three years' tour.

During this time Cockerell worked hard, and besides what he did which could only be of use to himself, he made himself so familiar with Pompeii that Gell proposed to him to join him in writing an itinerary of that place.

Altogether, leaving Athens on the 15th of January, it was six months before Cockerell got to Rome. Between Naples and Rome the country seems to have been in a very unquiet state, and Carl Rester, who was still with him, writes afterwards : " You remember how anxious about brigands we all were on the journey."

Soon after they arrived, Rester, who must by now have become an irksome burden, started from Rome to walk to his own home at Frankfort. He took a long time about it, but he got there at last in December, only to find his family so reduced by the wars that he determined, as he says, not to be a burden to them, but to show his gratitude to his benefactor by asking for more favours and throwing himself as a burden upon him. So he determined to extend his walk to England. Before leaving his native town, however, he says he published in the local newspaper the following strange tribute to Cockerell's generosity :

" Magna Britannia victoriosa, gloriosa, bene merens, felix. Carolus Robertus Cockerell nobilis Anglus et moribus et scientiis praeclarus me infelicem perditum Germaniae prolem, primis diebus 1815 e Morea barbaris deportavit. Ad Corfum deinde amicis meis Anglis restituit et patriae advicinavit per Napolem universum, Romae me secum ducentem [for ducens] humaniter semper et nobili amicitia me tractavit a London, Old Burlington Street, No. 8, nobilissimi parentes ipsum progenuerunt dignissimum membrum magnae nationis et hominem ubicunque aestimatissimum

Pro gratia universis Anglis et ipsi

Carolus Rester germanus.

Gallis merentibus, Britannia juncta Germanis felix Auspicium semper semperque erit." (Are these two last lines elegiacs ?—ED.)

He arrived at Bois le Duc early in March 1816, and after an illness there of seven weeks, writes to Cockerell to beg his assistance to get him over to England, that he might be the better able to sponge upon him there. I never heard what became of him afterwards.

Cockerell then was in Rome, and here he first began to enjoy the harvest of his labours. He says there were no English there at the time except Lady Westmoreland, mother of the British minister at Florence, but there was a large society of foreign artists, into which he threw himself. There were the brothers Riepenhausen, painters; Schadow, a sculptor from Berlin; Ingres, who drew his portrait;[1] Cornelius of Munich, and others of his school; Knoering, a Russian; Mazois, author of " Le Palais de Scaurus " and an itinerary of Pompeii; Catel, a French architect; Thorwaldsen, Overbeck, Vogel, portrait painter; Bartholdy, Prussian consul-general; Hess, a painter from Vienna; Canova, and Checcarini, who did the Neptune and Tritons in the Piazza del Popolo at the bottom of the drive up to the Pincio. The air of Rome was steeped in classicism. In this company every event was described in classical figures: their café was the Café Greco, which still exists; the front half was called the Pronaos. There all the artistic world collected and made acquaintance.

"If I were a little more vain I should be out of my wits at the attention paid me here. I have a daily levee of savants, artists and amateurs come to see my drawings; envoys and ambassadors beg to know when it will be convenient for me to show them some sketches; Prince Poniatowski and the Prince of Saxe-Gotha beg to be permitted to see them. I say they are slight, and in truth poor things, but at any rate they were done on the spot, and they, ' C'est la Grèce enfin, c'est là le véritable pays. Ah, Monsieur, que vous êtes heureux d'avoir parcouru ce beau pays!' Then I explain to them some constructions or beauties which they

---

[1] See frontispiece.

don't understand. ' Ah, que c'est merveilleux, mais vous les publierez, vous nous donnerez le bonheur de les posséder, mais ce sont des choses fort intéressantes, enfin c'est de la Grèce.' And in truth publishers and readers have been so long restricted to the Roman antiquities, which have been published and read over and over again a thousand times, that the avidity for novelty is beyond measure, and Greece is the fashion here as everywhere else.

There is not a single English artist here and only a few passengers. Lady Westmoreland is one. She is a very clever, well-bred, agreeable chatterer, who has been very civil to me, and made me lose several hours which might have been better employed. Fortunately she is going away. I have several letters for the Roman nobles, but I have not presented them that I may have my time to myself.

So Canova is gone to England. I hope it is not to execute the paltry monument of Lord Nelson which he has published here. It would be a disgrace to us all. Fancy the great Nelson as a Roman in petticoats ! I do trust whenever a monument is erected to him it may be as original, national, and characteristic as was the man and the great nation he sprang from. Every age hitherto has had ingenuity enough to make its costume interesting in sculpture ; we are the first who have shown such poverty of ideas as to despise our age and our dress.

T

I hope he will not be made too much of in England. It is true that nobody ever worked the marble as he does, and it is this finish of his which has deceived and captivated the world, but it is nothing but artificiality, and there is no nature about it. When he attempts the sublime he is ludicrous. In seeking grace he is more successful ; but, after all, his Terpsichore was conceived in the Palais Royal, and her headdress is exactly the latest hairdressers' fashion. It is exasperating to think of his success when Flaxman, as far his superior as Hyperion to a satyr, an artist looked up to by the schools of the Continent as a great and extraordinary genius, is neglected by us because he is not a foreigner.

It is exceedingly gratifying to me to find everything in my portfolio turning to account. I had the pleasure of showing to Colonel Catinelli, who lately fortified Genoa, my fortifications of Syracuse, and the sketches I made of that subject in Greece. He assures me that they are invaluable notices new to modern warfare, and that they prove that, compared to the ancients, we who imagine ourselves so well informed on the matter, know nothing at all.

Then I have above 150 inscriptions among my papers, and I find most of them are unpublished. I have had them copied fairly, and they are now in the hands of a great savant, M. Akerblad, for his perusal. He promises to give me his notes on them.

I do think I have not made a bad use of my opportunities, if I may judge by the interest taken in the various new notices on different subjects I have brought with me, and the flattering consideration everywhere shown me. I get so many invitations, and am so harassed to show distinguished persons of all nations my drawings, that I can get no time to myself. And in order to have something to show I have been obliged to finish up some of my sketches, which has occupied the whole of the last two months. I have now a portfolio of about fifteen of some of the most interesting scenes in Greece fit to show, and I generally find them as much as my visitors want to see.

Finding at last that my time and occupations were too much infringed upon by gaieties, I left Rome to seek more quiet in Florence. I found it at first, and for more than six weeks was as busy as it was possible to be. My life was a curious one. I rose early, and after working all day, dined alone at a trattoria, refusing frequently three or four invitations in a day. Then I slept three or four hours on a sofa, and rose in the night to work calmly until four or five in the morning, when I took another nap, and rose at seven. This odd life got wind; and as I was a great deal known here, either by reputation or by name and family, I occasioned a good deal of wonder, particularly among those who are astonished at anyone's occupying

himself earnestly except for a necessity.   The interest
in me was also increased rather than diminished by my
shyness when I did show in company.   I had so much
lost the habit of society by the long sojourn in Turkey,
and, looking on it with a new eye, was often so disgusted with the follies of it, and showed my disgust,
that I got a character for being a cynic.   But instead
of taking offence people only made the more of me,
and I was constantly invited out, more to gratify my
hosts' curiosity than to give pleasure to me.   To have
travelled in Greece, still more to have been a discoverer there, is enough to make a lion ; while the fame
of my drawings, which few of the many who saw them
understood and all were therefore willing to think
wonderful, completed the business.   It was at this
time that I brought out my drawing of the Niobe and
the etchings from it."

B. Bartholdy, Prussian consul-general in Rome,
an intelligent man and much interested in art, had
travelled up from Rome to Florence with Cockerell
and made himself one of his most intimate acquaint-
ances.   Walking together one day in the Uffizi, they
examined the group of the Niobe.   It is now neglected
and forgotten, but in those days it occupied, in the
estimation of artists, the place to-day held by the Elgin
Marbles.   With the Venus de' Medici, the Apollo Bel-
vedere, and the Torso in the Vatican, these statues
were regarded as the greatest remains antiquity had

bequeathed to the modern world. But, prized and studied as they were, the purpose of so many figures, evidently meant to stand together, had never yet dawned on the minds of their admirers. The figure of Niobe, which is the largest, had been placed in the middle, and the rest in a circle round her. It was felt indeed that this could not be right, but no one had anything better to suggest, and it remained one of the favourite puzzles for art lovers to wrangle over. Into the middle of this clouded state of intelligences Cockerell dropped as from another planet. The experience of the Æginetan statues, which he had arranged so laboriously, besides the constant sight of what remained of the Parthenon and other Greek monuments, made the notion of a pediment or ἀετός so familiar as to present itself to his mind at once as the only possible destination for so many statues. He says the first suggestion came on that occasion from Bartholdy. " I have told Schlegel and all parties that it was first proposed by you ; " to which Bartholdy replies : " J'aurai le plaisir de pouvoir dire que vous avez fait fructifier un petit grain tombé de la main d'un amateur des beaux arts qui sans cela serait resté stérile." But it was probably the company of Cockerell and the associations with Ægina &c. which suggested the notion to Bartholdy. At all events, beyond that first suggestion, Bartholdy did nothing. It was Cockerell who measured the statues, arranged them, proved the case, and made the etching which hangs to this day in the Niobe Room in the Uffizi Gallery, showing the arrangement which he proposed. In recognition, however, of the part Bartholdy had had in it, the plate was dedicated to him.

For the introduction of Cockerell as a lion into society—if that be a thing to be desired—this discovery was most opportune. He had arrived with a great reputation as a traveller, a discoverer, and unraveller of age-long puzzles, as in the case of the Temple of the Giants, and now here was a proof of his powers exhibited in the centre of artistic Europe.

" I had shown my drawing to several people and amongst the ambassadors and distinguished persons here—all of whom, *de rigueur*, more or less pretend to understand the arts—and it gained universal approbation. It was talked about by all, and written about by Demetrius Schinas and other obscure poets and prose writers. I was flattered, invited, and made much of. Our ambassador boasts that the solution has been proved by an Englishman; others bow and beg to be allowed to send copies of my etching to their Governments, to Metternich, &c. It was formally presented to the Grand Duke, and I have received from the Academy here a handsome letter and diploma of Academician of Florence. It is to be published in the official work on the Gallery. I have presented it myself to Madame de Staël, and my friends have sent it to all parts of the Continent."

He was now regularly launched in the fashionable society of Florence.

The reigning beauty at this time, the centre of all jollity and brightness, was Lady Dillon. All the young men were at her feet, and Cockerell was as deeply smitten as anybody. As already mentioned, during the time that he was in Syracuse he had learnt the art of cameo-cutting. He now made use of it—or at least of the preliminary stage, which is to make a model in wax—to execute a highly finished portrait of her, which still exists in the possession of her descendants. It shows a head of great beauty, and is executed with admirable skill and minuteness.

The whole English nation was now jubilant over the success of its army at Waterloo, and was considering the rewards to be offered to its idol, the Duke of Wellington. He was to have a magnificent palace, surpassing the glories of Blenheim, and architects were called upon to give reins to their imagination in preparing designs in competition. The celebrity which my father had by now made for himself obtained him, through the medium of Lord and Lady Burghersh, his fast friends, a formal invitation to send in designs for the Wellington Palace.

The opportunity was of course magnificent, but nothing he had been doing for years had in the least adapted him to take advantage of it.

" Although my occupation in the Wellington Palace

is a very honourable one, and the study and exercise
of invention in the course of it may be profitable, yet
I cannot help wishing I had never been invited to
give an idea for it, for I have spent a vast deal of time
over it, and it will add nothing to my reputation, even if
it does not detract from it.   If such a design was difficult to everyone, you may imagine what it was to me
who have never attempted anything original before.
I consulted every architectural work of Europe (they
are all in the library here), and I would have consulted
every professional man I could get at if there had been
any here whose opinion was worth having.   Then I
composed general ideas, and finally fixed on one
which pleased Mr. North and several other persons to
whom I showed it ; but when I went into detail I found
the difficulties increase immeasurably, and the notions
which were plausible while they were vague could not
be put into execution.   Plan would not agree with
elevation.   Doors and windows would not come into
their right places.   I invented roundabout ways for
simple ends.   In fact I worked furiously, and for the
first time realised the practical difficulties of the profession.   At last, when I had filled a portfolio with
sketches and schemes, I completed a set and showed
them to Lord and Lady Burghersh, who said they
were pleased with them.

I began to feel that I had too large an acquaintance in Florence—too many visits and invitations.

My wound [?], of which I did not get the better, confined me, and that made me generally unwell and .
obliged me to go through a course of physic.   Altogether I got out of heart with my work and determined
to get away.   I went to Pisa for the month of July,
and except for visits from Pigou I was quite alone.
There I undid all I had done before, and finding that
to do the thing well I should need more time than I
could possibly give, I determined to make some small
sketches which, prettily finished, might attract attention
and show that I was in some sort capable.   Finally, I
made some sketches and sent them with an explanation to Lady Burghersh and a request to forward them
to the proper quarter."

The difficulties he had encountered over these
drawings so disgusted him with architecture that he
seems to have even proposed to his father to throw it
up and become a painter, as that, he thought, was the
profession for which he was best suited.   But Mr.
Cockerell, who was a steady business man, had no
notion of his son becoming what he would have considered a bohemian, and refused to sanction any such
change.

The only thing to do, then, was to continue his
studies.   The Wellington Palace drawings had at any
rate weaned him of any idea that pure Greek architecture was applicable to modern architectural designing,
and he had little knowledge of any other.   He started

for a tour of the north of Italy. His letters contain few criticisms. Palladio, probably as being most akin to what he had hitherto studied, pleased him more than any other architect. In Venice he fell in with Stackelberg, who had been home to Russia while his travels in Greece were still fresh enough to claim attention, and had been received with every sort of distinction. He was now on his way back to Rome to settle there and bring out the various books he subsequently published.

The two joined forces, and having run through all the principal towns, returned southwards to Florence.

Shortly after, in company with Lord and Lady Dillon, he went to Rome. He was now a recognised lion, everywhere fêted and made much of. Bartholdy writes of him : " Cockerell est gâté par les femmes." Nevertheless he worked hard. Amongst other things he finished the drawing of the Forum Romanum, the engraving of which is well known. The Duchess of Devonshire wished to insert a reduction of it in her " Virgil," and writes to thank him for " the beautiful drawing you *was* so good as to do for me."

He had left also in Rome the bulk of his, and Haller's, drawings for the intended book on Greek architecture. These he picked up, and having seen all the architecture Italy had to show him, he started in March for England. In Paris he remained some

little time. A letter from his father during his stay
there is worth transcribing in part.

" I send a few hints as to what you should observe
in Paris ; not things of that high order to which you
have so long been used, but yet important to study in
order to supply the luxurious indulgence so much
coveted by the great here, by whom a complete
knowledge of them in their professors of architecture
is expected.

You have raised a name here so high that everything in perfection will be expected of you ; at least in
all that relates to taste in the arts, and in all the
subordinate degrees of contrivances, as well as in
decoration. The last is that which affords the most
extensive employment, and you will be surprised to
find more importance attached to the decorations of a
salon than to the building of a temple. If, therefore,
you can bend to the consideration of what is called the
' fittings up' of the interior of the best hotels and
palaces of Paris, the graces of their *meubles*, and the
harmony of their colours in hangings, painting, and
gilding, you may be the general arbiter of taste here ;
and as there are very few persons who are real judges
of compositions even classical, much less sublime, and
there must be few opportunities of exercising those
parts of your studies here, it will be really useful if you
allow yourself to look at those minor objects at Paris
which in truth they judge well of.

Percier[1] is the first architect in Paris; he will tell you what is worth seeing. Dismalter & Jacob are the first decorators in furniture &c., 57 Rue Meslée.

Your friends Lord Burghersh and Lord Dillon proclaim your name without·ceasing, and much is expected of you. The Duke of Gloucester has commanded me to introduce you to his acquaintance. You have been spoken of at Carlton House, where I have reason to think there is great likelihood of your being noticed advantageously; but you must not be disappointed to find very common things occupying the minds of a large majority of a nation of *boutiquiers*, and we must take the world as we find it, believing always that good sense, refined judgment, and true taste will ultimately prevail.

Do not imagine that I am thinking of money as the only thing worth your attention. I consider that as the last object. The first, a higher order of taste and information, you possess amply. The second is to learn to suit in some measure the times we live in and the objects which occupy the multitude, and it is worth attending to. The third and last is the profit which follows; but that must come of itself, and is not worth pursuing.

You will think me lecturing to the last, but I really

[1] Charles Percier (1764-1838), originator of the so-called "Empire" style in furniture, architect of the Arc de Triomphe du Carrousel, and of parts of the Louvre and of the Tuileries.

mean no more than to express my hope that you will
not despise trifles, if elegant, finding yourself for the
moment amongst a nation of triflers, because they have
long been considered and imitated by ourselves and
the rest of Europe as accomplished in matters of
ornament, though not in subjects of use.

Your family are now on tiptoe for your arrival, and
daily drink their affectionate good wishes to the homeward bound. None is behind another in their impatience ; for myself, it is always present to me.
Nevertheless, I am not selfish enough to wish you to
leave unseen, for the sake of a few days more, anything
which you ought to be acquainted with."

My father arrived in London on the 17th of June,
1817, having left it on the 10th of April, 1810. Besides
his own, he had brought with him all Haller's drawings
for the intended book which was to be the complete and
final authority on Greek architecture and the grand
result of his seven years of travel. Haller was to come
to England to see it through the press. Had it appeared
at once it would have been most *à propos*. Greek architecture was all the fashion. Unhappily, the intention
was thwarted by the sudden death of Haller, which
took place at Ambelakia, in the Vale of Tempe, of a
congestion of the lungs, caught while making excavations in the month of September 1818. The loss of
this valuable help disheartened my father, who had no
taste for the work. He was already busy in other

ways, and the task which should have had his first attention gradually sank into the background.   One by one those who had taken part in the discoveries died : Stackelberg in 1836, Linckh and Foster not many years after.   But the book remained a load on my father's conscience all his life, and it was not till 1859, more than forty years later, that it saw the light. The interest in the events and actors had died down, and the novelties had become common property.   His unfortunate dislike for writing lost him much of the credit he might have reaped, while others profited by his experience.   His collection of inscriptions was picked over by Walpole; Hughes fills out his pages with his letters ; Bronstedt uses his drawings.   It is Stackelberg who relates how he discovered the bas-reliefs at Phigaleia ; Beaufort anticipates anything he might have had to tell of Karamania ; Wordsworth plundered his portfolio ; and in the absence of any consecutive account of his own, it has been often only by the help of the writings of others that it has been possible for me to piece together his disjointed and often undated diaries.

PRINTED BY
SPOTTISWOODE AND CO LTD , NEW-STREET SQUARE
LONDON

A Classified Catalogue
OF WORKS IN
GENERAL LITERATURE
PUBLISHED BY
LONGMANS, GREEN, & CO.
39 PATERNOSTER ROW, LONDON, E.C.
91 AND 93 FIFTH AVENUE, NEW YORK, AND 32 HORNBY ROAD, BOMBAY

CONTENTS.

INDEX OF AUTHORS AND EDITORS.

History, Politics, Polity, Political Memoirs, &c.

Abbott.—*A History of Greece.*
By EVELYN ABBOTT, M A , LL D

Part I.—From the Earliest Times to the Ionian Revolt.   Crown 8vo., 10s. 6d.

Part II.—500-445 B.C.   Crown 8vo., 10s. 6d.

Part III.—From the Peace of 445 B C to the Fall of the Thirty at Athens in 403 B.C.   Crown 8vo., 10s 6d.

Abbott.—*Tommy Cornstalk* being Some Account of the Less Notable Features of the South African War from the Point of View of the Australian Ranks. By J. H M ABBOTT   Crown 8vo., 5s. net.

Acland and Ransome.—*A Hand-book in Outline of the Political History of England to* 1896   Chronologically Arranged   By the Right Hon. A H. DYKE ACLAND, and CYRIL RANSOME, M A   Crown 8vo , 6s.

Allgood. — *China War,* 1860 *Letters and Journals*   By Major-General G ALLGOOD, C B , formerly Lieut G ALLGOOD, 1st Division China Field Force.   With Maps, Plans, and Illustrations   Demy 4to   12s 6d net

Annual Register (The).   A Review of Public Events at Home and Abroad, for the year 1902.   8vo., 18s.

Volumes of the *ANNUAL REGISTER* for the years 1863-1901 can still be had.   18s each.

Arnold.—*Introductory Lectures on Modern History.*   By THOMAS ARNOLD, D D., formerly Head Master of Rugby School   8vo., 7s. 6d

Ashbourne.—*Pitt Some Chapters on His Life and Times.*   By the Right Hon EDWARD GIBSON, LORD ASHBOURNE, Lord Chancellor of Ireland.   With 11 Portraits.   8vo , gilt top, 21s.

Ashley (W. J.).

English Economic History and Theory.   Crown 8vo , Part I , 5s   Part II , 10s 6d

Surveys, Historic and Economic   Crown 8vo., 9s. net.

Bagwell.—*Ireland under the Tudors.*   By RICHARD BAGWELL, LL D   (3 vols)   Vols I and II. From the first invasion of the Northmen to the year 1578   8vo , 32s   Vol. III   1578-1603   8vo., 18s.

Baillie.—*The Oriental Club, and Hanover Square*   By ALEXANDER F. BAILLIE   With 6 Photogravure Portraits and 8 Full-page Illustrations.   Crown 4to., 25s. net.

Besant.—*The History of London.*   By Sir WALTER BESANT.   With 74 Illustrations.   Crown 8vo , 1s. 9d.   Or bound as a School Prize Book, gilt edges, 2s. 6d

Bright.—*A History of England.*   By the Rev. J. FRANCK BRIGHT, D.D.

Period I.   *Mediæval Monarchy*:   A D. 449-1485   Crown 8vo , 4s. 6d

Period II   *Personal Monarchy.*   1485-1688.   Crown 8vo , 5s.

Period III.   *Constitutional Monarchy*   1689-1837.   Crown 8vo , 7s 6d

Period IV.   *The Growth of Democracy*   1837-1880.   Crown 8vo., 6s

Bruce.—*The Forward Policy and its Results*; or, Thirty-five Years' Work amongst the Tribes on our North-Western Frontier of India   By RICHARD ISAAC BRUCE, C.I.E.   With 28 Illustrations and a Map   8vo , 15s. net.

Buckle.—*History of Civilisation in England.*   By HENRY THOMAS BUCKLE.

Cabinet Edition   3 vols   Crown 8vo , 24s

'*Silver Library' Edition*   3 vols   Crown 8vo., 10s 6d

Burke.—*A History of Spain,* *from the Earliest Times to the Death of Ferdinand the Catholic.*   By ULICK RALPH BURKE, M A.   Edited by MARTIN A S. HUME.   With 6 Maps. 2 vols   Crown 8vo., 16s. net.

Caroline, Queen.—*Caroline the Illustrious, Queen-Consort of George II and Sometime Queen Regent*   a Study of Her Life and Time.   By W H. WILKINS, M.A., F.S.A , Author of ' The Love of an Uncrowned Queen '   2 vols , 8vo., 36s.

Casserly. — *The Land of the Boxers*; or, China under the Allies   By Captain GORDON CASSERLY.   With 15 Illustrations and a Plan   8vo., 10s 6d. net.

Chesney.—*Indian Polity*: a View of the System of Administration in India   By General Sir GEORGE CHESNEY, K C B.   With Map showing all the Administrative Divisions of British India.   8vo., 21s.

History, Politics, Polity, Political Memoirs, &c.—*continued.*

Churchill (WINSTON SPENCER, M.P.).

THE RIVER WAR : an Historical Account of the Reconquest of the Soudan Edited by Colonel F. RHODES, D.S.O. With Photogravure Portrait of Viscount Kitchener of Khartoum, and 22 Maps and Plans. 8vo , 10s. 6d net

THE STORY OF THE MALAKAND FIELD FORCE, 1897. With 6 Maps and Plans Crown 8vo., 3s. 6d

LONDON TO LADYSMITH VIÂ PRETORIA. Crown 8vo., 6s

IAN HAMILTON'S MARCH. With Portrait of Major-General Sir Ian Hamilton, and 10 Maps and Plans. Crown 8vo., 6s.

Corbett (JULIAN S.).

DRAKE AND THE TUDOR NAVY, with a History of the Rise of England as a Maritime Power. With Portraits, Illustrations and Maps. 2 vols. Crown 8vo , 16s.

THE SUCCESSORS OF DRAKE. With 4 Portraits (2 Photogravures) and 12 Maps and Plans 8vo., 21s

Creighton (M., D.D., Late Lord Bishop of London).

A HISTORY OF THE PAPACY FROM THE GREAT SCHISM TO THE SACK OF ROME, 1378-1527 6 vols. Cr. 8vo , 5s. net each.

QUEEN ELIZABETH With Portrait Crown 8vo., 5s. net.

HISTORICAL ESSAYS AND REVIEWS. Edited by LOUISE CREIGHTON. Crown 8vo., 5s. net.

Dale.—*THE PRINCIPLES OF ENGLISH CONSTITUTIONAL HISTORY* By LUCY DALE, late Scholar of Somerville College, Oxford. Crown 8vo , 6s.

De Tocqueville.—*DEMOCRACY IN AMERICA.* By ALEXIS DE TOCQUEVILLE. Translated by HENRY REEVE, C.B., D.C L. 2 vols. Crown 8vo., 16s.

Falkiner.—*STUDIES IN IRISH HISTORY AND BIOGRAPHY,* Mainly of the Eighteenth Century. By C LITTON

Fitzmaurice. — *CHARLES WILLIAM FERDINAND, DUKE OF BRUNSWICK:* an Historical Study By Lord EDMUND FITZMAURICE With Map and 2 Portraits. 8vo , 6s net

Froude (JAMES A.)

THE HISTORY OF ENGLAND, from the Fall of Wolsey to the Defeat of the Spanish Armada. 12 vols. Crown 8vo , 3s. 6d each

THE DIVORCE OF CATHERINE OF ARAGON. Crown 8vo., 3s. 6d.

THE SPANISH STORY OF THE ARMADA, and other Essays. Cr. 8vo., 3s 6d.

THE ENGLISH IN IRELAND IN THE EIGHTEENTH CENTURY. 3 vols Cr. 8vo., 10s. 6d.

ENGLISH SEAMEN IN THE SIXTEENTH CENTURY.

Cabinet Edition Crown 8vo , 6s.

Illustrated Edition With 5 Photogravure Plates and 16 other Illustrations. Large Cr. 8vo , gilt top, 6s. net. '*Silver Library*' *Edition.* Cr. 8vo., 3s. 6d.

THE COUNCIL OF TRENT. Crown 8vo., 3s. 6d.

SHORT STUDIES ON GREAT SUBJECTS.

Cabinet Edition. 4 vols. 24s '*Silver Library*' *Edition* 4 vols. Crown 8vo., 3s 6d. each

CÆSAR. a Sketch Cr. 8vo, 3s. 6d.

SELECTIONS FROM THE WRITINGS OF JAMES ANTHONY FROUDE. Edited by P. S. ALLEN, M.A Crown 8vo , 3s 6d

Fuller.—*EGYPT AND THE HINTERLAND.* By FREDERIC W FULLER With Frontispiece and Map of Egypt and the Sudan Crown 8vo , 6s. net

Gardiner (SAMUEL RAWSON, D.C.L., LL D).

HISTORY OF ENGLAND, from the Accession of James I. to the Outbreak of the Civil War, 1603-1642 With 7 Maps. 10 vols. Crown 8vo , 5s net each.

A HISTORY OF THE GREAT CIVIL WAR, 1642-1649. With 54 Maps and Plans 4 vols. Cr. 8vo , 5s net each

History, Politics, Polity, Political Memoirs, &c.—*continued.*

Gardiner (SAMUEL RAWSON, D.C L., LL D)—*continued*

A HISTORY OF THE COMMONWEALTH AND THE PROTECTORATE 1649-1656. 4 vols Crown 8vo., 5s net each

THE STUDENT'S HISTORY OF ENGLAND With 378 Illustrations Crown 8vo , gilt top, 12s
Also in Three Volumes, price 4s. each.

WHAT GUNPOWDER PLOT WAS. With 8 Illustrations. Crown 8vo , 5s.

CROMWELL'S PLACE IN HISTORY. Founded on Six Lectures delivered in the University of Oxford Cr 8vo , 3s. 6d.

OLIVER CROMWELL With Frontispiece. Crown 8vo , 5s net

German Empire (The) of To-day : Outlines of its Formation and Development By ' VERITAS ' Crown 8vo , 6s. net

Graham.—*ROMAN AFRICA* an Outline of the History of the Roman Occupation of North Africa, based chiefly upon Inscriptions and Monumental Remains in that Country. By ALEXANDER GRAHAM, F S A , F R.I.B.A. With 30 reproductions of Original Drawings by the Author, and 2 Maps. 8vo., 16s. net

Greville.—*A JOURNAL OF THE REIGNS OF KING GEORGE IV , KING WILLIAM IV., AND QUEEN VICTORIA.* By CHARLES C F. GREVILLE, formerly Clerk of the Council 8 vols Crown 8vo , 3s 6d each.

Gross.—*THE SOURCES AND LITERATURE OF ENGLISH HISTORY, FROM THE EARLIEST TIMES TO ABOUT 1485* By CHARLES GROSS, Ph D 8vo., 18s net

Hamilton.—*HISTORICAL RECORD OF THE 14TH (KING'S) HUSSARS,* from A D 1715 to A D 1900 By Colonel HENRY BLACKBURNE HAMILTON, M.A., Christ Church, Oxford , late Commanding the Regiment With 15 Coloured Plates, 35 Portraits, etc , in Photogravure, and 10 Maps and Plans. Crown 4to., gilt edges, 42s. net.

Hill.—*LIBERTY DOCUMENTS* With Contemporary Exposition and Critical Comments drawn from various Writers Selected and Prepared by MABEL HILL Edited with an Introduction by ALBERT BUSHNELL HART, Ph.D Large Crown 8vo., 7s. 6d. net.

HARVARD HISTORICAL STUDIES.

THE SUPPRESSION OF THE AFRICAN SLAVE TRADE TO THE UNITED STATES OF AMERICA, 1638-1870. By W. E. B DU BOIS, Ph D. 8vo., 7s. 6d.

THE CONTEST OVER THE RATIFICATON OF THE FEDERAL CONSTITUTION IN MASSACHUSETTS By S B. HARDING, A, M. 8vo ,6s.

A CRITICAL STUDY OF NULLIFICATION IN SOUTH CAROLINA By D. F. HOUSTON, A.M. 8vo , 6s.

NOMINATIONS FOR ELECTIVE OFFICE IN THE UNITED STATES. By FREDERICK W DALLINGER, A.M. 8vo., 7s. 6d.

A BIBLIOGRAPHY OF BRITISH MUNICIPAL HISTORY, INCLUDING GILDS AND PARLIAMENTARY REPRESENTATION. By CHARLES GROSS, Ph D. 8vo , 12s.

THE LIBERTY AND FREE SOIL PARTIES IN THE NORTH WEST. By THEODORE C. SMITH, Ph D 8vo, 7s. 6d.

THE PROVINCIAL GOVERNOR IN THE ENGLISH COLONIES OF NORTH AMERICA. By EVARTS BOUTELL GREENE. 8vo., 7s. 6d.

THE COUNTY PALATINE OF DURHAM. a Study in Constitutional History. By GAILLARD THOMAS LAPSLEY, Ph.D. 8vo., 10s. 6d

THE ANGLICAN EPISCOPATE AND THE AMERICAN COLONIES. By ARTHUR LYON CROSS Ph D , Instructor in History in the University of Michigan. 8vo , 10s. 6d,

Hill.—*THREE FRENCHMEN IN BENGAL,* or, The Loss of the French Settlements. By S. C HILL, B.A , B.Sc , Officer in charge of the Records of the Government of India. With 4 Maps. 8vo

Historic Towns.—Edited by E. A. FREEMAN, D.C.L , and Rev. WILLIAM HUNT, M A With Maps and Plans Crown 8vo , 3s 6d each.

Bristol By Rev W. Hunt	Oxford By Rev C. W. Boase
Carlisle By Mandell Creighton, D D	Winchester By G W. Kitchin, D D
Cinque Ports By Montagu Burrows	York. By Rev James Raine
Colchester By Rev E L Cutts.	New York. By Theodore Roosevelt
Exeter By E A Freeman.	Boston (U S) By Henry Cabot Lodge
London By Rev W J Loftie	

History, Politics, Polity, Political Memoirs, &c.—*continued*

Hunter (Sir WILLIAM WILSON).

A HISTORY OF BRITISH INDIA. Vol I.—Introductory to the Overthrow of the English in the Spice Archipelago, 1623. With 4 Maps 8vo , 18s Vol. II.—To the Union of the Old and New Companies under the Earl of Godolphin's Award, 1708. 8vo., 16s.

THE INDIA OF THE QUEEN, and other Essays. Edited by Lady HUNTER. With an Introduction by FRANCIS HENRY SKRINE, Indian Civil Service (Retired). 8vo., 9s net

Ingram.—*A CRITICAL EXAMINATION OF IRISH HISTORY* From the Elizabethan Conquest to the Legislative Union of 1800 By T. DUNBAR INGRAM, LL D. 2 vols. 8vo , 24s

Joyce. —*A SHORT HISTORY OF IRELAND*, from the Earliest Times to 1603 By P W. JOYCE, LL.D. Crown 8vo., 10s. 6d.

Kaye and Malleson.—*HISTORY OF THE INDIAN MUTINY*, 1857-1858. By Sir JOHN W. KAYE and Colonel G B MALLESON With Analytical Index and Maps and Plans 6 vols Crown 8vo , 3s 6d each.

Lang (ANDREW)

THE MYSTERY OF MARY STUART With 6 Photogravure Plates (4 Portraits) and 15 other Illustrations 8vo , 18s net

JAMES THE SIXTH AND THE GOWRIE MYSTERY With Gowrie's Coat of Arms in colour, 2 Photogravure Portraits and other Illustrations 8vo , 12s 6d net.

PRINCE CHARLES EDWARD STUART, THE YOUNG CHEVALIER. With Photogravure Frontispiece Cr 8vo , 7s. 6d net

Laurie.—*HISTORICAL SURVEY OF PRE-CHRISTIAN EDUCATION* By S S. LAURIE, A.M., LL D Crown 8vo , 7s 6d.

Lecky (The Rt. Hon. WILLIAM E. H.)

HISTORY OF ENGLAND IN THE EIGHTEENTH CENTURY

Library Edition 8 vols 8vo. Vols I and II , 1700-1760, 36s. , Vols. III. and IV , 1760-1784, 36s. , Vols V and VI., 1784-1793, 36s.; Vols VII and VIII , 1793-1800, 36s

Cabinet Edition ENGLAND. 7 vols Crown 8vo., 5s. net each. IRELAND. 5 vols. Crown 8vo 5s net each

Lecky (The Rt. Hon. WILLIAM E H.) —*continued*

LEADERS OF PUBLIC OPINION IN IRELAND FLOOD—GRATTAN—O'CONNELL. 2 vols 8vo , 25s net

HISTORY OF EUROPEAN MORALS FROM AUGUSTUS TO CHARLEMAGNE 2 vols Crown 8vo , 10s net.

A SURVEY OF ENGLISH ETHICS · Being the First Chapter of the ' History of European Morals Edited, with Introduction and Notes, by W. A HIRST. Crown 8vo , 3s 6d

HISTORY OF THE RISE AND INFLUENCE OF THE SPIRIT OF RATIONALISM IN EUROPE. 2 vols. Crown 8vo , 10s. net.

DEMOCRACY AND LIBERTY. *Library Edition* 2 vols. 8vo., 36s. *Cabinet Edition.* 2 vols. Cr. 8vo., 10s. net.

Lieven. — *LETTERS OF DOROTHEA, PRINCESS LIEVEN, DURING HER RESIDENCE IN LONDON*, 1812-1834 Edited by LIONEL G ROBINSON With 2 Photogravure Portraits 8vo , 14s net

Lowell.—*GOVERNMENTS AND PARTIES IN CONTINENTAL EUROPE* By A. LAWRENCE LOWELL 2 vols 8vo , 21s.

Lumsden's Horse, Records of.— Edited by H. H. S. PEARSE. With a Map, and numerous Portraits and Illustrations in the Text. 4to , 21s. net

Lynch.—*THE WAR OF THE CIVILISATIONS . BEING A RECORD OF ' A FOREIGN DEVIL'S' EXPERIENCES WITH THE ALLIES IN CHINA.* By GEORGE LYNCH, Special Correspondent of the ' Sphere,' etc With Portrait and 21 Illustrations. Crown 8vo , 6s net

Macaulay (Lord).

THE LIFE AND WORKS OF LORD MACAULAY.

'*Edinburgh' Edition.* 10 vols 8vo , 6s each.

Vols I -IV *HISTORY OF ENGLAND*

Vols V.-VII. *ESSAYS, BIOGRAPHIES, INDIAN PENAL CODE, CONTRIBUTIONS TO KNIGHT'S 'QUARTERLY MAGAZINE'.*

Vol VIII *SPEECHES, LAYS OF ANCIENT ROME, MISCELLANEOUS POEMS.*

Vols IX and X. *THE LIFE AND LETTERS OF LORD MACAULAY* By Sir G O. Trevelyan, Bart

History, Politics, Polity, Political Memoirs, &c.—*continued.*

Macaulay (Lord)—*continued.*

THE WORKS

'*Albany*' *Edition*   With 12 Portraits
12 vols Large Crown 8vo , 3s 6d. each.

Vols. I.-VI. · HISTORY OF ENGLAND,
FROM THE ACCESSION OF JAMES THE
SECOND

Vols. VII.-X ESSAYS AND BIOGRAPHIES

Vols. XI.-XII. '' SPEECHES, LAYS OF
ANCIENT ROME, ETC., AND INDEX

Cabinet Edition.   16 vols.   Post 8vo.,
£4 16s.

Library Edition   5 vols.   8vo , £4.

HISTORY OF ENGLAND FROM THE
ACCESSION OF JAMES THE SECOND

Popular Edition.   2 vols   Cr 8vo , 5s.
Student's Edition   2 vols   Cr 8vo , 12s.
People's Edition.   4 vols.   8vo., 16s.
'*Albany*' *Edition*   With 6 Portraits   6
vols.   Large Crown 8vo., 3s. 6d. each.
Cabinet Edition.   8 vols.   Post 8vo., 48s.
'*Edinburgh*' *Edition.*   4 vols   8vo., 6s.
each.

CRITICAL AND HISTORICAL ESSAYS,
WITH LAYS OF ANCIENT ROME, etc., in 1
volume

Popular Edition   Crown 8vo., 2s. 6d.
'*Silver Library*' *Edition*   With Portrait
and 4 Illustrations to the '*Lays*'   Cr.
8vo., 3s. 6d

CRITICAL AND HISTORICAL ESSAYS.

Student's Edition.   1 vol   Cr. 8vo , 6s
'*Trevelyan*' *Edition.*   2 vols   Cr 8vo., 9s.
Cabinet Edition   4 vols.   Post 8vo., 24s.
'*Edinburgh*' *Edition.*   3 vols   8vo., 6s.
each.
Library Edition.   3 vols   8vo , 36s

ESSAYS, which may be had separately,
sewed, 6d. each , cloth, 1s each

Addison and Walpole	Frederick the Great.
Croker's Boswell's Johnson.	Ranke and Gladstone
Hallam's Constitutional	Lord Bacon
History	Lord Clive.
Warren Hastings.	Lord Byron, and The
The Earl of Chatham (Two	Comic Dramatists of
Essays)	the Restoration

MISCELLANEOUS   WRITINGS,
SPEECHES AND POEMS.
Popular Edition   Crown 8vo , 2s. 6d
Cabinet Edition.   4 vols.   Post 8vo., 24s.

SELECTIONS FROM THE WRITINGS OF
LORD MACAULAY   Edited, with Occa-
sional Notes, by the Right Hon. Sir G. O.
TREVELYAN. Bart.   Crown 8vo., 6s

Mackinnon (JAMES, Ph.D.)

THE HISTORY OF EDWARD THE
THIRD.   8vo., 18s

THE GROWTH AND DECLINE OF THE
FRENCH MONARCHY   8vo , 21s. net.

Mallet.—*MALLET DU PAN AND THE
FRENCH REVOLUTION*   By BERNARD
MALLET.   With Photogravure Portrait
8vo., 12s. 6d. net.

May.—*THE CONSTITUTIONAL HIS-
TORY OF ENGLAND* since the Accession
of George III. 1760-1870   By Sir THOMAS
ERSKINE MAY, K C B (Lord Farnborough).
3 vols. Cr 8vo , 18s.

Merivale (CHARLES, D.D.).

HISTORY OF THE ROMANS UNDER THE
EMPIRE. 8 vols. Crown 8vo , 3s. 6d. each

THE FALL OF THE ROMAN REPUBLIC:
a Short History of the Last Century of the
Commonwealth. 12mo , 7s 6d

GENERAL HISTORY OF ROME, from
the Foundation of the City to the Fall of
Augustulus, B.C 753-A.D. 476   With 5
Maps. Crown 8vo., 7s. 6d.

Montague. — *THE ELEMENTS OF
ENGLISH CONSTITUTIONAL HISTORY.* By
F. C MONTAGUE, M A   Crown 8vo., 3s. 6d.

Moran.—*THE THEORY AND PRAC-
TICE OF THE ENGLISH GOVERNMENT.* By
THOMAS FRANCIS MORAN, Ph D., Professor
of History and Economics in Purdue University, U.S. Crown 8vo , 5s. net.

Nash.—*THE GREAT FAMINE AND
ITS CAUSES* By VAUGHAN NASH. With
8 Illustrations from Photographs by the
Author, and a Map of India showing the
Famine Area   Crown 8vo , 6s

Owens College Essays.—Edited
by T F. TOUT, M.A., Professor of History
in the Owens College, Victoria University,
and JAMES TAIT, M.A , Assistant Lecturer
in History. With 4 Maps. 8vo , 12s 6d. net.

Pears.—*THE DESTRUCTION OF THE
GREEK EMPIRE AND THE STORY OF THE
CAPTURE OF CONSTANTINOPLE BY THE
TURKS. By EDWIN PEARS, LL.B. With
3 Maps and 4 Illustrations. 8vo., 18s. net.*

History, Politics, Polity, Political Memoirs, &c.—*continued.*

Powell and Trevelyan. — *THE PEASANTS' RISING AND THE LOLLARDS*. a Collection of Unpublished Documents. Edited by EDGAR POWELL and G. M. TREVELYAN. 8vo., 6s. net.

Randolph.—*THE LAW AND POLICY OF ANNEXATION*, with Special Reference to the Philippines, together with Observations on the Status of Cuba. By CARMAN F RANDOLPH   8vo, 9s. net

Rankin (REGINALD).

THE MARQUIS D'ARGENSON, AND RICHARD THE SECOND   8vo, 10s 6d net.

A SUBALTERN'S LETTERS TO HIS WIFE. (The Boer War)   Crown 8vo, 3s 6d.

Ransome.—*THE RISE OF CONSTITUTIONAL GOVERNMENT IN ENGLAND.* By CYRIL RANSOME, M.A.   Crown 8vo., 6s.

Seebohm (FREDERIC, LL D., F.S.A.).

THE ENGLISH VILLAGE COMMUNITY. With 13 Maps and Plates   8vo., 16s.
TRIBAL CUSTOM IN ANGLO-SAXON LAW. being an Essay supplemental to (1) 'The English Village Community,' (2) 'The Tribal System in Wales'. 8vo, 16s

Seton-Karr.—*THE CALL TO ARMS*, 1900-1901, or a Review of the Imperial Yeomanry Movement, and some subjects connected therewith. By Sir HENRY SETON-KARR, M.P.   With a Frontispiece by R. CATON-WOODVILLE.   Crown 8vo, 5s net

Shaw.—*A HISTORY OF THE ENGLISH CHURCH DURING THE CIVIL WARS AND UNDER THE COMMONWEALTH*, 1640-1660. By WILLIAM A. SHAW, Litt D   2 vols 8vo, 36s.

Sheppard. — *THE OLD ROYAL PALACE OF WHITEHALL*   By EDGAR SHEPPARD, D D, Sub-Dean of H M Chapels Royal, Sub-Almoner to the King. With 6 Photogravure Plates and 33 other Illustrations   Medium 8vo, 21s net

Smith.—*CARTHAGE AND THE CARTHAGINIANS.* By R BOSWORTH SMITH, M A. With Maps, Plans, etc.   Cr. 8vo., 3s 6d

Stephens. — *A HISTORY OF THE FRENCH REVOLUTION*   By H. MORSE STEPHENS   8vo   Vols I and II. 18s. each.

Sternberg. — *MY EXPERIENCES OF THE BOER WAR*   By ADALBERT COUNT STERNBERG   With Preface by Lieut.-Col. G. F. R. HENDERSON.   Crown 8vo., 5s net.

Stubbs.—*HISTORY OF THE UNIVERSITY OF DUBLIN.* By J. W STUBBS   8vo, 12s. 6d.

Stubbs. — *HISTORICAL INTRODUCTIONS TO THE 'ROLLS SERIES'.* By WILLIAM STUBBS, D D, formerly Bishop of Oxford, Regius Professor of Modern History in the University   Collected and Edited by ARTHUR HASSALL, M A   8vo, 12s 6d. net.

Sutherland. — *THE HISTORY OF AUSTRALIA AND NEW ZEALAND*, from 1606-1900.   By ALEXANDER SUTHERLAND, M A., and GEORGE SUTHERLAND, M.A.   Crown 8vo, 2s. 6d.

Taylor.—*A STUDENT'S MANUAL OF THE HISTORY OF INDIA.* By Colonel MEADOWS TAYLOR, C.S I   Cr 8vo., 7s 6d

Thomson.—*CHINA AND THE POWERS* a Narrative of the Outbreak of 1900.   By H C THOMSON   With 2 Maps and 29 Illustrations   8vo, 10s 6d net

Todd. — *PARLIAMENTARY GOVERNMENT IN THE BRITISH COLONIES*   By ALPHEUS TODD, LL D   8vo, 30s net

Trevelyan.—*THE AMERICAN REVOLUTION*   Part I   1766-1776.   By Sir G O TREVELYAN, Bart.   8vo, 16s.

Trevelyan.—*ENGLAND IN THE AGE OF WYCLIFFE*   By GEORGE MACAULAY TREVELYAN.   8vo, 15s

Wakeman and Hassall.—*ESSAYS INTRODUCTORY TO THE STUDY OF ENGLISH CONSTITUTIONAL HISTORY.*   Edited by HENRY OFFLEY WAKEMAN, M A, and ARTHUR HASSALL, M A   Crown 8vo, 6s.

Walpole.—*HISTORY OF ENGLAND FROM THE CONCLUSION OF THE GREAT WAR IN 1815 TO 1858.* By Sir SPENCER WALPOLE, K.C B   6 vols Cr 8vo, 6s each.

Wylie (JAMES HAMILTON, M.A.).

HISTORY OF ENGLAND UNDER HENRY IV   4 vols   Crown 8vo.   Vol. I., 1399-1404, 10s 6d.   Vol. II., 1405-1406, 15s. (*out of print*).   Vol. III, 1407-1411, 15s.   Vol IV., 1411-1413, 21s.

THE COUNCIL OF CONSTANCE TO THE DEATH OF JOHN HUS.   Cr. 8vo., 6s. net.

Biography, Personal Memoirs, &c.

Bacon.—*THE LETTERS AND LIFE OF FRANCIS BACON, INCLUDING ALL HIS OCCASIONAL WORKS.* Edited by JAMES SPEDDING. 7 vols. 8vo , £4 4*s*

Bagehot.—*BIOGRAPHICAL STUDIES* By WALTER BAGEHOT Crown 8vo , 3*s*. 6*d*

Blount. — *THE MEMOIRS OF SIR EDWARD BLOUNT, K C.B , ETC* Edited by STUART J REID, Author of 'The Life and Times of Sydney Smith,' etc With 3 Photogravure Plates. 8vo., 10*s*. 6*d* net.

Bowen.—*EDWARD BOWEN · A MEMOIR* By the Rev. the Hon. W. E. BOWEN. With Appendices, 3 Photogravure Portraits and 2 other Illustrations. 8vo., 12*s*. 6*d* net

Carlyle.—*THOMAS CARLYLE* A History of his Life. By JAMES ANTHONY FROUDE

1795-1835	2 vols	Crown 8vo , 7*s*
1834-1881	2 vols	Crown 8vo., 7*s*

Crozier.—*MY INNER LIFE* : being a Chapter in Personal Evolution and Autobiography. By JOHN BEATTIE CROZIER, LL.D 8vo., 14*s*.

Dante.—*THE LIFE AND WORKS OF DANTE ALLIGHIERI* : being an Introduction to the Study of the 'Divina Commedia' By the Rev J F HOGAN, D.D With Portrait 8vo , 12*s*. 6*d*.

Danton.—*LIFE OF DANTON.* By A. H. BEESLY. With Portraits Cr. 8vo., 6*s*.

De Bode.—*THE BARONESS DE BODE,* 1775-1803 By WILLIAM S. CHILDE-PEMBERTON. With 4 Photogravure Portraits and other Illustrations. 8vo , gilt top, 12*s* 6*d*. net.

Erasmus.

LIFE AND LETTERS OF ERASMUS By JAMES ANTHONY FROUDE. Crown 8vo., 3*s*. 6*d*.

THE EPISTLES OF ERASMUS, from his Earliest Letters to his Fifty-first Year, arranged in Order of Time. English Translations, with a Commentary By FRANCIS MORGAN NICHOLS. 8vo., 18*s*. net.

Faraday.—*FARADAY AS A DISCOVERER.* By JOHN TYNDALL Crown 8vo., 3*s* 6*d*

Fénelon : his Friends and his Enemies, 1651-1715. By E. K. SANDERS. With Portrait. 8vo., 10*s*. 6*d*.

Fox. — *THE EARLY HISTORY OF CHARLES JAMES FOX.* By the Right Hon Sir G. O. TREVELYAN, Bart. Crown 8vo , 3*s*. 6*d*.

Granville.—*SOME RECORDS OF THE LATER LIFE OF HARRIET, COUNTESS GRANVILLE* By her Granddaughter, the Hon Mrs OLDFIELD With 17 Portraits 8vo , gilt top, 16*s*. net.

Grey. — *MEMOIR OF SIR GEORGE GREY, BART, G C.B.,* 1799-1882. By MANDELL CREIGHTON, D.D., late Lord Bishop of London. With 3 Portraits. Crown 8vo , 6*s*. net

Hamilton.—*LIFE OF SIR WILLIAM HAMILTON.* By R. P. GRAVES. 8vo. 3 vols. 15*s* each ADDENDUM 8vo , 6*d*. sewed

Harrow School Register (The), 1801-1900. Second Edition, 1901. Edited by M. G DAUGLISH, Barrister-at Law 8vo. 10*s*. net.

Havelock.—*MEMOIRS OF SIR HENRY HAVELOCK, K C B* By JOHN CLARK MARSHMAN. Crown 8vo , 3*s* 6*d*

Haweis.—*MY MUSICAL LIFE.* By the Rev.H R HAWEIS With Portrait of Richard Wagner and 3 Illustrations. Cr. 8vo., 6*s*. net.

Higgins.—*THE BERNARDS OF ABINGTON AND NETHER WINCHENDON.* A Family History By Mrs. NAPIER HIGGINS 2 Vols 8vo , 21*s* net

Hunter.—*THE LIFE OF SIR WILLIAM WILSON HUNTER, K.C.S.I., M.A., LL.D.* Author of 'A History of British India,' etc. By FRANCIS HENRY SKRINE, F.S.S. With 6 Portraits (2 Photogravures) and 4 other Illustrations. 8vo., 16*s*. net.

Jackson.—*STONEWALL JACKSON AND THE AMERICAN CIVIL WAR* By Lieut.-Col. G. F R HENDERSON With 2 Portraits and 33 Maps and Plans. 2 vols. Cr. 8vo , 16*s*. net

Kielmansegge.—*DIARY OF A JOURNEY TO ENGLAND IN THE YEARS* 1761-1762. By Count FREDERICK KIELMANSEGGE. With 4 Illustrations. Crown 8vo. 5*s*. net

Luther. — *LIFE OF LUTHER.* By JULIUS KOSTLIN. With 62 Illustrations and 4 Facsimiles of MSS. Cr. 8vo., 3*s*. 6*d*.

Biography, Personal Memoirs, &c.—*continued*.

Macaulay.—*THE LIFE AND LETTERS OF LORD MACAULAY.* By the Right Hon Sir G O TREVELYAN, Bart
   Popular Edition 1 vol Cr 8vo , 2s. 6d.
   Student's Edition 1 vol. Cr 8vo., 6s.
   Cabinet Edition 2 vols Post 8vo , 12s.
   'Edinburgh' Edition 2 vols 8vo ,6s. each.
   Library Edition 2 vols 8vo , 36s

Marbot. — *THE MEMOIRS OF THE BARON DE MARBOT.* 2 vols Cr. 8vo , 7s.

Max Müller (F.)

THE LIFE AND LETTERS OF THE RIGHT HON FRIEDRICH MAX MÜLLER Edited by his Wife With Photogravure Portraits and other Illustrations 2 vols , 8vo., 32s net

MY AUTOBIOGRAPHY. a Fragment. With 6 Portraits 8vo , 12s. 6d.

AULD LANG SYNE. Second Series. 8vo , 10s. 6d.

CHIPS FROM A GERMAN WORKSHOP. Vol II. Biographical Essays. Cr. 8vo , 5s

Meade.—*GENERAL SIR RICHARD MEADE AND THE FEUDATORY STATES OF CENTRAL AND SOUTHERN INDIA* By THOMAS HENRY THORNTON. With Portrait, Map and Illustrations. 8vo., 10s. 6d. net.

Morris. — *THE LIFE OF WILLIAM MORRIS.* By J W. MACKAIL With 2 Portraits and 8 other Illustrations by E. H. NEW, etc. 2 vols. Large Crown 8vo , 10s. net.

On the Banks of the Seine. By A. M. F , Author of 'Foreign Courts and Foreign Homes'. Crown 8vo., 6s

Paget.—*MEMOIRS AND LETTERS OF SIR JAMES PAGET.* Edited by STEPHEN PAGET, one of his sons With Portrait. 8vo , 6s net.

Place.—*THE LIFE OF FRANCIS PLACE,* 1771-1854. By GRAHAM WALLAS, M A. With 2 Portraits. 8vo., 12s.

Powys.—*PASSAGES FROM THE DIARIES OF MRS. PHILIP LYBBE POWYS, OF HARDWICK HOUSE, OXON* 1756-1808 Edited by EMILY J CLIMENSON 8vo , gilt top, 16s.

Râmakrishna : *HIS LIFE AND SAYINGS* By the Right Hon. F. MAX MULLER. Crown 8vo , 5s

Rich.—*MARY RICH, COUNTESS OF WARWICK* (1625-1678) Her Family and Friends By C FELL SMITH. With 7 Photogravure Portraits and 9 other Illustra

Rochester, and other Literary Rakes of the Court of Charles II., with some Account of their Surroundings By the Author of 'The Life of Sir Kenelm Digby,' The Life of a Prig,' etc With 15 Portraits. 8vo , 16s

Romanes.—*THE LIFE AND LETTERS OF GEORGE JOHN ROMANES, M.A., LL D , F R.S.* Written and Edited by his WIFE With Portrait and 2 Illustrations Cr. 8vo , 5s. net

Russell. — *SWALLOWFIELD AND ITS OWNERS* By CONSTANCE LADY RUSSELL, of Swallowfield Park. With 15 Photogravure Portraits and 36 other Illustrations 4to , gilt edges, 42s net.

Seebohm.—*THE OXFORD REFORMERS —JOHN COLET, ERASMUS, AND THOMAS MORE :* a History of their Fellow-Work By FREDERIC SEEBOHM. 8vo , 14s.

Shakespeare. — *OUTLINES OF THE LIFE OF SHAKESPEARE.* By J. O HALLIWELL-PHILLIPPS. With Illustrations and Facsimiles. 2 vols. Royal 8vo., 21s.

Tales of my Father.—By A. M F Crown 8vo., 6s.

Tallentyre.—*THE WOMEN OF THE SALONS,* and other French Portraits By S. G. TALLENTYRE With 11 Photogravure Portraits. 8vo , 10s 6d net

Victoria, Queen, 1819-1901. By RICHARD R. HOLMES, M.V.O., F.S.A. With Photogravure Portrait Crown 8vo , gilt top, 5s net

Walpole.—*SOME UNPUBLISHED LETTERS OF HORACE WALPOLE.* Edited by Sir SPENCER WALPOLE, K.C.B With 2 Portraits Crown 8vo., 4s 6d. net

Wellington.—*LIFE OF THE DUKE OF WELLINGTON* By the Rev G. R. GLEIG, M A. Crown 8vo , 3s 6d

Wilkins (W. H.).

CAROLINE THE ILLUSTRIOUS, QUEEN-CONSORT OF GEORGE II AND SOMETIME QUEEN-REGENT a Study of Her Life and Time 2 vols 8vo , 36s

THE LOVE OF AN UNCROWNED QUEEN Sophie Dorothea, Consort of George I , and her Correspondence with Philip Christopher, Count Königsmarck. With Portraits and Illustrations 8vo ,

Travel and Adventure, the Colonies, &c.

Arnold.—*SEAS AND LANDS.* By Sir EDWIN ARNOLD. With 71 Illustrations. Crown 8vo., 3*s* 6*d.*

Baker (Sir S. W.).

EIGHT YEARS IN CEYLON. With 6 Illustrations. Crown 8vo., 3*s* 6*d.*

THE RIFLE AND THE HOUND IN CEYLON. With 6 Illusts Cr 8vo , 3*s* 6*d*

Ball (JOHN).

THE ALPINE GUIDE. Reconstructed and Revised on behalf of the Alpine Club, by W A. B COOLIDGE.

Vol I , *THE WESTERN ALPS* the Alpine Region, South of the Rhone Valley, from the Col de Tenda to the Simplon Pass. With 9 New and Revised Maps Crown 8vo , 12*s* net

HINTS AND NOTES, PRACTICAL AND SCIENTIFIC, FOR TRAVELLERS IN THE ALPS being a Revision of the General Introduction to the ' Alpine Guide ' Crown 8vo , 3*s.* net

Bent.—*THE RUINED CITIES OF MA-SHONALAND* being a Record of Excavation and Exploration in 1891 By J THEODORE BENT With 117 Illustrations. Crown 8vo , 3*s* 6*d*

Brassey (The Late Lady)

A VOYAGE IN THE ' SUNBEAM ' ; OUR HOME ON THE OCEAN FOR ELEVEN MONTHS.

Cabinet Edition With Map and 66 Illustrations. Cr. 8vo., gilt edges, 7*s.* 6*d.*
' *Silver Library* ' *Edition.* With 66 Illustrations. Crown 8vo., 3*s.* 6*d*
Popular Edition. With 60 Illustrations. 4to , 6*d.* sewed, 1*s.* cloth.
School Edition With 37 Illustrations, Fcp., 2*s* cloth, or 3*s* white parchment.

SUNSHINE AND STORM IN THE EAST

Popular Edition. With 103 Illustrations. 4to., 6*d* sewed, 1*s.* cloth.

IN THE TRADES, THE TROPICS, AND THE ' ROARING FORTIES '.

Cabinet Edition With Map and 220 Illustrations Cr 8vo., gilt edges, 7*s.* 6*d.*

Cockerell.—*TRAVELS IN SOUTHERN EUROPE AND THE LEVANT*, 1810-1817. By C R COCKERELL, Architect, R A. Edited by his Son, SAMUEL PEPYS COCKERELL With Portrait, 8vo

Fountain (PAUL).

THE GREAT DESERTS AND FORESTS OF NORTH AMERICA With a Preface by W H. HUDSON, Author of ' The Naturalist in La Plata,' etc. 8vo , 9*s.* 6*d* net'

THE GREAT MOUNTAINS AND FORESTS OF SOUTH AMERICA With Portrait and 7 Illustrations 8vo , 10*s* 6*d* net.

Froude (JAMES A).

OCEANA : or England and her Colonies With 9 Illustrations. Cr. 8vo , 3*s.* 6*d*

THE ENGLISH IN THE WEST INDIES : or, the Bow of Ulysses With 9 Illustrations Crown 8vo., 2*s.* boards, 2*s.* cloth.

Grove.—*SEVENTY-ONE DAYS' CAMPING IN MOROCCO* By Lady GROVE With Photogravure Portrait and 32 Illustrations from Photographs 8vo., 7*s* 6*d* net.

Haggard.—*A WINTER PILGRIMAGE* Being an Account of Travels through Palestine, Italy and the Island of Cyprus, undertaken in the year 1900. By H. RIDER HAGGARD With 31 Illustrations from Photographs. Cr. 8vo., gilt top, 12*s.* 6*d.* net.

Hardwick.—*AN IVORY TRADER IN NORTH KENIA* the Record of an Expedition to the Country North of Mount Kenia in East Equatorial Africa, with an account of the Nomads of Galla-Land By A ARKELL-HARDWICK, F.R.G.S. With 23 Illustrations from Photographs, and a Map. 8vo , 12*s* 6*d.* net

Heathcote.—*ST. KILDA.* By NORMAN HEATHCOTE. With 80 Illustrations from Sketches and Photographs of the People, Scenery and Birds by the Author. 8vo., 10*s* 6*d.* net.

Howitt.—*VISITS TO REMARKABLE PLACES.* Old Halls, Battle-Fields, Scenes, illustrative of Striking Passages in English History and Poetry. By WILLIAM HOWITT. With 80 Illustrations Crown 8vo., 3*s.* 6*d.*

Knight (E. F.).

WITH THE ROYAL TOUR , a Narrative of the Recent Tour of the Duke and Duchess of Cornwall and York through Greater Britain. With 16 Illustrations and a Map Crown 8vo., 5*s.* net.

THE CRUISE OF THE ' ALERTE' : the Narrative of a Search for Treasure on the Desert Island of Trinidad. With 2 Maps and 23 Illustrations. Crown 8vo., 3*s.* 6*d.*

Travel and Adventure, the Colonies, &c.—*continued.*

Knight (E. F.)—*continued.*

WHERE THREE EMPIRES MEET: a Narrative of Recent Travel in Kashmir, Western Tibet, Baltistan, Ladak, Gilgit, and the adjoining Countries. With a Map and 54 Illustrations. Cr. 8vo , 3s. 6d.

THE 'FALCON' ON THE BALTIC: a Voyage from London to Copenhagen in a Three-Tonner. With 10 Full-page Illustrations. Crown 8vo , 3s. 6d.

Lees.—*PEAKS AND PINES:* another Norway Book. By J A. LEES With 63 Illustrations and Photographs. Cr. 8vo , 6s.

Lees and Clutterbuck.—B.C. 1887 : *A RAMBLE IN BRITISH COLUMBIA.* By J. A. LEES and W J CLUTTERBUCK With Map and 75 Illustrations. Crown 8vo , 3s 6d.

Lynch. — *ARMENIA :* Travels and Studies. By H. F. B. LYNCH. With 197 Illustrations (some in tints) reproduced from Photographs and Sketches by the Author, 16 Maps and Plans, a Bibliography, and a Map of Armenia and adjacent countries. 2 vols Medium 8vo., gilt top, 42s. net.

Nansen.—*THE FIRST CROSSING OF GREENLAND* By FRIDTJOF NANSEN. With 143 Illustrations and a Map. Crown 8vo , 3s 6d

Rice.—*OCCASIONAL ESSAYS ON NATIVE SOUTH INDIAN LIFE.* By STANLEY P. RICE, Indian Civil Service. 8vo , 10s 6d.

Smith,—*CLIMBING IN THE BRITISH ISLES* By W P. HASKETT SMITH. With Illustrations and Numerous Plans.

Part I. *ENGLAND*   16mo , 3s. net.

Part II *WALES AND IRELAND.*   16mo , 3s. net.

Spender.—*TWO WINTERS IN NORWAY* being an Account of Two Holidays spent on Snow-shoes and in Sleigh Driving, and including an Expedition to the Lapps By A. EDMUND SPENDER   With 40 Illustrations from Photographs   8vo , 10s. 6d. net

Stephen. — *THE PLAY-GROUND OF EUROPE* (The Alps). By Sir LESLIE STEPHEN, K C B. With 4 Illustrations. Crown 8vo., 3s. 6d.

Three in Norway.   By Two of Them   With a Map and 59 Illustrations Crown 8vo., 2s. boards, 2s. 6d. cloth.

Tyndall.—(JOHN).

THE GLACIERS OF THE ALPS With 61 Illustrations. Crown 8vo., 6s. 6d. net.

HOURS OF EXERCISE IN THE ALPS. With 7 Illustrations. Cr. 8vo , 6s. 6d. net

---

Sport and Pastime.

THE BADMINTON LIBRARY.

Edited by HIS GRACE THE (EIGHTH) DUKE OF BEAUFORT, K.G., and A. E. T. WATSON.

ARCHERY. By C. J. LONGMAN and Col. H. WALROND. With Contributions by Miss LEGH, Viscount DILLON, etc. With 2 Maps, 23 Plates and 172 Illustrations in the Text. Crown 8vo., cloth, 6s. net ; half-bound, with gilt top, 9s. net.

ATHLETICS.   By MONTAGUE SHEARMAN. With Chapters on Athletics at School by W. BEACHER THOMAS, Athletic Sports in America by C. H. SHERRILL ; a Contribution on Paper-chasing by W. RYE, and an Introduction by Sir RICHARD WEBSTER (Lord ALVERSTONE).   With 12 Plates and 37 Illustrations in the Text. Cr. 8vo.,
cloth 6s. net; half bound with gilt top 9s. net

BIG GAME SHOOTING   By CLIVE PHILLIPPS-WOLLEY.

Vol. I.   AFRICA AND AMERICA With Contributions by Sir SAMUEL W. BAKER, W C OSWELL, F. C SELOUS, etc   With 20 Plates and 57 Illustrations in the Text. Crown 8vo., cloth, 6s. net , half-bound, with gilt top, 9s net

Vol. II.   EUROPE, ASIA, AND THE ARCTIC REGIONS.   With Contributions by Lieut.-Colonel R HEBER PERCY, Major ALGERNON C HEBER PERCY, etc.   With 17 Plates and 56 Illustrations in the Text   Crown 8vo., cloth
6s. net half bound with gilt top or net

Sport and Pastime—*continued.*

THE BADMINTON LIBRARY—*continued.*

Edited by HIS GRACE THE (EIGHTH) DUKE OF BEAUFORT, K G.,
and A. E. T. WATSON.

BILLIARDS. By Major W. BROAD-FOOT, R E With Contributions by A H BOYD, SYDENHAM DIXON, W J FORD, etc With 11 Plates, 19 Illustrations in the Text, and numerous Diagrams. Crown 8vo , cloth, 6s. net , half-bound, with gilt top, 9s net.

COURSING AND FALCONRY. By HARDING COX, CHARLES RICHARDSON, and the Hon GERALD LASCELLES. With 20 Plates and 55 Illustrations in the Text Crown 8vo , cloth, 6s. net , half-bound, with gilt top, 9s net

CRICKET. By A. G. STEEL and the Hon R H. LYTTELTON. With Contributions by ANDREW LANG, W G GRACE, F. GALE, etc With 13 Plates and 52 Illustrations in the Text. Crown 8vo , cloth, 6s. net , half-bound, with gilt top, 9s net

CYCLING. By the EARL OF ALBEMARLE and G. LACY HILLIER. With 19 Plates and 44 Illustrations in the Text Crown 8vo., cloth, 6s net , half-bound, with gilt top, 9s net

DANCING. By Mrs LILLY GROVE. With Contributions by Miss MIDDLETON, The Hon. Mrs. ARMYTAGE, etc With Musical Examples, and 38 Full-page Plates and 93 Illustrations in the Text. Crown 8vo , cloth, 6s. net , half-bound, with gilt top, 9s net.

DRIVING By His Grace the (Eighth) DUKE of BEAUFORT, K G With Contributions by A E. T. WATSON the EARL OF ONSLOW, etc. With 12 Plates and 54 Illustrations in the Text. Crown 8vo , cloth, 6s. net , half-bound, with gilt top, 9s. net.

FENCING, BOXING, AND WRESTLING. By WALTER H. POLLOCK, F C GROVE, C PREVOST, E B MITCHELL, and WALTER ARMSTRONG. With 18 Plates and 24 Illustrations in the Text. Crown 8vo., cloth, 6s. net , half-bound, with gilt top, 9s net.

FISHING. By H. CHOLMONDELEY-PENNELL

Vol. I SALMON AND TROUT. With Contributions by H R. FRANCIS, Major JOHN P. TRAHERNE, etc With 9 Plates and numerous Illustrations of Tackle, etc. Crown 8vo , cloth, 6s. net , half-bound, with gilt top, 9s net

Vol. II PIKE AND OTHER' COARSE FISH. With Contributions by the MARQUIS OF EXETER, WILLIAM SENIOR, G. CHRISTOPHER DAVIS, etc. With 7 Plates and numerous Illustrations or Tackle, etc. Crown 8vo., cloth, 6s net ; half-bound, with gilt top, 9s net

FOOTBALL HISTORY, by MONTAGUE SHEARMAN ; *THE ASSOCIATION GAME*, by W. J OAKLEY and G. O. SMITH , *THE RUGBY UNION GAME*, by FRANK MITCHELL. With other Contributions by R E. MACNAGHTEN, M. C. KEMP, J E VINCENT, WALTER CAMP and A SUTHERLAND With 19 Plates and 35 Illustrations in the Text. Crown 8vo , cloth, 6s net , half-bound, with gilt top, 9s. net.

GOLF. By HORACE G. HUTCHINSON. With Contributions by the Rt Hon A. J BALFOUR, M P , Sir WALTER SIMPSON, Bart., ANDREW LANG, etc. With 34 Plates and 56 Illustrations in the Text. Crown 8vo., cloth, 6s. net , half-bound, with gilt top, 9s. net.

HUNTING. By His Grace the (Eighth) DUKE OF BEAUFORT, K.G , and MOWBRAY MORRIS With Contributions by the EARL OF SUFFOLK AND BERKSHIRE, Rev. E. W L. DAVIES, G. H. LONGMAN, etc. With 5 Plates and 54 Illustrations in the Text Crown 8vo., cloth, 6s net , half-bound, with gilt top, 9s. net.

MOTORS AND MOTOR-DRIVING. By ALFRED C HARMSWORTH, the MARQUIS DE CHASSELOUP-LAUBAT, the Hon. JOHN SCOTT-MONTAGU, R J MECREDY, the Hon C S ROLLS, Sir DAVID SALOMONS, Bart , etc. With 13 Plates and 136 Illustrations in the Text. Crown 8vo , cloth, 9s. net , half-bound, 12s. net.

A Cloth Box for use when Motoring, 2s. net.

Sport and Pastime—*continued.*

THE BADMINTON LIBRARY—*continued.*

Edited by HIS GRACE THE (EIGHTH) DUKE OF BEAUFORT, K G.,
and A E. T. WATSON

MOUNTAINEERING. By C. T. DENT. With Contributions by the Right Hon. J BRYCE, M P , Sir MARTIN CONWAY, D W FRESHFIELD, C E MATTHEWS, etc. With 13 Plates and 91 Illustrations in the Text. Crown 8vo., cloth, 6s net; half-bound, with gilt top, 9s net

POETRY OF SPORT (THE)—Selected by HEDLEY PEEK With a Chapter on Classical Allusions to Sport by ANDREW LANG, and a Special Preface to the BADMINTON LIBRARY by A. E T. WATSON. With 32 Plates and 74 Illustrations in the Text. Crown 8vo., cloth, 6s net; half-bound, with gilt top, 9s net

RACING AND STEEPLE-CHASING By the EARL OF SUFFOLK AND BERKSHIRE, W. G. CRAVEN, the Hon F. LAWLEY, ARTHUR COVENTRY, and A E. T WATSON. With Frontispiece and 56 Illustrations in the Text Crown 8vo , cloth, 6s. net; half-bound, with gilt top, 9s net.

RIDING AND POLO. By Captain ROBERT WEIR, J. MORAY BROWN, T. F. DALE, THE LATE DUKE OF BEAUFORT, THE EARL OF SUFFOLK AND BERKSHIRE, etc. With 18 Plates and 41 Illusts. in the Text. Crown 8vo., cloth, 6s. net, half-bound, with gilt top, 9s. net.

ROWING. By R. P. P. ROWE and C. M PITMAN With Chapters on Steering by C. P. SEROCOLD and F. C. BEGG, Metropolitan Rowing by S LE BLANC SMITH, and on PUNTING by P. W. SQUIRE. With 75 Illustrations. Crown 8vo., cloth, 6s. net, half-bound, with gilt top, 9s. net.

SHOOTING.

Vol I. FIELD AND COVERT By Lord WALSINGHAM and Sir RALPH PAYNE-GALLWEY, Bart With Contributions by the Hon GERALD LASCELLES and A. J STUART-WORTLEY With 11 Plates and 95 Illustrations in the Text. Crown 8vo., cloth, 6s. net, half-bound, with gilt top, 9s. net

Vol II MOOR AND MARSH. By LORD WALSINGHAM and Sir RALPH PAYNE-GALLWEY, Bart. With Contributions by LORD LOVAT and Lord CHARLES LENNOX KERR. With 8 Plates and 57 Illustrations in the Text. Crown 8vo , cloth, 6s. net; half-bound, with gilt top, 9s. net.

SEA FISHING. By JOHN BICKERDYKE, Sir H. W. GORE-BOOTH, ALFRED C HARMSWORTH, and W SENIOR With 22 Full-page Plates and 175 Illusts in the Text Crown 8vo , cloth, 6s. net, half-bound, with gilt top, 9s net.

SKATING, CURLING, TOBOGANING By J. M. HEATHCOTE, C G. TEBBUTT, T. MAXWELL WITHAM, Rev. JOHN KERR, ORMOND HAKE, HENRY A BUCK, etc. With 12 Plates and 272 Illustrations in the Text. Crown 8vo , cloth, 6s net, half-bound, with gilt top, 9s. net.

SWIMMING By ARCHIBALD SINCLAIR and WILLIAM HENRY, Hon. Secs. of the Life-Saving Society With 13 Plates and 112 Illustrations in the Text Crown 8vo , cloth, 6s net; half-bound, with gilt top, 9s. net

TENNIS, LAWN TENNIS, RACKETS AND FIVES By J. M. and C. G. HEATHCOTE, E. O. PLEYDELL-BOUVERIE, and A. C. AINGER With Contributions by the Hon A. LYTTELTON, W C. MARSHALL, Miss L DOD, etc With 14 Plates and 65 Illustrations in the Text. Crown 8vo., cloth, 6s. net; half-bound, with gilt top, 9s net

YACHTING.

Vol I CRUISING, CONSTRUCTION OF YACHTS, YACHT RACING RULES, FITTING-OUT, etc By Sir EDWARD SULLIVAN, Bart., THE EARL OF PEMBROKE, LORD BRASSEY, K C B, C. E SETH-SMITH, C B , G L. WATSON, R T. PRITCHETT, E. F KNIGHT, etc With 21 Plates and 93 Illustrations in the Text. Crown 8vo., cloth, 6s net, half-bound, with gilt top, 9s. net

Vol. II YACHT CLUBS, YACHTING IN AMERICA AND THE COLONIES, YACHT RACING, etc By R T. PRITCHETT, THE MARQUIS OF DUFFERIN AND AVA, K.P , THE EARL OF ONSLOW, JAMES MCFERRAN, etc. With 35 Plates and 160 Illustrations in the Text. Crown 8vo., cloth, 9s. net; half-bound, with gilt top, 9s. net.

Sport and Pastime—*continued.*
FUR, FEATHER, AND FIN SERIES.
Edited by A. E. T. WATSON
Crown 8vo , price 5s. each Volume, cloth.

₊ *The Volumes are also issued half-bound in Leather, with gilt top. Price 7s 6d. net each*

THE PARTRIDGE. Natural History, by the Rev. H. A. MACPHERSON; Shooting, by A J. STUART-WORTLEY; Cookery, by GEORGE SAINTSBURY. With 11 Illustrations and various Diagrams Crown 8vo , 5s

THE GROUSE. Natural History, by the Rev H. A. MACPHERSON, Shooting, by A. J STUART-WORTLEY, Cookery, by GEORGE SAINTSBURY With 13 Illustrations and various Diagrams Crown 8vo , 5s

THE PHEASANT. Natural History, by the Rev H. A. MACPHERSON, Shooting, by A. J STUART-WORTLEY; Cookery, by ALEXANDER INNES SHAND With 10 Illustrations and various Diagrams Crown 8vo., 5s.

THE HARE Natural History, by the Rev H. A MACPHERSON , Shooting, by the Hon. GERALD LASCELLES, Coursing, by CHARLES RICHARDSON, Hunting, by J. S GIBBONS and G H LONGMAN, Cookery, by Col KENNEY HERBERT With 9 Illustrations. Crown 8vo , 5s.

RED DEER.—Natural History, by the Rev. H. A. MACPHERSON; Deer Stalking, by CAMERON OF LOCHIEL; Stag Hunting, by Viscount EBRINGTON, Cookery, by ALEXANDER INNES SHAND With 10 Illustrations Crown 8vo., 5s

THE SALMON. By the Hon. A. E. GATHORNE-HARDY With Chapters on the Law of Salmon Fishing by CLAUD DOUGLAS PENNANT; Cookery, by ALEXANDER INNES SHAND. With 8 Illustrations Cr 8vo , 5s

THE TROUT. By the MARQUESS OF GRANBY. With Chapters on the Breeding of Trout by Col. H. CUSTANCE ; and Cookery, by ALEXANDER INNES SHAND With 12 Illustrations Crown 8vo , 5s.

THE RABBIT. By JAMES EDMUND HARTING Cookery, by ALEXANDER INNES SHAND With 10 Illustrations Cr. 8vo., 5s

PIKE AND PERCH. By WILLIAM SENIOR ('Redspinner,' Editor of the 'Field'). With Chapters by JOHN BICKERDYKE and W. H POPE, Cookery, by ALEXANDER INNES SHAND. With 12 Illustrations Crown 8vo., 5s.

Alverstone and Alcock.—*SURREY CRICKET* its History and Associations. Edited by the Right Hon LORD ALVERSTONE, L C J., President, and C W. ALCOCK, Secretary, of the Surrey County Cricket Club With 48 Illustrations. 8vo., 16s. net

Bickerdyke.—*DAYS OF MY LIFE ON WATER, FRESH AND SALT;* and other Papers. By JOHN BICKERDYKE. With Photo-etching Frontispiece and 8 Full-page Illustrations. Crown 8vo , 3s. 6d.

Blackburne. — *MR. BLACKBURNE'S GAMES AT CHESS* Selected, Annotated and Arranged by Himself Edited, with a Biographical Sketch and a brief History of Blindfold Chess, by P ANDERSON GRAHAM With Portrait of Mr Blackburne 8vo , 7s 6d net

Dead Shot (The) · or, Sportsman's Complete Guide Being a Treatise on the Use of the Gun, with Rudimentary and Finishing Lessons in the Art of Shooting Game of all kinds Also Game-driving, Wildfowl and Pigeon-shooting, Dog-breaking, etc. By MARKSMAN With numerous Illustrations Crown 8vo 10s 6d

Ellis.—*CHESS SPARKS;* or, Short and Bright Games of Chess Collected and Arranged by J. H ELLIS, M.A. 8vo., 4s 6d.

Folkard.—*THE WILD-FOWLER .* A Treatise on Fowling, Ancient and Modern, descriptive also of Decoys and Flight-ponds, Wild-fowl Shooting, Gunning-punts, Shooting-yachts, etc Also Fowling in the Fens and in Foreign Countries, Rock-fowling, etc., etc , by H. C FOLKARD. With 13 Engravings on Steel, and several Woodcuts. 8vo , 12s 6d

Ford.—*THE THEORY AND PRACTICE OF ARCHERY* By HORACE FORD. New Edition, thoroughly Revised and Re-written by W BUTT, M A With a Preface by C. J. LONGMAN, M.A 8vo , 14s

Francis.—*A BOOK ON ANGLING:* or, Treatise on the Art of Fishing in every Branch , including full Illustrated List of Salmon Flies. By FRANCIS FRANCIS. With Portrait and Coloured Plates Crown 8vo , 15s.

Fremantle. — *THE BOOK OF THE RIFLE* By the Hon T. F FREMANTLE, V D , Major, 1st Bucks V.R.C With 54 Plates and 107 Diagrams in the Text. 8vo., 12s 6d net

Sport and Pastime—*continued.*

Gathorne - Hardy. — *AUTUMNS IN ARGYLESHIRE WITH ROD AND GUN.* By the Hon. A. E. GATHORNE-HARDY. With 8 Illustrations by ARCHIBALD THORBURN. 8vo., 6s. net.

Graham.—*COUNTRY PASTIMES FOR BOYS.* By P. ANDERSON GRAHAM. With 252 Illustrations from Drawings and Photographs. Cr. 8vo., gilt edges, 3s. net.

Hutchinson.—*THE BOOK OF GOLF AND GOLFERS.* By HORACE G. HUTCHINSON. With Contributions by Miss AMY PASCOE, H. H. HILTON, J. H. TAYLOR, H. J. WHIGHAM, and Messrs. SUTTON & SONS. With 71 Portraits from Photographs. Large crown 8vo., gilt top, 7s. 6d. net.

Lang.—*ANGLING SKETCHES.* By ANDREW LANG. With 20 Illustrations. Crown 8vo., 3s. 6d.

Lillie.—*CROQUET UP TO DATE.* Containing the Ideas and Teachings of the Leading Players and Champions. By ARTHUR LILLIE. With Contributions by Lieut.-Col. the Hon. H. NEEDHAM, C. D. LOCOCK, etc. With 19 Illustrations (15 Portraits), and numerous Diagrams. 8vo., 10s. 6d. net.

Locock.—*SIDE AND SCREW:* being Notes on the Theory and Practice of the Game of Billiards. By C. D. LOCOCK. With Diagrams. Crown 8vo., 5s. net.

Longman.—*CHESS OPENINGS.* By FREDERICK W. LONGMAN. Fcp. 8vo., 2s. 6d.

Mackenzie.—*NOTES FOR HUNTING MEN.* By Captain CORTLANDT GORDON MACKENZIE. Crown 8vo., 2s. 6d. net.

Madden.—*THE DIARY OF MASTER WILLIAM SILENCE:* a Study of Shakespeare and of Elizabethan Sport. By the Right Hon. D. H. MADDEN, Vice-Chancellor of the University of Dublin. 8vo., gilt top, 16s.

Maskelyne.—*SHARPS AND FLATS:* a Complete Revelation of the Secrets of Cheating at Games of Chance and Skill. By JOHN NEVIL MASKELYNE, of the Egyptian Hall. With 62 Illustrations. Crown 8vo., 6s.

Millais (JOHN GUILLE).

THE WILD-FOWLER IN SCOTLAND. With a Frontispiece in Photogravure by Sir J. E. MILLAIS, Bart., P.R.A., 8 Photogravure Plates, 2 Coloured Plates and 50 Illustrations from the Author's Drawings and from Photographs. Royal 4to., gilt top, 30s. net.

Millais (JOHN GUILLE)—*continued.*

THE NATURAL HISTORY OF THE BRITISH SURFACE-FEEDING DUCKS. With 6 Photogravures and 66 Plates (41 in Colours) from Drawings by the Author, ARCHIBALD THORBURN, and from Photographs. Royal 4to., cloth, gilt top, £6 6s. net.

Modern Bridge.—By 'Slam'. With a Reprint of the Laws of Bridge, as adopted by the Portland and Turf Clubs. 18mo., gilt edges, 3s. 6d. net.

Park.—*THE GAME OF GOLF.* By WILLIAM PARK, Jun., Champion Golfer, 1887-89. With 17 Plates and 26 Illustrations in the Text. Crown 8vo., 7s. 6d.

Payne-Gallwey (Sir RALPH, Bart.).

THE CROSS-BOW: Mediæval and Modern; Military and Sporting; its Construction, History and Management, with a Treatise on the Balista and Catapult of the Ancients. With 220 Illustrations. Royal 4to., £3 3s. net.

LETTERS TO YOUNG SHOOTERS (First Series). On the Choice and use of a Gun. With 41 Illustrations. Crown 8vo., 7s. 6d.

LETTERS TO YOUNG SHOOTERS (Second Series). On the Production, Preservation, and Killing of Game. With Directions in Shooting Wood-Pigeons and Breaking-in Retrievers. With Portrait and 103 Illustrations. Crown 8vo., 12s. 6d.

LETTERS TO YOUNG SHOOTERS. (Third Series.) Comprising a Short Natural History of the Wildfowl that are Rare or Common to the British Islands, with complete directions in Shooting Wildfowl on the Coast and Inland. With 200 Illustrations. Crown 8vo., 18s.

Pole.—*THE THEORY OF THE MODERN SCIENTIFIC GAME OF WHIST.* By WILLIAM POLE, F.R.S. Fcp. 8vo., gilt edges, 2s. net.

Proctor.—*HOW TO PLAY WHIST: WITH THE LAWS AND ETIQUETTE OF WHIST.* By RICHARD A. PROCTOR. Crown 8vo., gilt edges, 3s. net.

Ronalds.—*THE FLY-FISHER'S ENTOMOLOGY.* By ALFRED RONALDS. With 20 coloured Plates. 8vo., 14s.

Selous.—*SPORT AND TRAVEL, EAST AND WEST.* By FREDERICK COURTENEY SELOUS. With 18 Plates and 35 Illustrations in the Text. Medium 8vo., 12s. 6d. net.

Warner.—*CRICKET IN AUSTRALASIA:* being Record of the Tour of the English Team, 1902-3. By PELHAM F. WARNER. With numerous Illustrations from Photographs. Crown 8vo.

Mental, Moral, and Political Philosophy.

LOGIC, RHETORIC, PSYCHOLOGY, &C.

Abbott.—*THE ELEMENTS OF LOGIC.* By T K ABBOTT, B.D. 12mo., 3s.

Aristotle.

THE ETHICS: Greek Text, Illustrated with Essay and Notes. By Sir ALEXANDER GRANT, Bart. 2 vols. 8vo., 32s.

AN INTRODUCTION TO ARISTOTLE'S ETHICS. Books I.-IV. (Book X. c. vi.-ix. in an Appendix). With a continuous Analysis and Notes. By the Rev. E. MOORE, D.D. Crown 8vo., 10s. 6d

Bacon (FRANCIS).

COMPLETE WORKS. Edited by R. L ELLIS, JAMES SPEDDING and D. D. HEATH. 7 vols. 8vo., £3 13s 6d

LETTERS AND LIFE, including all his occasional Works. Edited by JAMES SPEDDING. 7 vols. 8vo., £4 4s.

THE ESSAYS. with Annotations. By RICHARD WHATELY, D.D. 8vo., 10s. 6d.

THE ESSAYS: with Notes. By F. STORR and C H GIBSON Cr. 8vo , 3s. 6d

THE ESSAYS: with Introduction, Notes, and Index By E A ABBOTT, D D 2 Vols Fcp 8vo , 6s The Text and Index only, without Introduction and Notes, in One Volume. Fcp 8vo , 2s 6d.

Bain (ALEXANDER).

MENTAL AND MORAL SCIENCE a Compendium of Psychology and Ethics. Crown 8vo , 10s. 6d.
Or separately,
Part I. *PSYCHOLOGY AND HISTORY OF PHILOSOPHY* Crown 8vo., 6s. 6d.
Part II. *THEORY OF ETHICS AND ETHICAL SYSTEMS.* Crown 8vo , 4s. 6d.

LOGIC. Part I. *DEDUCTION* Cr. 8vo., 4s. Part II *INDUCTION.* Cr. 8vo , 6s. 6d

THE SENSES AND THE INTELLECT. 8vo , 15s.

THE EMOTIONS AND THE WILL 8vo., 15s

PRACTICAL ESSAYS. Cr. 8vo., 2s.

DISSER· T·ONS ·N LF ·D ·· PH·C·

Baldwin.—*A COLLEGE MANUAL OF RHETORIC* By CHARLES SEARS BALDWIN A M , Ph D. Crown 8vo., 4s. 6d.

Brooks.—*THE ELEMENTS OF MIND :* being an Examination into the Nature of the First Division of the Elementary Substances of Life. By H. JAMYN BROOKS 8vo , 10s 6d. net.

Brough.—*THE STUDY OF MENTAL SCIENCE.* Five Lectures on the Uses and Characteristics of Logic and Psychology. By J. BROUGH, LL.D Crown 8vo, 2s. net.

Crozier (JOHN BEATTIE).

CIVILISATION AND PROGRESS. being the Outlines of a New System of Political, Religious and Social Philosophy. 8vo ,14s.

HISTORY OF INTELLECTUAL DEVELOPMENT: on the Lines of Modern Evolution.

Vol. I. 8vo , 14s.

Vol II. (*In preparation*)

Vol. III. 8vo., 10s 6d.

Davidson.—*THE LOGIC OF DEFINITION,* Explained and Applied By WILLIAM L DAVIDSON, M.A Crown 8vo., 6s

Green (THOMAS HILL).—THE WORKS OF. Edited by R. L. NETTLESHIP.

Vols I and II. Philosophical Works. 8vo. 16s. each.

Vol. III Miscellanies. With Index to the three Volumes, and Memoir 8vo., 21s.

LECTURES ON THE PRINCIPLES OF POLITICAL OBLIGATION With Preface by BERNARD BOSANQUET. 8vo , 5s.

Gurnhill.—*THE MORALS OF SUICIDE.* By the Rev J GURNHILL. B.A. Vol. I., Crown 8vo., 5s. net. Vol. II., Crown 8vo., 5s. net.

Mental, Moral and Political Philosophy—*continued.*

LOGIC, RHETORIC, PSYCHOLOGY, &C.

Hodgson (SHADWORTH H.).

TIME AND SPACE · A Metaphysical Essay. 8vo., 16s.

THE THEORY OF PRACTICE: an Ethical Inquiry. 2 vols. 8vo , 24s

THE PHILOSOPHY OF REFLECTION. 2 vols 8vo , 21s

THE METAPHYSIC OF EXPERIENCE. Book I. General Analysis of Experience ; Book II. Positive Science ; Book III Ana ysis of Conscious Action ; Book IV. The Real Universe. 4 vols. 8vo , 36s. net.

Hume.—*THE PHILOSOPHICAL WORKS OF DAVID HUME.* Edited by T H. GREEN and T H GROSE 4 vols. 8vo , 28s. Or separately, ESSAYS. 2 vols. 14s. TREATISE OF HUMAN NATURE. 2 vols 14s.

James (WILLIAM, M D., LL D.).

THE WILL TO BELIEVE, and Other Essays in Popular Philosophy. Crown 8vo., 7s 6d

THE VARIETIES OF RELIGIOUS EXPERIENCE a Study in Human Nature. Being the Gifford Lectures on Natural Religion delivered at Edinburgh in 1901-1902 8vo , 12s net

TALKS TO TEACHERS ON PSYCHOLOGY, AND TO STUDENTS ON SOME OF LIFE'S IDEALS Crown 8vo , 4s. 6d

Justinian.—*THE INSTITUTES OF JUSTINIAN* Latin Text, chiefly that of Huschke, with English Introduction, Translation, Notes, and Summary. By THOMAS C SANDARS, M.A 8vo , 18s

Kant (IMMANUEL)

CRITIQUE OF PRACTICAL REASON, AND OTHER WORKS ON THE THEORY OF ETHICS. Translated by T. K. ABBOTT, B D. With Memoir. 8vo., 12s 6d

FUNDAMENTAL PRINCIPLES OF THE METAPHYSIC OF ETHICS Translated by T. K. ABBOTT, B.D. Crown 8vo, 3s.

INTRODUCTION TO LOGIC, AND HIS ESSAY ON THE MISTAKEN SUBTILTY OF THE FOUR FIGURES Translated by T. K. ABBOTT 8vo., 6s

Kelly.—*GOVERNMENT OR HUMAN EVOLUTION.* By EDMOND KELLY, M A , F G S Vol I Justice Crown 8vo , 7s. 6d net. Vol. II. Collectivism and Individualism Crown 8vo., 10s 6d net

Killick. —*HANDBOOK TO MILL'S SYSTEM OF LOGIC.* By Rev. A. H.

Ladd (GEORGE TRUMBULL).

PHILOSOPHY OF CONDUCT: a Treatise of the Facts, Principles and Ideals of Ethics. 8vo., 21s.

ELEMENTS OF PHYSIOLOGICAL PSYCHOLOGY. 8vo , 21s

OUTLINES OF DESCRIPTIVE PSYCHOLOGY. a Text-Book of Mental Science for Colleges and Normal Schools 8vo., 12s.

OUTLINES OF PHYSIOLOGICAL PSYCHOLOGY. 8vo., 12s.

PRIMER OF PSYCHOLOGY. Cr. 8vo., 5s. 6d

Lecky (WILLIAM EDWARD HARTPOLE)

THE MAP OF LIFE : Conduct and Character Crown 8vo , 5s net.

HISTORY OF EUROPEAN MORALS FROM AUGUSTUS TO CHARLEMAGNE. 2 vols. Crown 8vo., 10s net.

A SURVEY OF ENGLISH ETHICS : being the First Chapter of W. E. H Lecky's 'History of European Morals' Edited, with Introduction and Notes, by W. A. HIRST Crown 8vo., 3s. 6d. ;

HISTORY OF THE RISE AND INFLUENCE OF THE SPIRIT OF RATIONALISM IN EUROPE 2 vols. Cr 8vo , 10s net.

DEMOCRACY AND LIBERTY
Library Edition. 2 vols. 8vo., 36s.
Cabinet Edition. 2 vols Cr 8vo , 10s. net.

Lutoslawski.—*THE ORIGIN AND GROWTH OF PLATO'S LOGIC* With an Account of Plato s Style and of the Chronology of his Writings. By WINCENTY LUTOSLAWSKI. 8vo., 21s.

Max Müller (F.).

THE SCIENCE OF THOUGHT. 8vo., 21s.

THE SIX SYSTEMS OF INDIAN PHILOSOPHY. 8vo., 18s.

THREE LECTURES ON THE VEDANTA PHILOSOPHY. Crown 8vo , 5s.

Mill (JOHN STUART).

A SYSTEM OF LOGIC. Cr 8vo , 3s 6d.

ON LIBERTY. Crown 8vo , 1s. 4d.

CONSIDERATIONS ON REPRESENTATIVE GOVERNMENT Crown 8vo , 2s

UTILITARIANISM 8vo., 2s. 6d

EXAMINATION OF SIR WILLIAM HAMILTON'S PHILOSOPHY 8vo., 16s.

NATURE, THE UTILITY OF RELIGION,

Mental, Moral, and Political Philosophy—*continued.*

LOGIC, RHETORIC, PSYCHOLOGY, &C.

Monck. — *An Introduction to Logic* By William Henry S Monck, M A   Crown 8vo , 5s

Myers.—*Human Personality and its Survival of Bodily Death* By Frederic W H. Myers. 2 vols. 8vo , 42s net.

Pierce.—*Studies in Auditory and Visual Space Perception* Essays on Experimental Psychology. By A H Pierce   Crown 8vo , 6s 6d. net

Richmond.—*The Mind of a Child* By Ennis Richmond   Cr. 8vo., 3s. 6d net

Romanes.—*Mind and Motion and Monism.* By George John Romanes, Cr 8vo , 4s. 6d

Sully (James).

An Essay on Laughter its Forms, its Cause, its Development and its Value   8vo , 12s. 6d. net.

The Human Mind : a Text-book of Psychology. 2 vols 8vo , 21s

Outlines of Psychology   Crown 8vo , 9s

The Teacher's Handbook of Psychology. Crown 8vo., 6s. 6d.

Studies of Childhood. 8vo.,10s 6d

Children's Ways · being Selections from the Author's ' Studies of Childhood ' With 25 Illustrations Crown 8vo , 4s 6d

Sutherland. — *The Origin and Growth of the Moral Instinct* By Alexander Sutherland, M A. 2 vols. 8vo , 28s.

Swinburne. — *Picture Logic :* an Attempt to Popularise the Science of Reasoning. By Alfred James Swinburne, M A   With 23 Woodcuts Cr. 8vo., 2s 6d

Thomas. — *Intuitive Suggestion* By J. W. Thomas, Author of ' Spiritual Law in the Natural World,' etc   Crown 8vo , 3s. 6d. net.

Webb.—*The Veil of Isis* a Series of Essays on Idealism.   By Thomas E. Webb, LL D , Q C   8vo , 10s 6d

Weber.—*History of Philosophy* By Alfred Weber, Professor in the University of Strasburg.   Translated by Frank Thilly, Ph D. 8vo , 16s.

Whately (Archbishop)

Bacon's Essays. With Annotations. 8vo , 10s. 6d

Elements of Logic Cr. 8vo , 4s. 6d

Elements of Rhetoric.   Cr. 8vo , 4s. 6d

Zeller (Dr. Edward).

The Stoics, Epicureans, and Sceptics Translated by the Rev. O J Reichel, M.A Crown 8vo., 15s.

Outlines of the History of Greek Philosophy Translated by Sarah F Alleyne and Evelyn Abbott, M A., LL D Crown 8vo , 10s 6d

Plato and the Older Academy. Translated by Sarah F. Alleyne and Alfred Goodwin, B A Crown 8vo , 18s

Socrates and the Socratic Schools Translated by the Rev. O J Reichel, M.A. Crown 8vo , 10s 6d

Aristotle and the Earlier Peripatetics. Translated by B F C. Costelloe, M A , and J H Muirhead, M A 2 vols Crown 8vo , 24s

---

STONYHURST PHILOSOPHICAL SERIES.

A Manual of Political Economy. By C. S. Devas, M.A. Crown 8vo , 7s. 6d.

First Principles of Knowledge By John Rickaby, S.J. Crown 8vo., 5s.

General Metaphysics. By John Rickaby, S J Crown 8vo., 5s.

Logic. By Richard F. Clarke, S.J. : Crown 8vo ...

Moral Philosophy (Ethics and Natural Law) By Joseph Rickaby, S J Crown 8vo , 5s

Natural Theology By Bernard Boedder, S J. Crown 8vo., 6s. 6d.

Psychology. By Michael Maher, S J D Litt M A (Lond) Cr 8vo 6s 6d

History and Science of Language, &c.

Davidson.—*LEADING AND IMPORT-ANT ENGLISH WORDS :* Explained and Exemplified. By WILLIAM L. DAVIDSON, M.A. Fcp. 8vo., 3s. 6d.

Farrar.—*LANGUAGE AND LANGUAGES.* By F. W. FARRAR, D.D., late Dean of Canterbury. Crown 8vo., 6s.

Graham. — *ENGLISH SYNONYMS,* Classified and Explained: with Practical Exercises. By G. F. GRAHAM. Fcp. 8vo., 6s.

Max Müller (F.).

THE SCIENCE OF LANGUAGE. 2 vols. Crown 8vo., 10s.

Max Müller (F.)—*continued.*

BIOGRAPHIES OF WORDS, AND THE HOME OF THE ARYAS. Crown 8vo., 5s.

CHIPS FROM A GERMAN WORKSHOP. Vol. III. *ESSAYS ON LANGUAGE AND LITERATURE.* Crown 8vo., 5s.

LAST ESSAYS. First Series. Essays on Language, Folk-lore and other Subjects. Crown 8vo., 5s.

Roget.—*THESAURUS OF ENGLISH WORDS AND PHRASES.* Classified and Arranged so as to Facilitate the Expression of Ideas and assist in Literary Composition. By PETER MARK ROGET, M.D., F.R.S. With full Index. Crown 8vo., 9s. net.

Political Economy and Economics.

Ashley (W. J.).

ENGLISH ECONOMIC HISTORY AND THEORY. Crown 8vo., Part I., 5s. Part II., 10s. 6d.

SURVEYS, HISTORIC AND ECONOMIC. Crown 8vo., 9s. net.

THE ADJUSTMENT OF WAGES : a Study on the Coal and Iron Industries of Great Britain and the United States. With 4 Maps. 8vo.

Bagehot.—*ECONOMIC STUDIES.* By WALTER BAGEHOT. Crown 8vo., 3s. 6d.

Barnett.—*PRACTICABLE SOCIALISM :* Essays on Social Reform. By SAMUEL A. and HENRIETTA BARNETT. Crown 8vo., 6s.

Devas.—*A MANUAL OF POLITICAL ECONOMY.* By C. S. DEVAS, M.A. Cr. 8vo., 7s. 6d. (*Stonyhurst Philosophical Series.*)

Dewey.—*FINANCIAL HISTORY OF THE UNITED STATES.* By DAVIS RICH DEWEY. Crown 8vo., 7s. 6d. net.

Lawrence.—*LOCAL VARIATIONS IN WAGES.* By F. W. LAWRENCE, M.A. With Index and 18 Maps and Diagrams. 4to.,8s.6d.

Leslie.—*ESSAYS ON POLITICAL ECONOMY.* By T. E. CLIFFE LESLIE, Hon. LL.D., Dubl. 8vo., 10s. 6d.

Macleod (HENRY DUNNING).

BIMETALLISM. 8vo., 5s. net.

THE ELEMENTS OF BANKING. Cr.

Macleod (HENRY DUNNING)—*contd.*

THE THEORY AND PRACTICE OF BANKING. Vol. I. 8vo., 12s. Vol. II. 14s.

THE THEORY OF CREDIT. 8vo. In 1 Vol., 30s. net; or separately, Vol. I., 10s. net. Vol. II., Part I., 10s. net. Vol II., Part II. 10s. net.

INDIAN CURRENCY. 8vo., 2s. 6d. net.

Mill.—*POLITICAL ECONOMY.* By JOHN STUART MILL. *Popular Edition.* Cr. 8vo.,3s.6d. *Library Edition.* 2 vols. 8vo.,30s.

Mulhall.—*INDUSTRIES AND WEALTH OF NATIONS.* By MICHAEL G. MULHALL, F.S.S. With 32 Diagrams. Cr. 8vo., 8s. 6d.

Symes. — *POLITICAL ECONOMY :* a Short Text-book of Political Economy. With Problems for Solution, Hints for Supplementary Reading, and a Supplementary Chapter on Socialism. By J. E. SYMES, M.A. Crown 8vo., 2s. 6d.

Toynbee.—*LECTURES ON THE INDUSTRIAL REVOLUTION OF THE 18TH CENTURY IN ENGLAND.* By ARNOLD TOYNBEE. 8vo., 10s. 6d.

Webb (SIDNEY and BEATRICE).

THE HISTORY OF TRADE UNIONISM. With Map and Bibliography. 8vo., 7s. 6d. net.

INDUSTRIAL DEMOCRACY : a Study in Trade Unionism. 2 vols. 8vo., 12s. net.

PROBLEMS OF MODERN INDUSTRY,

Evolution, Anthropology, &c.

Avebury.—*THE ORIGIN OF CIVILISA-TION*, and the Primitive Condition of Man By the Right Hon. LORD AVEBURY. With 6 Plates and 20 Illustrations   8vo , 18s

Clodd (EDWARD).

THE STORY OF CREATION a Plain Account of Evolution. With 77 Illustrations   Crown 8vo., 3s. 6d.

A PRIMER OF EVOLUTION · being a Popular Abridged Edition of 'The Story of Creation'. With Illustrations. Fcp 8vo , 1s 6d.

Lang and Atkinson. — *SOCIAL ORIGINS.* By ANDREW LANG, M.A ,LL D. , and *PRIMAL LAW.* By J J ATKINSON 8vo., 10s 6d. net

Packard.—*LAMARCK, THE FOUNDER OF EVOLUTION* his Life and Work, with Translations of his Writings on Organic Evolution   By ALPHEUS S PACKARD, M D , LL D   With 10 Portrait and other Illustrations.   Large Crown 8vo , 9s. net

Romanes (GEORGE JOHN)

ESSAYS. Ed. by C. LLOYD MORGAN Crown 8vo., 5s net

AN EXAMINATION OF WEISMANN-ISM   Crown 8vo , 6s

DARWIN, AND AFTER DARWIN: an Exposition of the Darwinian Theory, and a Discussion on Post-Darwinian Questions.

Part I   THE DARWINIAN THEORY.   With Portrait of Darwin and 125 Illustrations. Crown 8vo., 10s 6d

Part II   POST-DARWINIAN QUESTIONS: Heredity and Utility   With Portrait of the Author and 5 Illustrations   Cr. 8vo , 10s. 6d

Part III   Post-Darwinian Questions Isolation and Physiological Selection Crown 8vo., 5s.

The Science of Religion, &c.

Balfour. — *THE FOUNDATIONS OF BELIEF* being Notes Introductory to the Study of Theology. By the Right Hon. ARTHUR JAMES BALFOUR   Cr 8vo , 6s. net.

Baring-Gould —*THE ORIGIN AND DEVELOPMENT OF RELIGIOUS BELIEF.* By the Rev S. BARING-GOULD   2 vols Crown 8vo., 3s 6d each

Campbell.—*RELIGION IN GREEK LITERATURE*   By the Rev. LEWIS CAMPBELL, M.A., LL.D   8vo , 15s

Davidson.—*THEISM,* as Grounded in Human Nature, Historically and Critically Handled.   Being the Burnett Lectures for 1892 and 1893, delivered at Aberdeen. By W. L DAVIDSON, M.A., LL.D. 8vo , 15s.

James.—*THE VARIETIES OF RELIGIOUS EXPERIENCE* a Study in Human Nature   Being the Gifford Lectures on Natural Religion delivered at Edinburgh in 1901-1902   By WILLIAM JAMES, LL D , etc.   8vo , 12s net.

Lang (ANDREW).

MAGIC AND RELIGION. 8vo , 10s 6d

CUSTOM AND MYTH .   Studies of Early Usage and Belief   With 15 Illustrations   Crown 8vo , 3s 6d

MYTH, RITUAL, AND RELIGION.   2 vols   Crown 8vo   7s

Lang (ANDREW)—*continued.*

MODERN MYTHOLOGY : a Reply to Professor Max Muller. 8vo., 9s.

THE MAKING OF RELIGION. Cr. 8vo., 5s net.

Leighton.—*TYPICAL MODERN CONCEPTIONS OF GOD;* or, The Absolute of German Romantic Idealism and of English Evolutionary Agnosticism.   By JOSEPH ALEXANDER LEIGHTON, Professor of Philosophy in Hobart College, U.S   Crown 8vo , 3s. 6d net

Max Müller (The Right Hon. F.).

THE SILESIAN HORSEHERD (' *DAS PFERDEBÜRLA* ')   Questions of the Day answered by F. MAX MÜLLER.   Translated by OSCAR A. FECHTER, Mayor of North Jakima, U S.A.   With a Preface by J. ESTLIN CARPENTER.

CHIPS FROM A GERMAN WORKSHOP. Vol. IV. Essays on Mythology and Folklore   Crown 8vo., 5s.

THE SIX SYSTEMS OF INDIAN PHILOSOPHY. 8vo , 18s.

CONTRIBUTIONS TO THE SCIENCE OF MYTHOLOGY. 2 vols.   8vo., 32s.

THE ORIGIN AND GROWTH OF RELIGION, as illustrated by the Religions of India.   The Hibbert Lectures, delivered at the Chapter House, Westminster Abbey in 1878.   Crown 8vo.   5s

The Science of Religion, &c.—*continued.*

Max Müller (The Right Hon. F.)—
continued.

INTRODUCTION TO THE SCIENCE OF RELIGION. Four Lectures delivered at the Royal Institution. Crown 8vo., 5s.

NATURAL RELIGION. The Gifford Lectures, delivered before the University of Glasgow in 1888. Crown 8vo., 5s

PHYSICAL RELIGION. The Gifford Lectures, delivered before the University of Glasgow in 1890. Crown 8vo., 5s.

ANTHROPOLOGICAL RELIGION. The Gifford Lectures, delivered before the University of Glasgow in 1891. Cr 8vo , 5s

THEOSOPHY, OR PSYCHOLOGICAL RELIGION. The Gifford Lectures, delivered before the University of Glasgow in 1892. Crown 8vo., 5s

Max Müller (The Right Hon F)—
continued

THREE LECTURES ON THE VEDÂNTA PHILOSOPHY, delivered at the Royal Institution in March, 1894. Cr. 8vo , 5s

LAST ESSAYS. Second Series—Essays on the Science of Religion Crown 8vo , 5s

Oakesmith. — *THE RELIGION OF PLUTARCH* a Pagan Creed of Apostolic Times An Essay By JOHN OAKESMITH, D Litt , M A Crown 8vo , 5s net

Wood-Martin (W G)

TRACES OF THE ELDER FAITHS OF IRELAND a Folk-lore Sketch A Handbook of Irish Pre-Christian Traditions. With 192 Illustrations. 2 vols 8vo , 30s net

PAGAN IRELAND. an Archæological Sketch. A Handbook of Irish Pre-Christian Antiquities With 512 Illustrations 8vo , 15s.

Classical Literature, Translations, &c.

Abbott.—*HELLENICA* A Collection of Essays on Greek Poetry, Philosophy, History, and Religion. Edited by EVELYN ABBOTT, M A , LL.D. Crown 8vo., 7s 6d

Æschylus.—*EUMENIDES OF ÆSCHYLUS* With Metrical English Translation. By J F. DAVIES 8vo , 7s

Aristophanes. — *THE ACHARNIANS OF ARISTOPHANES,* translated into English Verse. By R. Y TYRRELL Crown 8vo., 1s.

Becker (W. A.), Translated by the Rev. F. METCALFE, B.D

GALLUS : or, Roman Scenes in the Time of Augustus. With Notes and Excursuses With 26 Illustrations. Crown 8vo , 3s. 6d

CHARICLES : or, Illustrations of the Private Life of the Ancient Greeks. With Notes and Excursuses. With 26 Illustrations. Crown 8vo , 3s. 6d

Campbell.—*RELIGION IN GREEK LITERATURE.* By the Rev. LEWIS CAMPBELL, M.A , LL.D., Emeritus Professor of Greek, University of St. Andrews 8vo , 15s.

Cicero.—*CICERO'S CORRESPONDENCE* By R Y. TYRRELL. Vols I , II , III., 8vo , each 12s. Vol. IV , 15s Vol V., 14s

Harvard Studies in Classical Philology. Edited by a Committee of the Classical Instructors of Harvard University. Vols. XI , 1900 , XII , 1901 , XIII , 1902 8vo., 6s 6d net each

Hime.—*LUCIAN, THE SYRIAN SATIRIST* By Lieut.-Col. HENRY W. L. HIME, (late) Royal Artillery. 8vo , 5s. net

Homer. — *THE ODYSSEY OF HOMER.* Done into English Verse. By WILLIAM MORRIS Crown 8vo., 5s net

Horace.—*THE WORKS OF HORACE,* RENDERED INTO ENGLISH PROSE. With Life, Introduction and Notes. By WILLIAM COUTTS, M.A Crown 8vo., 5s. net.

Lang.—*HOMER AND THE EPIC.* By ANDREW LANG Crown 8vo , 9s net.

Lucian. — *TRANSLATIONS FROM LUCIAN.* By AUGUSTA M CAMPBELL DAVIDSON, M A Edin Crown 8vo , 5s net.

Ogilvie.—*HORAE LATINAE :* Studies in Synonyms and Syntax. By the late ROBERT OGILVIE, M A., LL D., H M Chief Inspector of Schools for Scotland. Edited by ALEXANDER SOUTER, M.A. With a Memoir by JOSEPH OGILVIE, M A., LL,D,

Classical Literature, Translations, &c.—*continued.*

Rich.—*A DICTIONARY OF ROMAN AND GREEK ANTIQUITIES*   By A RICH, B.A. With 2000 Woodcuts   Crown 8vo., 6s. net.

Sophocles.—Translated into English Verse.   By ROBERT WHITELAW, M.A, Assistant Master in Rugby School   Cr 8vo , 8s. 6d

Theophrastus.—*THE CHARACTERS OF THEOPHRASTUS*. a Translation, with Introduction   By CHARLES E BENNETT and WILLIAM A HAMMOND, Professors in Cornell University.   Fcp 8vo , 2s. 6d. net.

Tyrrell. — *DUBLIN TRANSLATIONS INTO GREEK AND LATIN VERSE.*   Edited by R Y. TYRRELL.   8vo., 6s.

Virgil.

THE POEMS OF VIRGIL.   Translated into English Prose by JOHN CONINGTON. Crown 8vo., 6s.

Virgil—*continued*

THE ÆNEID OF VIRGIL   Translated into English Verse by JOHN CONINGTON. Crown 8vo , 6s

THE ÆNEIDS OF VIRGIL.   Done into English Verse.   By WILLIAM MORRIS. Crown 8vo., 5s. net.

THE ÆNEID OF VIRGIL, freely translated into English Blank Verse.   By W. J. THORNHILL.   Crown 8vo., 6s. net

THE ÆNEID OF VIRGIL.   Translated into English Verse by JAMES RHOADES. Books I.-VI.   Crown 8vo., 5s. Books VII -XII.   Crown 8vo , 5s

THE ECLOGUES AND GEORGICS OF VIRGIL   Translated into English Prose by J. W. MACKAIL, Fellow of Balliol College, Oxford.   16mo., 5s.

Wilkins.—*THE GROWTH OF THE HOMERIC POEMS.*   By G. WILKINS. 8vo., 6s.

Poetry and the Drama.

Arnold.—*THE LIGHT OF THE WORLD* or, The Great Consummation   By Sir EDWIN ARNOLD   With 14 Illustrations after HOLMAN HUNT   Crown 8vo., 5s. net

Bell (MRS. HUGH)

CHAMBER COMEDIES : a Collection of Plays and Monologues for the Drawing Room   Crown 8vo , 5s. net.

FAIRY TALE PLAYS, AND HOW TO ACT THEM   With 91 Diagrams and 52 Illustrations   Crown 8vo., 3s net

RUMPELSTILTZKIN a Fairy Play in Five Scenes (Characters, 7 Male; 1 Female)   From 'Fairy Tale Plays and How to Act Them'.   With Illustrations, Diagrams and Music. Cr. 8vo., sewed, 6d.

Bird. — *RONALD'S FAREWELL*, and other Verses.   By GEORGE BIRD, M.A., Vicar of Bradwell, Derbyshire.   Fcp. 8vo. 1s. 6d. net.

Cochrane.—*COLLECTED VERSES.*   By ALFRED COCHRANE, Author of ' The Kestrel's Nest, and other Verses,' ' Leviore Plectro,' etc   With a Frontispiece by H. J. FORD   Fcp 8vo

Dabney.—*THE MUSICAL BASIS OF VERSE*   a Scientific Study of the Principles of Poetic Composition.   By J. P. DABNEY.   Crown 8vo., 6s. 6d. net.

Graves. — *CLYTÆMNESTRA : A TRAGEDY.*   By ARNOLD F. GRAVES.   With a Preface by ROBERT Y TYRRELL, Litt D. Crown 8vo , 5s. net.

Hither and Thither : Songs and Verses.   By the Author of ' Times and Days,' etc.   Fcp 8vo , 5s.

Ingelow (JEAN).

POETICAL WORKS.   Complete in One Volume. Crown 8vo , gilt top, 6s. net.

LYRICAL AND OTHER POEMS.   Selected from the Writings of JEAN INGELOW. Fcp 8vo 2s 6d cloth plain 3s cloth gilt

Poetry and the Drama—*continued.*

Keary.—*THE BROTHERS :* a Fairy Masque. By C. F. KEARY. Cr. 8vo., 4s. net

Lang (ANDREW).

GRASS OF PARNASSUS. Fcp. 8vo., 2s 6d net.

THE BLUE POETRY BOOK. Edited by ANDREW LANG With 100 Illustrations. Crown 8vo., gilt edges, 6s.

Lecky.—*POEMS* By the Right Hon W. E. H. LECKY. Fcp. 8vo., 5s.

Lytton (The Earl of), (OWEN MEREDITH).

THE WANDERER Cr. 8vo , 10s. 6d.

LUCILE. Crown 8vo., 10s. 6d.

SELECTED POEMS. Cr. 8vo., 10s. 6d.

Macaulay.—*LAYS OF ANCIENT ROME, WITH 'IVRY' AND 'THE ARMADA'.* By Lord MACAULAY Illustrated by G. SCHARF. Fcp 4to., 10s. 6d.

———————————— Bijou Edition 18mo , 2s 6d gilt top.

———————————— Popular Edition. Fcp. 4to , 6d. sewed, 1s. cloth

Illustrated by J. R. WEGUELIN Crown 8vo., 3s. net.

Annotated Edition. Fcp. 8vo , 1s sewed, 1s. 6d cloth

MacDonald.—*A BOOK OF STRIFE, IN THE FORM OF THE DIARY OF AN OLD SOUL* Poems By GEORGE MACDONALD, LL.D 18mo., 6s.

Morris (WILLIAM).

POETICAL WORKS—LIBRARY EDITION. Complete in 11 volumes. Crown 8vo., price 5s. net each

THE EARTHLY PARADISE. 4 vols. Crown 8vo., 5s. net each.

THE LIFE AND DEATH OF JASON. Crown 8vo , 5s. net.

THE DEFENCE OF GUENEVERE, and other Poems Crown 8vo , 5s net.

THE STORY OF SIGURD THE VOLSUNG, AND THE FALL OF THE NIBLUNGS. Cr.

Morris (WILLIAM)—*continued*

POEMS BY THE WAY, AND LOVE IS ENOUGH Crown 8vo., 5s. net

THE ODYSSEY OF HOMER. Done into English Verse. Crown 8vo., 5s. net.

THE ÆNEIDS OF VIRGIL. Done into English Verse. Crown 8vo , 5s. net.

THE TALE OF BEOWULF, SOMETIME KING OF THE FOLK OF THE WEDERGEATS. Translated by WILLIAM MORRIS and A. J. WYATT. Crown 8vo , 5s. net

Certain of the POETICAL WORKS may also be had in the following Editions :—

THE EARTHLY PARADISE.

Popular Edition 5 vols. 12mo , 25s , or 5s. each, sold separately.

The same in Ten Parts, 25s., or 2s. 6d· each, sold separately.

Cheap Edition. in 1 vol Crown 8vo., 6s net

POEMS BY THE WAY. Square crown 8vo., 6s.

‚ For Mr. William Morris's other Works, see pp. 27, 28, 37 and 40

Morte Arthur : an Alliterative Poem of the Fourteenth Century. Edited from the Thornton MS., with Introduction, Notes and Glossary. By MARY MACLEOD BANKS. Fcp. 8vo., 3s 6d.

Nesbit.—*LAYS AND LEGENDS.* By E. NESBIT (Mrs. HUBERT BLAND). First Series. Crown 8vo., 3s. 6d. Second Series. With Portrait. Crown 8vo , 5s.

Ramal.—*SONGS OF CHILDHOOD.* By WALTER RAMAL. With a Frontispiece from a Drawing by RICHARD DOYLE Fcp. 8vo , 3s. 6d net

Riley. — *OLD FASHIONED ROSES :* Poems. By JAMES WHITCOMB RILEY 12mo , gilt top, 5s

Romanes.—*A SELECTION FROM THE POEMS OF GEORGE JOHN ROMANES, M.A., LL.D., F.R S.* With an Introduction by T. HERBERT WARREN, President of Mag-

Poetry and the Drama—*continued.*

Savage-Armstrong.—*BALLADS OF DOWN* By G F SAVAGE-ARMSTRONG, M A, D Litt Crown 8vo., 7s. 6d.

Shakespeare.

BOWDLER'S FAMILY SHAKESPEARE With 36 Woodcuts. 1 vol. 8vo, 14s Or in 6 vols Fcp 8vo, 21s.

THE SHAKESPEARE BIRTHDAY BOOK. By MARY F. DUNBAR. 32mo., 1s. 6d.

Stevenson.—*A CHILD'S GARDEN OF VERSES.* By ROBERT LOUIS STEVENSON. Fcp. 8vo, gilt top, 5s.

Trevelyan.—*CECILIA GONZAGA* a Drama. By R C TREVELYAN. Fcp 8vo, 2s 6d net

Wagner.—*THE NIBELUNGEN RING* Done into English Verse by REGINALD RANKIN, B A, of the Inner Temple, Barrister-at-Law

Vol I Rhine Gold, The Valkyrie. Fcp. 8vo, gilt top, 4s. 6d.

Vol. II. Siegfried, The Twilight of th Gods. Fcp. 8vo., gilt top, 4s. 6d.

Fiction, Humour, &c.

Anstey (F.).

VOCES POPULI. (Reprinted from 'Punch')

First Series With 20 Illustrations by J. BERNARD PARTRIDGE Cr. 8vo, gilt top, 3s. net

Second Series. With 25 Illustrations by J. BERNARD PARTRIDGE Cr. 8vo, gilt top, 3s. net.

THE MAN FROM BLANKLEY'S, and other Sketches. (Reprinted from 'Punch'.) With 25 Illustrations by J BERNARD PARTRIDGE Cr 8vo, gilt top, 3s net

Bailey (H. C.).

MY LADY OF ORANGE a Romance of the Netherlands in the Days of Alva. With 8 Illustrations Crown 8vo., 6s

KARL OF ERBACH : a Tale of the Thirty Years' War Crown 8vo, 6s.

Beaconsfield (The Earl of).

NOVELS AND TALES Complete in 11 vols. Crown 8vo, 1s. 6d each, or in sets, 11 vols., gilt top, 15s. net.

Vivian Grey	Contarini Fleming,
The Young Duke;	The Rise of Iskander.
Count Alarcos a	
Tragedy	Sybil.
Alroy ; Ixion in	Henrietta Temple.
Heaven, The In-	Venetia
fernal Marriage;	Coningsby
Popanilla	Lothair.
Tancred	Endymion.

NOVELS AND TALES. THE HUGHENDEN EDITION. With 2 Portraits and ... Vignettes ... vols. Crown 8vo ...

Bottome.—*LIFE, THE INTERPRETER.* By PHYLLIS BOTTOME Crown 8vo, 6s.

Churchill.—*SAVROLA* a Tale of the Revolution in Laurania By WINSTON SPENCER CHURCHILL, M P Cr. 8vo, 6s.

Crawford.—*THE AUTOBIOGRAPHY OF A TRAMP.* By J H. CRAWFORD. With a Photogravure Frontispiece 'The Vagrants,' by FRED. WALKER, and 8 other Illustrations Crown 8vo, 5s. net.

Creed.—*THE VICAR OF ST. LUKE'S.* By SIBYL CREED. Crown 8vo, 6s

Davenport.—*BY THE RAMPARTS OF JEZREEL :* a Romance of Jehu, King of Israel By ARNOLD DAVENPORT. With Frontispiece by LANCELOT SPEED. Crown 8vo, 6s

Dougall.—*BEGGARS ALL.* By L. DOUGALL Crown 8vo., 3s 6d

Doyle (Sir A. CONAN).

MICAH CLARKE: A Tale of Monmouth's Rebellion. With 10 Illustrations. Cr. 8vo., 3s. 6d.

THE REFUGEES: A Tale of the Huguenots With 25 Illustrations. Cr. 8vo, 3s 6d

THE STARK MUNRO LETTERS. Cr. 8vo, 3s 6d.

THE CAPTAIN OF THE POLESTAR, and other Tales. Cr 8vo., 3s. 6d.

Fiction, Humour, &c.—*continued.*

Dyson.—*THE GOLD-STEALERS*. a Story of Waddy. By EDWARD DYSON, Author of 'Rhymes from the Mines,' etc. Crown 8vo , 6s

Farrar (F. W., late DEAN OF CANTERBURY).

DARKNESS AND DAWN· or, Scenes in the Days of Nero An Historic Tale Cr. 8vo , gilt top, 6s net

GATHERING CLOUDS · a Tale of the Days of St. Chrysostom. Cr. 8vo , gilt top, 6s net.

Fowler (EDITH H.)

THE YOUNG PRETENDERS. A Story of Child Life. With 12 Illustrations by Sir PHILIP BURNE-JONES, Bart. Crown 8vo., 6s.

THE PROFESSOR'S CHILDREN With 24 Illustrations by ETHEL KATE BURGESS. Crown 8vo , 6s

Francis (M. E.)

FIANDER'S WIDOW. Cr. 8vo , 6s

YEOMAN FLEETWOOD. With Frontispiece Crown 8vo , 3s net.

PASTORALS OF DORSET. With 8 Illustrations Crown 8vo., 6s.

THE MANOR FARM With Frontispiece by CLAUD C. DU PRÉ COOPER. Crown 8vo , 6s

Froude.—*THE TWO CHIEFS OF DUNBOY.* an Irish Romance of the Last Century. By JAMES A FROUDE Cr 8vo , 3s 6d.

Haggard (H. RIDER).

ALLAN QUATERMAIN. With 31 Illustrations Crown 8vo., 3s. 6d.

ALLAN'S WIFE. With 34 Illustra-

Haggard (H. RIDER)—*continued*

BEATRICE With Frontispiece and Vignette Crown 8vo , 3s. 6d.

BLACK HEART AND WHITE HEART, AND OTHER STORIES. With 33 Illustrations Crown 8vo , 3s 6d.

CLEOPATRA With 29 Illustrations. Crown 8vo , 3s 6d.

COLONEL QUARITCH, V.C With Frontispiece and Vignette Cr 8vo , 3s 6d

DAWN. With 16 Illustrations Cr. 8vo., 3s. 6d

DR. THERNE. Crown 8vo , 3s 6d.

ERIC BRIGHTEYES. With 51 Illustrations Crown 8vo , 3s 6d

HEART OF THE WORLD. With 15 Illustrations Crown 8vo , 3s. 6d.

JOAN HASTE. With 20 Illustrations Crown 8vo , 3s. 6d.

LYSBETH With 26 Illustrations Crown 8vo., 6s.

MAIWA'S REVENGE. Cr 8vo., 1s. 6d.

MONTEZUMA'S DAUGHTER. With 24 Illustrations Crown 8vo , 3s. 6d.

MR. MEESON'S WILL With 16 Illustrations Crown 8vo. 3s 6d

NADA THE LILY. With 23 Illustrations. Crown 8vo , 3s 6d

PEARL-MAIDEN. a Tale of the Fall of Jerusalem With 16 Illustrations. Crown 8vo., 6s

SHE. With 32 Illustrations. Crown 8vo , 3s 6d.

SWALLOW · a Tale of the Great Trek. With 8 Illustrations. Crown 8vo., 3s. 6d

THE PEOPLE OF THE MIST. With 16 Illustrations. Crown 8vo., 3s. 6d.

THE WITCH'S HEAD. With 16 Illustrations Crown 8vo 3s 6d

Fiction, Humour, &c.—*continued*

Haggard and Lang.—*THE WORLD'S DESIRE.* By H RIDER HAGGARD and ANDREW LANG. With 27 Illustrations Crown 8vo , 3s 6d

Harte.—*IN THE CARQUINEZ WOODS.* By BRET HARTE. Crown 8vo , 3s 6d.

Hope.—*THE HEART OF PRINCESS OSRA* By ANTHONY HOPE. With 9 Illustrations Crown 8vo., 3s 6d.

Howard.—*THE FAILURE OF SUCCESS.* By Lady MABEL HOWARD Crown 8vo., 6s.

Hutchinson.—*A FRIEND OF NELSON.* By HORACE G. HUTCHINSON Cr. 8vo., 6s.

Jerome.—*SKETCHES IN LAVENDER: BLUE AND GREEN.* By JEROME K. JEROME, Author of ' Three Men in a Boat,' etc Crown 8vo , 3s 6d.

Joyce.—*OLD CELTIC ROMANCES.* Twelve of the most beautiful of the Ancient Irish Romantic Tales Translated from the Gaelic. By P. W JOYCE, LL.D Crown 8vo , 3s 6d.

Lang (ANDREW)

A MONK OF FIFE ; a Story of the Days of Joan of Arc. With 13 Illustrations by SELWYN IMAGE. Crown 8vo , 3s 6d.

THE DISENTANGLERS With 7 Full-page Illustrations by H. J. FORD. Crown 8vo., 6s.

Lyall (EDNA).

THE HINDERERS. Crown 8vo , 2s.6d

THE AUTOBIOGRAPHY OF A SLANDER. Fcp. 8vo., 1s. sewed.
Presentation Edition With 20 Illustrations by LANCELOT SPEED. Crown 8vo , 2s. 6d net

DOREEN. The Story of a Singer. Crown 8vo., 6s

WAYFARING MEN. Crown 8vo., 6s.

HOPE THE HERMIT : a Romance of Borrowdale. Crown 8vo., 6s.

Marchmont.—*IN THE NAME OF A WOMAN:* a Romance By ARTHUR W MARCHMONT. With 8 Illustrations Crown 8vo , 6s.

Mason and Lang.—*PARSON KELLY* By A E. W MASON and ANDREW LANG Crown 8vo , 3s. 6d.

Max Muller. — *DEUTSCHE LIEBE (GERMAN LOVE)* Fragments from the Papers of an Alien Collected by F. MAX MULLER. Translated from the German by G. A. M. Crown 8vo , gilt top, 5s

Melville (G J. WHYTE).

The Gladiators	Holmby House
The Interpreter	Kate Coventry.
Good for Nothing	Digby Grand.
The Queen's Maries.	General Bounce

Crown 8vo., 1s. 6d. each.

Merriman.—*FLOTSAM ·* A Story of the Indian Mutiny By HENRY SETON MERRIMAN. With Frontispiece and Vignette by H G MASSEY Cr 8vo , 3s. 6d

Morris (WILLIAM).

THE SUNDERING FLOOD. Cr. 8vo , 7s. 6d.

THE WATER OF THE WONDROUS ISLES. Crown 8vo , 7s 6d.

THE WELL AT THE WORLD'S END 2 vols 8vo , 28s

THE WOOD BEYOND THE WORLD Crown 8vo., 6s. net.

THE STORY OF THE GLITTERING PLAIN, which has been also called The Land of the Living Men, or The Acre of the Undying Square post 8vo , 5s net

THE ROOTS OF THE MOUNTAINS, wherein is told somewhat of the Lives of the Men of Burgdale, their Friends, their Neighbours, their Foemen, and their Fellows-in-Arms. Written in Prose and Verse. Square crown 8vo , 8s.

Fiction, Humour, &c.—*continued.*

Morris (WILLIAM)—*continued.*

A TALE OF THE HOUSE OF THE WOLFINGS, and all the Kindreds of the Mark. Written in Prose and Verse. Square crown 8vo , 6s

A DREAM OF JOHN BALL, AND A KING'S LESSON 16mo , 2s. net.

NEWS FROM NOWHERE, or, An Epoch of Rest Being some Chapters from an Utopian Romance Post 8vo , 1s 6d

THE STORY OF GRETTIR THE STRONG. Translated from the Icelandic by EIRÍKR MAGNÚSSON and WILLIAM MORRIS Cr. 8vo., 5s. net.

THREE NORTHERN LOVE STORIES, AND OTHER TALES Translated from the Icelandic by EIRIKR MAGNÚSSON and WILLIAM MORRIS. Crown 8vo., 6s net

. For Mr. William Morris's other Works, see pp. 24, 37 and 40

Newman (Cardinal).

LOSS AND GAIN: The Story of a Convert. Crown 8vo , 3s. 6d.

CALLISTA: A Tale of the Third Century Crown 8vo., 3s. 6d.

Phillipps-Wolley.—*SNAP·* a Legend of the Lone Mountain. By C PHILLIPPS-WOLLEY. With 13 Illustrations. Crown 8vo , 3s. 6d.

Portman.—*STATION STUDIES ·* being the Jottings of an African Official. By LIONEL PORTMAN Crown 8vo , 5s. net.

Sewell (ELIZABETH M.).

A Glimpse of the World.	Amy Herbert.
Laneton Parsonage.	Cleve Hall.
Margaret Percival.	Gertrude.
Katharine Ashton	Home Life.
The Earl's Daughter.	After Life
The Experience of Life.	Ursula. Ivors.

Cr. 8vo., cloth plain, 1s. 6d. each. Cloth extra gilt edges 2s 6d each

Sheehan. — *LUKE DELMEGE.* By the Rev. P A SHEEHAN, P.P., Author of 'My New Curate'. Crown 8vo , 6s

Somerville (E. Œ.) **and Ross** (MARTIN).

SOME EXPERIENCES OF AN IRISH R M. With 31 Illustrations by E. Œ. SOMERVILLE. Crown 8vo., 6s.

ALL ON THE IRISH SHORE Irish Sketches. With Illustrations by E. Œ. SOMERVILLE. Crown 8vo , 6s.

THE REAL CHARLOTTE Crown 8vo., 3s 6d

THE SILVER FOX. Cr. 8vo , 3s 6d.

Stebbing.—*RACHEL WULFSTAN*, and other Stories By W STEBBING, author of 'Probable Tales' Crown 8vo., 4s. 6d.

Stevenson (ROBERT LOUIS).

THE STRANGE CASE OF DR. JEKYLL AND MR HYDE. Fcp. 8vo., 1s sewed. 1s 6d. cloth.

THE STRANGE CASE OF DR JEKYLL AND MR HYDE; WITH OTHER FABLES. Crown 8vo., bound in buckram, with gilt top, 5s. net.

'Silver Library' Edition Crown 8vo., 3s. 6d.

MORE NEW ARABIAN NIGHTS—THE DYNAMITER By ROBERT LOUIS STEVENSON and FANNY VAN DE GRIFT STEVENSON. Crown 8vo , 3s. 6d.

THE WRONG BOX. By ROBERT LOUIS STEVENSON and LLOYD OSBOURNE. Crown 8vo., 3s. 6d.

Fiction, Humour, &c.—*continued.*

Suttner.—*LAY DOWN YOUR ARMS* (*Die Waffen Nieder*) : The Autobiography of Martha von Tilling. By BERTHA VON SUTTNER. Translated by T. HOLMES. Cr. 8vo., 1s. 6d.

Trollope (ANTHONY).

THE WARDEN. Cr. 8vo., 1s. 6d.

BARCHESTER TOWERS. Cr. 8vo., 1s. 6d.

Walford (L. B.).

STAY-AT-HOMES. Crown 8vo., 6s.

CHARLOTTE. Crown 8vo., 6s.

ONE OF OURSELVES. Cr. 8vo., 6s.

THE INTRUDERS. Crown 8vo., 2s. 6d.

LEDDY MARGET. Crown 8vo., 2s. 6d.

IVA KILDARE : a Matrimonial Problem. Crown 8vo., 2s. 6d.

MR. SMITH : a Part of his Life. Crown 8vo., 2s. 6d.

THE BABY'S GRANDMOTHER. Cr. 8vo., 2s. 6d.

COUSINS. Crown 8vo., 2s. 6d.

TROUBLESOME DAUGHTERS. Cr. 8vo., 2s. 6d.

PAULINE. Crown 8vo., 2s. 6d.

DICK NETHERBY. Cr. 8vo., 2s. 6d.

THE HISTORY OF A WEEK. Cr. 8vo. 2s. 6d.

A STIFF-NECKED GENERATION. Cr. 8vo. 2s. 6d.

NAN, and other Stories. Cr. 8vo., 2s. 6d.

Walford (L. B.)—*continued.*

THE MISCHIEF OF MONICA. Cr. 8vo., 2s. 6d.

THE ONE GOOD GUEST. Cr. 8vo. 2s. 6d.

' *PLOUGHED,*' and other Stories. Crown 8vo., 2s. 6d.

THE MATCHMAKER. Cr. 8vo., 2s. 6d.

Ward.—*ONE POOR SCRUPLE.* By Mrs. WILFRID WARD. Crown 8vo., 6s.

Weyman (STANLEY).

THE HOUSE OF THE WOLF. With Frontispiece and Vignette. Crown 8vo., 3s. 6d.

A GENTLEMAN OF FRANCE. With Frontispiece and Vignette. Cr. 8vo., 6s.

THE RED COCKADE. With Frontispiece and Vignette. Crown 8vo., 6s.

SHREWSBURY. With 24 Illustrations by CLAUDE A. SHEPPERSON. Cr. 8vo., 6s.

SOPHIA. With Frontispiece. Crown 8vo., 6s.

Yeats (S. LEVETT).

THE CHEVALIER D'AURIAC. Crown 8vo., 3s. 6d.

THE TRAITOR'S WAY. Cr. 8vo., 6s.

Yoxall.—*THE ROMMANY STONE.* By J. H. YOXALL, M.P. Crown 8vo., 6s.

Popular Science (Natural History, &c.).

Butler.—*Our Household Insects.* An Account of the Insect-Pests found in Dwelling-Houses By EDWARD A. BUTLER, B.A., B Sc (Lond). With 113 Illustrations. Crown 8vo., 3s. 6d.

Furneaux (W.).

The Outdoor World; or The Young Collector's Handbook. With 18 Plates (16 of which are coloured), and 549 Illustrations in the Text. Crown 8vo., gilt edges, 6s. net

Butterflies and Moths (British). With 12 coloured Plates and 241 Illustrations in the Text. Crown 8vo., gilt edges, 6s. net.

Life in Ponds and Streams. With 8 coloured Plates and 331 Illustrations in the Text Crown 8vo., gilt edges, 6s. net.

Hartwig (GEORGE).

The Sea and its Living Wonders. With 12 Plates and 303 Woodcuts 8vo., gilt top, 7s. net.

The Tropical World. With 8 Plates and 172 Woodcuts. 8vo., gilt top, 7s. net.

The Polar World. With 3 Maps, 8 Plates and 85 Woodcuts. 8vo., gilt top, 7s. net

The Subterranean World. With 3 Maps and 80 Woodcuts. 8vo., gilt top, 7s. net

Helmholtz.—*Popular Lectures on Scientific Subjects.* By HERMANN VON HELMHOLTZ. With 68 Woodcuts. 2 vols.

Hudson (W. H.)

Hampshire Days. With numerous Illustrations from Drawings by BRYAN HOOK, etc. 8vo., 10s. 6d. net

Birds and Man. Large crown 8vo., 6s net

Nature in Downland. With 12 Plates and 14 Illustrations in the Text by A D McCORMICK. 8vo., 10s. 6d. net.

British Birds. With a Chapter on Structure and Classification by FRANK E BEDDARD, F R.S With 16 Plates (8 of which are Coloured), and over 100 Illustrations in the Text. Crown 8vo., gilt edges, 6s. net.

Millais.—*The Natural History of the British Surface Feeding-Ducks.* By JOHN GUILLE MILLAIS, F Z S, etc. With 6 Photogravures and 66 Plates (41 in Colours) from Drawings by the Author, ARCHIBALD THORBURN, and from Photographs. Royal 4to, £6 6s.

Proctor (RICHARD A.).

Light Science for Leisure Hours. Familiar Essays on Scientific Subjects Crown 8vo., 3s 6d

Rough Ways made Smooth. Familiar Essays on Scientific Subjects Crown 8vo, 3s. 6d.

Pleasant Ways in Science Crown 8vo., 3s. 6d.

Nature Studies. By R. A. PROCTOR, GRANT ALLEN, A. WILSON, T. FOSTER and E CLODD. Cr 8vo., 3s. 6d.

Leisure Readings. By R. A. PROCTOR, E. CLODD, A. WILSON, T. FOSTER and A C. RANYARD Cr 8vo, 3s. 6d.

** *For Mr. Proctor's other books see pp.* 16 *and* 35, *and Messrs. Longmans & Co.'s Catalogue of Scientific Works*

Popular Science (Natural History, &c.)—*continued.*

Stanley.—*A FAMILIAR HISTORY OF BIRDS.* By E STANLEY, D D., formerly Bishop of Norwich. With 160 Illustrations Cr. 8vo , 3s. 6d

Wood (Rev J G.).

HOMES WITHOUT HANDS: A Description of the Habitations of Animals, classed according to their Principle of Construction With 140 Illustrations 8vo., gilt top, 7s. net.

INSECTS AT HOME : A Popular Account of British Insects, their Structure, Habits and Transformations With 700 Illustrations 8vo , gilt top, 7s net

Wood (Rev J. G.)—*continued.*

INSECTS ABROAD A Popular Account of Foreign Insects, their Structure, Habits and Transformations. With 600 Illustrations 8vo , 7s. net

OUT OF DOORS; a Selection of Original Articles on Practical Natural History. With 11 Illustrations. Cr. 8vo , 3s. 6d.

PETLAND REVISITED. With 33 Illustrations Cr. 8vo., 3s 6d.

STRANGE DWELLINGS: a Description of the Habitations of Animals, abridged from 'Homes without Hands' With 60 Illustrations Cr 8vo., 3s. 6d.

Works of Reference.

Gwilt.—*AN ENCYCLOPÆDIA OF ARCHITECTURE.* By JOSEPH GWILT, F S.A. With 1700 Engravings Revised (1888), with Alterations and Considerable Additions by WYATT PAPWORTH 8vo , 21s. net.

Longmans' *GAZETTEER OF THE WORLD.* Edited by GEORGE G. CHISHOLM, M A , B.Sc. Imperial 8vo., 18s net cloth ; 21s. half-morocco

Maunder (SAMUEL)

BIOGRAPHICAL TREASURY. With Supplement brought down to 1889. By Rev. JAMES WOOD Fcp 8vo., 6s

THE TREASURY OF BIBLE KNOWLEDGE. By the Rev. J. AYRE, M.A. With 5 Maps, 15 Plates, and 300 Woodcuts. Fcp. 8vo., 6s.

TREASURY OF KNOWLEDGE AND LIBRARY OF REFERENCE Fcp 8vo 6s

Maunder (SAMUEL)—*continued.*

THE TREASURY OF BOTANY. Edited by J. LINDLEY, F.R.S., and T. MOORE, F.L S. With 274 Woodcuts and 20 Steel Plates. 2 vols. Fcp. 8vo., 12s.

Roget. — *THESAURUS OF ENGLISH WORDS AND PHRASES.* Classified and Arranged so as to Facilitate the Expression of Ideas and assist in Literary Composition. By PETER MARK ROGET, M D , F.R S. Recomposed throughout, enlarged and improved, partly from the Author's Notes, and with a full Index, by the Author's Son, JOHN LEWIS ROGET. Crown 8vo , 9s. net.

Willich.--*POPULAR TABLES* for giving information for ascertaining the value of Lifehold, Leasehold, and Church Property, the Public Funds, etc. By CHARLES M. WILLICH Edited by H. BENCE JONES. Crown 8vo 10s 6d

Children's Books.

Adelborg.—*CLEAN PETER AND THE CHILDREN OF GRUBBYLEA.* By OTTILIA ADELBORG. Translated from the Swedish by Mrs. GRAHAM WALLAS With 23 Coloured Plates. Oblong 4to, boards, 3s. 6d. net.

Alick's Adventures. — By G. R. With 8 Illustrations by JOHN HASSALL. Crown 8vo, 3s 6d

Brown.—*THE BOOK OF SAINTS AND FRIENDLY BEASTS.* By ABBIE FARWELL BROWN With 8 Illustrations by FANNY Y. CORY. Crown 8vo., 4s. 6d. net.

Buckland.—*TWO LITTLE RUNAWAYS.* Adapted from the French of LOUIS DESNOYERS. By JAMES BUCKLAND. With 110 Illustrations by CECIL ALDIN Cr 8vo, 6s

Crake (Rev. A. D.).

EDWY THE FAIR , or, The First Chronicle of Æscendune. Cr. 8vo., silver top, 2s. net.

ALFGAR THE DANE , or, The Second Chronicle of Æscendune Cr. 8vo , silver top, 2s net

THE RIVAL HEIRS being the Third and Last Chronicle of Æscendune. Cr. 8vo., silver top, 2s. net.

THE HOUSE OF WALDERNE. A Tale of the Cloister and the Forest in the Days of the Barons' Wars. Crown 8vo , silver top, 2s net

BRIAN FITZ-COUNT. A Story of Wallingford Castle and Dorchester Abbey. Cr. 8vo., silver top, 2s. net.

Henty (G. A).—EDITED BY.

YULE LOGS . A Story-Book for Boys. By VARIOUS AUTHORS. With 61 Illustrations. Crown 8vo., gilt edges, 3s. net.

YULE TIDE YARNS : a Story-Book for Boys. By VARIOUS AUTHORS With 45 Illustrations. Cr. 8vo , gilt edges, 3s. net.

Lang (ANDREW).—EDITED BY.

THE BLUE FAIRY BOOK. With 138 Illustrations Crown 8vo., gilt edges, 6s

ThE RED FAIRY BOOK. With 100 Illustrations. Crown 8vo , gilt edges, 6s.

THE GREEN FAIRY BOOK. With 99 Illustrations. Crown 8vo., gilt edges, 6s.

THE GREY FAIRY BOOK With 65 Illustrations Crown 8vo , gilt edges, 6s.

THE YELLOW FAIRY BOOK. With 104 Illustrations. Cr. 8vo., gilt edges, 6s

THE PINK FAIRY BOOK. With 67 Illustrations Crown 8vo , gilt edges, 6s

THE VIOLET FAIRY BOOK. With 8 Coloured Plates and 54 other Illustrations. Crown 8vo , gilt edges, 6s.

THE BLUE POETRY BOOK With 100 Illustrations. Crown 8vo., gilt edges, 6s.

THE TRUE STORY BOOK. With 66 Illustrations. Crown 8vo, gilt edges, 6s.

THE RED TRUE STORY BOOK. With 100 Illustrations. Cr. 8vo., gilt edges, 6s.

THE ANIMAL STORY BOOK. With 67 Illustrations. Cr. 8vo , gilt edges, 6s.

THE RED BOOK OF ANIMAL STORIES. With 65 Illustrations. Crown 8vo., gilt edges, 6s.

THE ARABIAN NIGHTS ENTERTAINMENTS With 66 Illustrations Cr. 8vo , gilt edges, 6s

THE BOOK OF ROMANCE. With 8 Coloured Plates and 44 other Illustrations. Crown 8vo., gilt edges, 6s.

Lyall.—*THE BURGES LETTERS :* a Record of Child Life in the Sixties. By EDNA LYALL. With Coloured Frontispiece and 8 other Full-page Illustrations by WALTER S. STACEY. Crown 8vo., 2s. 6d.

Meade (L. T.).

DADDY'S BOY. With 8 Illustrations. Crown 8vo., gilt edges, 3s. net.

DEB AND THE DUCHESS. With 7 Illustrations. Cr 8vo , gilt edges, 3s. net

THE BERESFORD PRIZE. With 7 Illustrations. Cr. 8vo., gilt edges, 3s. net

THE HOUSE OF SURPRISES. With 6 Illustrations Cr. 8vo., gilt edges, 3s. net.

Children's Books—*continued.*

Murray. — *FLOWER LEGENDS FOR CHILDREN* By HILDA MURRAY (the Hon. Mrs MURRAY of Elibank). Pictured by J. S ELAND. With numerous Coloured and other Illustrations Oblong 4to, 6s.

Penrose. — *CHUBBY: A NUISANCE.* By Mrs PENROSE With 8, Illustrations by G G MANTON Crown 8vo., 3s 6d

Praeger (ROSAMOND).

THE ADVENTURES OF THE THREE BOLD BABES HECTOR, HONORIA AND ALISANDER A Story in Pictures. With 24 Coloured Plates and 24 Outline Pictures Oblong 4to, 3s 6d

THE FURTHER DOINGS OF THE THREE BOLD BABES With 24 Coloured Pictures and 24 Outline Pictures. Oblong 4to, 3s 6d

Roberts. — *THE ADVENTURES OF CAPTAIN JOHN SMITH* Captain of Two Hundred and Fifty Horse, and sometime President of Virginia By E. P. ROBERTS With 17 Illustrations and 3 Maps. Crown 8vo., 5s. net

Stevenson. — *A CHILD'S GARDEN OF VERSES.* By ROBERT LOUIS STEVENSON. Fcp. 8vo., gilt top, 5s.

Tappan. — *OLD BALLADS IN PROSE* By EVA MARCH TAPPAN With 4 Illustrations by FANNY Y. CORY. Crown 8vo, gilt top, 4s 6d net

Upton (FLORENCE K. AND BERTHA)

THE ADVENTURES OF TWO DUTCH DOLLS AND A 'GOLLIWOGG' With 31 Coloured Plates and numerous Illustrations in the Text. Oblong 4to., 6s.

THE GOLLIWOGG'S BICYCLE CLUB With 31 Coloured Plates and numerous Illustrations in the Text. Oblong 4to, 6s.

THE GOLLIWOGG AT THE SEASIDE. With 31 Coloured Plates and numerous Illustrations in the Text Oblong 4to, 6s.

THE GOLLIWOGG IN WAR With 31 Coloured Plates Oblong 4to, 6s

THE GOLLIWOGG'S POLAR ADVENTURES. With 31 Coloured Plates Oblong 4to, 6s.

THE GOLLIWOGG'S AUTO-GO-CART. With 31 Coloured Plates and numerous Illustrations in the Text Oblong 4to., 6s

THE GOLLIWOGG'S AIR-SHIP. With 30 Coloured Pictures and numerous Illustrations in the Text. Oblong 4to, 6s

THE VEGE-MEN'S REVENGE. With 31 Coloured Plates and numerous Illustrations in the Text Oblong 4to, 6s.

Wemyss. —'*THINGS WE THOUGHT OF*'· Told from a Child's Point of View By MARY C E WEMYSS, Author of 'All About All of Us' With 8 Illustrations in Colour by S R PRAEGER. Crown 8vo, 3s 6d

The Silver Library.

CROWN 8vo. 3s. 6d. EACH VOLUME.

Arnold's (Sir Edwin) Seas and Lands. With 71 Illustrations 3s 6d

Bagehot's (W.) Biographical Studies. 3s 6d

Bagehot's (W.) Economic Studies. 3s 6d

Bagehot's (W.) Literary Studies. With Portrait 3 vols, 3s 6d. each.

Baker's (Sir S. W.) Eight Years in Ceylon. With 6 Illustrations. 3s 6d.

Baker's (Sir S. W.) Rifle and Hound in Ceylon. With 6 Illustrations 3s 6d

Baring-Gould's (Rev. S.) Curious Myths of the Middle Ages. 3s 6d.

Baring-Gould's (Rev. S.) Origin and Development of Religious Belief. 2 vols 3s 6d. each

Becker's (W. A.) Gallus: or, Roman Scenes in the Time of Augustus. With 26 Illus. 3s 6d.

Becker's (W. A.) Charicles: or, Illustrations of the Private Life of the Ancient Greeks With 26 Illustrations. 3s. 6d.

Bent's (J. T.) The Ruined Cities of Mashonaland With 117 Illustrations 3s 6d

Brassey's (Lady) A Voyage in the 'Sunbeam'. With 66 Illustrations 3s. 6d

Buckle's (H. T.) History of Civilisation in England. 3 vols 10s. 6d.

Churchill's (Winston S.) The Story of the Malakand Field Force, 1897. With 6 Maps and Plans. 3s 6d

Clodd's (E.) Story of Creation: a Plain Account of Evolution With 77 Illustrations 3s 6d

Conybeare (Rev. W. J.) and Howson's (Very Rev. J. S.) Life and Epistles of St. Paul. With 46 Illustrations. 3s. 6d

Dougall's (L.) Beggars All: a Novel 3s 6d

Doyle's (Sir A. Conan) Micah Clarke. A Tale of Monmouth's Rebellion. With 10 Illusts. 3s. 6d.

The Silver Library—*continued.*

Doyle's (Sir A. Conan) The Captain of the Polestar, and other Tales 3s 6d

Doyle's (Sir A. Conan) The Refugees. A Tale of the Huguenots. With 25 Illustrations. 3s 6d

Doyle's (Sir A. Conan) The Stark Munro Letters. 3s 6d

Froude's (J. A.) The History of England, from the Fall of Wolsey to the Defeat of the Spanish Armada. 12 vols. 3s. 6d. each.

Froude's (J. A.) The English in Ireland. 3 vols 10s 6d.

Froude's (J. A.) The Divorce of Catherine of Aragon. 3s 6d.

Froude's (J. A.) The Spanish Story of the Armada, and other Essays. 3s 6d

Froude's (J. A) English Seamen in the Sixteenth Century. 3s. 6d.

Froude's (J. A.) Short Studies on Great Subjects. 4 vols 3s 6d each

Froude's (J. A.) Oceana, or England and Her Colonies. With 9 Illustrations 3s 6d

Froude's (J. A.) The Council of Trent. 3s 6d

Froude's (J. A.) The Life and Letters of Erasmus. 3s. 6d

Froude's (J. A.) Thomas Carlyle. a History of his Life 1795-1835 2 vols 7s 1834-1881. 2 vols. 7s

Froude's (J. A) Cæsar: a Sketch 3s 6d

Froude's (J. A.) The Two Chiefs of Dunboy · an Irish Romance of the Last Century 3s 6d.

Froude's (J. A.) Writings, Selections from. 3s. 6d

Gleig's (Rev. G. R.) Life of the Duke of Wellington. With Portrait 3s 6d.

Greville's (C. C. F.) Journal of the Reigns of King George IV., King William IV., and Queen Victoria. 8 vols , 3s 6d each

Haggard's (H. R.) She : A History of Adventure With 32 Illustrations. 3s 6d

Haggard's (H. R.) Allan Quatermain. With 20 Illustrations 3s 6d

Haggard's (H. R.) Colonel Quaritch, V C . a Tale of Country Life With Frontispiece and Vignette. 3s 6d

Haggard's (H. R.) Cleopatra. With 29 Illustrations 3s 6d

Haggard's (H. R.) Eric Brighteyes. With 51 Illustrations 3s 6d.

Haggard's (H. R.) Beatrice. With Frontispiece and Vignette 3s 6d

Haggard's (H. R.) Black Heart and White Heart. With 33 Illustrations 3s. 6d.

Haggard's (H. R.) Allan's Wife. With 34 Illustrations. 3s. 6d

Haggard (H. R.) Heart of the World. With 15 Illustrations 3s. 6d

Haggard's (H. R.) Montezuma's Daughter. With 25 Illustrations 3s 6d

Haggard's (H R) Swallow · a Tale of the Great Trek With 8 Illustrations 3s 6d

Haggard's (H. R.) The Witch's Head. With 16 Illustrations. 3s. 6d.

Haggard's (H. R.) Mr. Meeson's Will. With 16 Illustrations. 3s. 6d.

Haggard's (H. R.) Nada the Lily. With 23 Illustrations 3s 6d.

Haggard's (H. R.) Dawn. With 16 Illusts. 3s 6d

Haggard's (H. R.) The People of the Mist. With 16 Illustrations 3s 6d.

Haggard's (H. R.) Joan Haste. With 20 Illustrations. 3s. 6d.

Haggard (H. R.) and Lang's (A.) The World's Desire. With 27 Illustrations 3s 6d

Harte's (Bret) In the Carquinez Woods and other Stories. 3s 6d

Helmholtz's (Hermann von) Popular Lectures on Scientific Subjects With 68 Illustrations 2 vols 3s 6d each

Hope's (Anthony) The Heart of Princess Osra. With 9 Illustrations 3s 6d

Howitt's (W.) Visits to Remarkable Places. With 80 Illustrations 3s 6d

Jefferies' (R.) The Story of My Heart: My Autobiography. With Portrait. 3s 6d

Jefferies' (R.) Field and Hedgerow. With Portrait. 3s. 6d.

Jefferies' (R.) Red Deer. With 17 Illusts 3s 6d.

Jefferies' (R.) Wood Magic. a Fable. With Frontispiece and Vignette by E. V B 3s. 6d

Jefferies (R.) The Toilers of the Field. With Portrait from the Bust in Salisbury Cathedral 3s 6d

Kaye (Sir J.) and Malleson's (Colonel) History of the Indian Mutiny of 1857-8. 6 vols 3s. 6d each.

Knight's (E. F.) The Cruise of the 'Alerte': the Narrative of a Search for Treasure on the Desert Island of Trinidad. With 2 Maps and 23 Illustrations 3s 6d

The Silver Library—*continued.*

Knight's (E. F.) Where Three Empires Meet: a Narrative of Recent Travel in Kashmir, Western Tibet, Baltistan, Gilgit. With a Map and 54 Illustrations   3s 6d

Knight's (E. F.) The 'Falcon' on the Baltic: a Coasting Voyage from Hammersmith to Copenhagen in a Three-Ton Yacht   With Map and 11 Illustrations   3s 6d

Kostlin's (J.) Life of Luther.   With 62 Illustrations and 4 Facsimiles of MSS   3s 6d

Lang's (A.) Angling Sketches.   With 20 Illustrations   3s 6d

Lang's (A.) Custom and Myth: Studies of Early Usage and Belief   3s 6d

Lang's (A.) Cock Lane and Common-Sense. 3s 6d

Lang's (A.) The Book of Dreams and Ghosts. 3s 6d

Lang's (A.) A Monk of Fife a Story of the Days of Joan of Arc   With 13 Illustrations 3s 6d

Lang's (A.) Myth, Ritual, and Religion. 2 vols 7s

Lees (J. A.) and Clutterbuck's (W. J.) B.C. 1887, A Ramble in British Columbia. With Maps and 75 Illustrations   3s 6d

Levett-Yeats' (S.) The Chevalier D'Auriac. 3s 6d

Macaulay's (Lord) Complete Works. 'Albany' Edition   With 12 Portraits   12 vols   3s 6d each

Macaulay's (Lord) Essays and Lays of Ancient Rome, etc   With Portrait and 4 Illustrations to the 'Lays'   3s 6d

Macleod's (H. D.) Elements of Banking.   3s 6d

Marshman's (J. C.) Memoirs of Sir Henry Havelock.   3s 6d.

Mason (A. E. W.) and Lang's (A.) Parson Kelly. 3s. 6d

Merivale's (Dean) History of the Romans under the Empire. 8 vols   3s 6d each

Merriman's (H. S. Flotsam: A Tale of the Indian Mutiny.   4s 6d.

Mill's (J. S.) Political Economy.   3s 6d.

Mill's (J. S.) System of Logic.   3s 6d

Milner's (Geo.) Country Pleasures: the Chronicle of a Year chiefly in a Garden   3s 6d

Nansen's (F.) The First Crossing of Greenland. With 142 Illustrations and a Map   3s 6d.

Phillipps-Wolley's (C.) Snap: a Legend of the Lone Mountain   With 12 Illustrations   3s 6d

Proctor's (R. A.) The Orbs Around Us.   3s 6d.

Proctor's (R. A.) The Expanse of Heaven. 3s 6d.

Proctor's (R. A.) Light Science for Leisure Hours.   3s. 6d.

Proctor's (R. A.) The Moon.   3s 6d

Proctor's (R. A.) Other Worlds than Ours. 3s 6d.

Proctor's (R. A.) Our Place among Infinities: a Series of Essays contrasting our Little Abode in Space and Time with the Infinities around us.   3s. 6d

Proctor's (R. A.) Other Suns than Ours. 3s 6d.

Proctor's (R. A.) Rough Ways made Smooth. 3s 6d

Proctor's (R A.) Pleasant Ways in Science. 3s 6d.

Proctor's (R. A.) Myths and Marvels of Astronomy.   3s 6d

Proctor's (R. A.) Nature Studies.   3s 6d.

Proctor's (R. A.) Leisure Readings. By R A PROCTOR, EDWARD CLODD, ANDREW WILSON, THOMAS FOSTER, and A C RANYARD   With Illustrations   3s 6d.

Rossetti's (Maria F.) A Shadow of Dante. 3s. 6d.

Smith's (R. Bosworth) Carthage and the Carthaginians.   With Maps, Plans, etc.   3s 6d.

Stanley's (Bishop) Familiar History of Birds. With 160 Illustrations   3s 6d

Stephen's (Sir Leslie) The Playground of Europe (The Alps).   With 4 Illustrations   3s. 6d.

Stevenson's (R. L.) The Strange Case of Dr. Jekyll and Mr. Hyde; with other Fables 3s 6d.

Stevenson (R. L.) and Osbourne's (Ll.) The Wrong Box.   3s. 6d.

Stevenson (Robert Louis) and Stevenson's (Fanny van de Grift) More New Arabian Nights.—The Dynamiter   3s. 6d

Trevelyan's (Sir G. O.) The Early History of Charles James Fox.   3s 6d

Weyman's (Stanley J.) The House of the Wolf: a Romance.   3s. 6d.

Wood's (Rev. J. G.) Petland Revisited. With 33 Illustrations   3s 6d

Wood's (Rev. J. G.) Strange Dwellings. With 60 Illustrations   3s 6d

Wood's (Rev. J. G.) Out of Doors. With 11 Illustrations   3s 6d

Cookery, Domestic Management, &c.

Acton. — *Modern Cookery.* By ELIZA ACTON With 150 Woodcuts Fcp 8vo , 4*s* 6*d*

Angwin.—*Simple Hints on Choice of Food*, with Tested and Economical Recipes. For Schools, Homes, and Classes for Technical Instruction. By M C ANGWIN, Diplomate (First Class) of the National Union for the Technical Training of Women, etc. Crown 8vo., 1*s*

Ashby.—*Health in the Nursery.* By HENRY ASHBY, M.D., F R.C.P , Physician to the Manchester Children's Hospital With 25 Illustrations. Crown 8vo., 3*s* net.

Bull (THOMAS, M.D.).

Hints to Mothers on the Management of their Health during the Period of Pregnancy. Fcp. 8vo., sewed, 1*s*. 6*d*.; cloth, gilt edges, 2*s*. net.

The Maternal Management of Children in Health and Disease. Fcp. 8vo., sewed, 1*s*. 6*d*. , cloth, gilt edges, 2*s* net

De Salis (Mrs.)

À la Mode Cookery . Up-to-date Recipes With 24 Plates (16 in Colour) Crown 8vo , 5*s* net.

Cakes and Confections À la Mode Fcp 8vo., 1*s*. 6*d*

Dogs . A Manual for Amateurs. Fcp 8vo., 1*s* 6*d*

Dressed Game and Poultry À la Mode. Fcp. 8vo., 1*s*. 6*d*.

Dressed Vegetables À la Mode Fcp 8vo., 1*s* 6*d*.

Drinks À la Mode. Fcp 8vo., 1*s*.6*d*.

De Salis (Mrs.)—*continued*

Entrées À la Mode. Fcp. 8vo , 1*s*. 6*d*

Floral Decorations Fcp. 8vo., 1*s* 6*d*

Gardening À la Mode. Fcp. 8vo Part I , Vegetables, 1*s*. 6*d*. Part II , Fruits, 1*s*. 6*d*

National Viands À la Mode. Fcp 8vo., 1*s*. 6*d*.

New-laid Eggs. Fcp. 8vo., 1*s*. 6*d*

Oysters À la Mode Fcp. 8vo., 1*s* 6*d*

Puddings and Pastry À la Mode. Fcp. 8vo., 1*s* 6*d*.

Savouries À la Mode. Fcp. 8vo., 1*s*.6*d*

Soups and Dressed Fish À la Mode. Fcp 8vo., 1*s* 6*d*.

Sweets and Supper Dishes À la Mode. Fcp. 8vo., 1*s* 6*d*

Tempting Dishes for Small Incomes. Fcp. 8vo., 1*s*. 6*d*

Wrinkles and Notions for Every Household Crown 8vo , 1*s*. 6*d*.

Lear.—*Maigre Cookery* By H. L. SIDNEY LEAR. 16mo , 2*s*.

Poole.—*Cookery for the Diabetic.* By W. H. and Mrs POOLE. With Preface by Dr PAVY Fcp 8vo , 2*s*. 6*d*

Rotheram. — *Household Cookery Recipes* By M A. ROTHERAM, First Class Diplomée, National Training School of Cookery, London ; Instructress to the Bedfordshire County Council. Crown 8vo., 2*s*.

The Fine Arts and Music.

Burne-Jones.—*The Beginning of the World* Twenty-five Pictures by Sir EDWARD BURNE-JONES, Bart Medium 4to., Boards, 7*s* 6*d* net

Burns and Colenso.—*Living Anatomy* By CECIL L. BURNS, R B A , and ROBERT J COLENSO, M A , M.D 40 Plates, 11¼ by 8¾ ins , each Plate containing Two Figures—(*a*) A Natural Male or Female Figure, (*b*) The same Figure Anatomised.

Hamlin.—*A Text-Book of the History of Architecture* By A D. F. HAMLIN, A M With 229 Illustrations Crown 8vo , 7*s*. 6*d*

Haweis (Rev. H. R.).

Music and Morals. With Portrait of the Author. Crown 8vo., 6*s*. net

My Musical Life. With Portrait of Richard Wagner and 3 Illustrations.

The Fine Arts and Music—*continued.*

Huish, Head, and Longman.—
SAMPLERS AND TAPESTRY EMBROIDERIES.
By MARCUS B HUISH, LL.B , also 'The
Stitchery of the Same,' by Mrs. HEAD,
and 'Foreign Samplers,' by Mrs C J.
LONGMAN   With 30 Reproductions in
Colour, and 40 Illustrations in Mono-
chrome. 4to , £2 2s. net.

Hullah.—*THE HISTORY OF MODERN
MUSIC* By JOHN HULLAH   8vo , 8s 6d

Jameson (Mrs. ANNA).

SACRED AND LEGENDARY ART, containing Legends of the Angels and Arch-
angels, the Evangelists, the Apostles, the
Doctors of the Church, St. Mary Mag-
dalene, the Patron Saints, the Martyrs,
the Early Bishops, the Hermits, and the
Warrior-Saints of Christendom, as represented in the Fine Arts. With 19 Etchings
and 187 Woodcuts 2 vols. 8vo., 20s. net.

LEGENDS OF THE MONASTIC ORDERS,
as represented in the Fine Arts, comprising the Benedictines and Augustines,
and Orders derived from their Rules, the
Mendicant Orders, the Jesuits, and the
Order of the Visitation of St. Mary. With
11 Etchings and 88 Woodcuts. 1 vol.
8vo., 10s. net.

*LEGENDS OF THE MADONNA, OR
BLESSED VIRGIN MARY.* Devotional with
and without the Infant Jesus, Historical
from the Annunciation to the Assumption,
as represented in Sacred and Legendary
Christian Art   With 27 Etchings and
165 Woodcuts   1 vol 8vo , 10s. net

THE HISTORY OF OUR LORD, as exemplified in Works of Art, with that of
His Types, St John the Baptist, and
other persons of the Old and New Testa-
ment.   Commenced by the late Mrs.
JAMESON ; continued and completed by
LADY EASTLAKE. With 31 Etchings
and 281 Woodcuts. 2 vols 8vo., 20s. net.

Kristeller. — *ANDREA MANTEGNA.*
By PAUL KRISTELLER   English Edition by
S. ARTHUR STRONG, M A., Librarian to the
House of Lords, and at Chatsworth. With
26 Photogravure Plates and 162 Illustrations
in the Text   4to , gilt top, £3 10s net.

Macfarren. — *LECTURES ON HAR-
MONY.* By Sir GEORGE A. MACFARREN
8vo 12s.

Morris (WILLIAM).
*ARCHITECTURE,   INDUSTRY   AND
WEALTH*   Collected Papers.   Crown
8vo , 6s net
HOPES AND FEARS FOR ART. Five
Lectures delivered in Birmingham, Lon-
don, etc , in 1878-1881. Cr 8vo , 4s 6d
*AN ADDRESS DELIVERED AT THE
DISTRIBUTION OF PRIZES TO STUDENTS
OF THE BIRMINGHAM MUNICIPAL SCHOOL
OF ART ON 21ST FEBRUARY,* 1894   8vo.,
2s 6d net. (*Printed in* 'Golden' Type)
*SOME HINTS ON PATTERN-DESIGN-
ING .* a Lecture delivered at the Working
Men's College, London, on 10th Decem-
ber, 1881. 8vo., 2s 6d. net (*Printed in
'Golden' Type.*)
ARTS AND ITS PRODUCERS (1888)
AND THE ARTS AND CRAFTS OF TO-DAY
(1889).   8vo., 2s. 6d. net.   (*Printed in
'Golden' Type*)
*ARCHITECTURE AND HISTORY, AND
WESTMINSTER ABBEY.*   Two Papers
read before the Society for the Protection
of Ancient Buildings   8vo , 2s. 6d net.
(*Printed in 'Golden' Type.*)
ARTS AND CRAFTS ESSAYS.   By
Members of the Arts and Crafts Exhibition
Society. With a Preface by WILLIAM
MORRIS. Crown 8vo., 2s. 6d net.
⁎⁎ For Mr William Morris's other
Works, see pp. 24, 27, 28 and 40.

Robertson.—*OLD ENGLISH SONGS
AND DANCES*   Decorated in Colour by W.
GRAHAM ROBERTSON. Royal 4to., 42s. net.

Vanderpoel. — *COLOUR PROBLEMS .*
a Practical Manual for the Lay Student of
Colour. By EMILY NOYES VANDERPOEL
With 117 Plates in Colour   Square 8vo ,
21s net.

Van Dyke.—*A TEXT-BOOK ON THE
HISTORY OF PAINTING* By JOHN C VAN
DYKE With 110 Illustrations Cr. 8vo., 6s

Wellington.—*A DESCRIPTIVE AND
HISTORICAL CATALOGUE OF THE COLLEC-
TIONS OF PICTURES AND SCULPTURE AT
APSLEY HOUSE, LONDON*   By EVELYN,
Duchess of Wellington. Illustrated by 52
Photo-Engravings, specially executed by
BRAUN, CLÉMENT, & Co , of Paris   2 vols ,
royal 4to., £6 6s. net

Willard. — *HISTORY OF MODERN
ITALIAN ART.*   By ASHTON ROLLINS
WILLARD. Part I. Sculpture.   Part II
Painting. Part III Architecture. With
Photogravure Frontispiece and numerous
full-page Illustrations. 8vo., 21s. net.

Miscellaneous and Critical Works.

Auto da Fé and other Essays: some being Essays in Fiction By the Author of 'Essays in Paradox' and 'Exploded Ideas' Crown 8vo., 5s.

Bagehot.—*LITERARY STUDIES* By WALTER BAGEHOT With Portrait. 3 vols. Crown 8vo., 3s 6d each

Baker. — *EDUCATION AND LIFE* · Papers and Addresses. By JAMES H. BAKER, M.A., LL.D. Crown 8vo., 4s. 6d

Baring-Gould.—*CURIOUS MYTHS OF THE MIDDLE AGES* By Rev S. BARING-GOULD. Crown 8vo, 3s 6d.

Baynes. — *SHAKESPEARE STUDIES*, and other Essays By the late THOMAS SPENCER BAYNES, LL.B , LL.D. With a Biographical Preface by Professor LEWIS CAMPBELL Crown 8vo, 7s 6d.

Bonnell. — *CHARLOTTE BRONTË, GEORGE ELIOT, JANE AUSTEN* · Studies in their Works. By HENRY H. BONNELL Crown 8vo., 7s. 6d. net.

Booth.—*THE DISCOVERY AND DECIPHERMENT OF THE TRILINGUAL CUNEIFORM INSCRIPTIONS* By ARTHUR JOHN BOOTH, M A With a Plan of Persepolis 8vo 14s net

Charities Register, The Annual, *AND DIGEST*. being a Classified Register of Charities in or available in the Metropolis 8vo , 5s. net.

Christie.—*SELECTED ESSAYS.* By RICHARD COPLEY CHRISTIE, M A , Oxon Hon. LL.D , Vict With 2 Portraits and 3 other Illustrations. 8vo , 12s net.

Dickinson.—*KING ARTHUR IN CORNWALL.* By W HOWSHIP DICKINSON, M.D. With 5 Illustrations. Crown 8vo , 4s. 6d.

Essays in Paradox. By the Author of 'Exploded Ideas ' and 'Times and Days' Crown 8vo , 5s

Evans.—*THE ANCIENT STONE IMPLEMENTS, WEAPONS AND ORNAMENTS OF GREAT BRITAIN* By Sir JOHN EVANS, K.C B With 537 Illustrations. 8vo , 10s 6d net

Exploded Ideas, *AND OTHER ESSAYS.* By the Author of 'Time, and Days'. Cr. 8vo. ...

Frost. — *A MEDLEY BOOK.* By GEORGE FROST. Crown 8vo., 3s. 6d net

Geikie.—*THE VICAR AND HIS FRIENDS* Reported by CUNNINGHAM GEIKIE, D D., LL D Crown 8vo , 5s. net.

Gilkes. — *THE NEW REVOLUTION.* By A. H. GILKES, Master of Dulwich College Fcp 8vo , 1s net

Haggard (H. RIDER).

A FARMER'S YEAR : being his Commonplace Book for 1898 With 36 Illustrations. Crown 8vo., 7s. 6d. net.

RURAL ENGLAND. With 23 Agricultural Maps and 56 Illustrations from Photographs 2 vols., 8vo., 36s net

Hoenig. — *INQUIRIES CONCERNING THE TACTICS OF THE FUTURE* By FRITZ HOENIG. With 1 Sketch in the Text and 5 Maps Translated by Captain H M BOWER 8vo , 15s. net

Hutchinson —*DREAMS AND THEIR MEANINGS* By HORACE G HUTCHINSON. 8vo , gilt top, 9s. 6d. net.

Jefferies (RICHARD).

FIELD AND HEDGEROW. With Portrait Crown 8vo., 3s. 6d.

THE STORY OF MY HEART : my Autobiography. Crown 8vo., 3s. 6d.

RED DEER. With 17 Illustrations. Crown 8vo., 3s. 6d.

THE TOILERS OF THE FIELD Crown 8vo , 3s. 6d.

WOOD MAGIC. a Fable. Crown 8vo , 3s 6d

Jekyll (GERTRUDE).

HOME AND GARDEN Notes and Thoughts, Practical and Critical, of a Worker in both With 53 Illustrations from Photographs. 8vo., 10s 6d. net.

WOOD AND GARDEN · Notes and Thoughts, Practical and Critical, of a Working Amateur. With 71 Photographs. 8vo , 10s 6d net.

Miscellaneous and Critical Works—*continued.*

Johnson (J. & J H.)

The Patentee's Manual . a Treatise on the Law and Practice of Letters Patent 8vo., 10s. 6d.

An Epitome of the Law and Practice connected with Patents for Inventions, with a reprint of the Patents Acts of 1883, 1885, 1886 and 1888 Crown 8vo , 2s. 6d.

Joyce.— *The Origin and History of Irish Names of Places.* By P. W. Joyce, LL.D 2 vols. Crown 8vo , 5s each

Lang (Andrew).

Letters to Dead Authors Fcp. 8vo , 2s 6d net

Books and Bookmen. With 2 Coloured Plates and 17 Illustrations. Fcp. 8vo , 2s. 6d net

Old Friends. Fcp. 8vo., 2s. 6d. net

Letters on Literature Fcp. 8vo , 2s. 6d net

Essays in Little. With Portrait of the Author. Crown 8vo , 2s 6d

Cock Lane and Common-Sense. Crown 8vo , 3s 6d

The Book of Dreams and Ghosts. Crown 8vo , 3s. 6d

Maryon.—*How the Garden Grew.* By Maud Maryon With 4 Illustrations Crown 8vo , 5s net

Matthews.—*Notes on Speech-Making.* By Brander Matthews. Fcp 8vo., 1s. 6d. net.

Max Müller (The Right Hon. F.).

Collected Works. 18 vols. Crown 8vo., 5s. each.

Vol I *Natural Religion* the Gifford Lectures, 1888

Vol. II. *Physical Religion* the Gifford Lectures, 1890.

Vol III *Anthropological Religion.* the Gifford Lectures, 1891.

Vol IV *Theosophy,* or, Psychological Religion the Gifford Lectures, 1892

Chips from a German Workshop.

Vol V. Recent Essays and Addresses.

Vol. VI. Biographical Essays

Vol. VII Essays on Language and Literature

Vol. VIII Essays on Mythology and Folk-lore

Vol. IX. *The Origin and Growth of Religion,* as Illustrated by the Religions of India . the Hibbert Lectures, 1878

Vol. X. *Biographies of Words, and the Home of the Aryas.*

Vols XI , XII *The Science of Language.* Founded on Lectures delivered at the Royal Institution in 1861 and 1863 2 vols 10s

Vol XIII *India* What can it Teach Us ?

Vol. XIV *Introduction to the Science of Religion.* Four Lectures, 1870.

Vol. XV. *Rámakrishna* his Life and Sayings

Vol. XVI. *Three Lectures on the Vedánta Philosophy,* 1894.

Vol XVII. *Last Essays.* First Series Essays on Language, Folk-lore, etc.

Vol XVIII *Last Ess ii s.* Second Series. Essays on the Science of Religion.

Miscellaneous and Critical Works—*continued*

Milner.—*COUNTRY PLEASURES:* the Chronicle of a Year chiefly in a Garden. By GEORGE MILNER   Crown 8vo , 3s 6d.

Morris.—*SIGNS OF CHANGE.* Seven Lectures delivered on various Occasions. By WILLIAM MORRIS. Post 8vo., 4s. 6d.

Parker and Unwin.—*THE ART OF BUILDING A HOME* a Collection of Lectures and Illustrations   By BARRY PARKER and RAYMOND UNWIN   With 68 Full-page Plates   8vo , 10s. 6d net.

Pollock.—*JANE AUSTEN* her Contemporaries and Herself   By WALTER HERRIES POLLOCK.   Cr. 8vo., 3s. 6d. net.

Poore (GEORGE VIVIAN, M.D.).

ESSAYS ON RURAL HYGIENE With 13 Illustrations   Crown 8vo , 6s 6d

THE DWELLING HOUSE. With 36 Illustrations   Crown 8vo , 3s 6d

THE EARTH IN RELATION TO THE PRESERVATION AND DESTRUCTION OF CONTAGIA being the Milroy Lectures delivered at the Royal College of Physicians in 1899, together with other Papers on Sanitation   With 13 Illustrations Crown 8vo , 5s

COLONIAL AND CAMP SANITATION. With 11 Illustrations.   Cr. 8vo., 2s. net

Rossetti. – *A SHADOW OF DANTE* being an Essay towards studying Himself, his World and his Pilgrimage   By MARIA FRANCESCA ROSSETTI.   Crown 8vo , 3s 6d.

Seria Ludo.   By a DILETTANTE Post 4to , 5s net

** *Sketches and Verses, mainly reprinted from the St James's Gazette*

Shadwell. — *DRINK   TEMPERANCE AND LEGISLATION*   By ARTHUR SHADWELL, M.A., M D.   Crown 8vo , 5s net

Soulsby (LUCY H. M.).

STRAY THOUGHTS ON READING. Fcp 8vo., 2s. 6d. net.

STRAY THOUGHTS FOR GIRLS   16mo.,

Soulsby (LUCY H. M)—*continued.*

STRAY THOUGHTS FOR MOTHERS AND TEACHERS   Fcp 8vo , 2s 6d net

STRAY THOUGHTS FOR INVALIDS. 16mo., 2s net

STRAY THOUGHTS ON CHARACTER. Fcp 8vo., 2s 6d. net.

Southey.—*THE CORRESPONDENCE OF ROBERT SOUTHEY WITH CAROLINE BOWLES.* Edited by EDWARD DOWDEN   8vo , 14s

Stevens.—*ON THE STOWAGE OF SHIPS AND THEIR CARGOES*   With Information regarding Freights, Charter-Parties, etc   By ROBERT WHITE STEVENS.   8vo., 21s.

Thuillier.—*THE PRINCIPLES OF LAND DEFENCE, AND THEIR APPLICATION TO THE CONDITIONS OF TO-DAY.* By Captain H. F THUILLIER, R.E.   With Maps and Plans. 8vo , 12s. 6d. net

Turner and Sutherland.—*THE DEVELOPMENT OF AUSTRALIAN LITERATURE* By HENRY GYLES TURNER and ALEXANDER SUTHERLAND   With Portraits and Illustrations   Crown 8vo , 5s.

Warwick.—*PROGRESS IN WOMEN'S EDUCATION IN THE BRITISH EMPIRE* being the Report of Conferences and a Congress held in connection with the Educational Section, Victorian Era Exhibition   Edited by the COUNTESS OF WARWICK   Cr 8vo 6s

Weathers.—*A PRACTICAL GUIDE TO GARDEN PLANTS*   By JOHN WEATHERS, F.R.H S   With 159 Diagrams   8vo , 21s net.

Whittall —*FREDERICK THE GREAT ON KINGCRAFT*, from the Original Manuscript ; with Reminiscences and Turkish Stories. By Sir J. WILLIAM WHITTALL, President of the British Chamber of Commerce at Turkey.   8vo., 7s 6d. net.

Lightning Source UK Ltd.
Milton Keynes UK
UKHW022057110521
383564UK00003B/187